Zoom- 893

password- 487175

FREE FROM DEPENDENCY

The Grace of Letting Go

NATTI RONEL

- Living in the Truth
- Doing the Next right thing
- Live Honestly
- Results in Peace *
- do you beliv God love you worth

Producer & International Distributor
eBookPro Publishing
www.ebook-pro.com

Free from Dependency
Natti Ronel

Translation: Avi Woolf

Contact: Natti.Ronel@biu.ac.il
ISBN 9798829108717

FREE FROM DEPENDENCY

The Grace of Letting Go

NATTI RONEL

CONTENTS

PREFACE

This unique book by Professor Natti Ronel is being published during challenging global times. A time when 'quarantine,' 'lockdowns' and 'social distancing' have become part of our daily routine. The poet Nathan Alterman's "Endless Meeting" line keeps running through my mind: "On iron streets, empty and long." It seems as though with the physical distance, the whole world has become alienated and metallic, a world whose grace and compassion have vanished.

Yet, something amazing and wonderful has happened: It turns out that grace did not, in fact, disappear. On the contrary, it was precisely in these challenging times that we have witnessed so much grace, and people full of grace – good people who felt that they could not sit back and do nothing. Who felt they must, even at their own personal cost, act in order to bring change, and prevent the suffering, physical and emotional harm so many have suffered by helping out anyone they can.

This is the essence of grace, and the main topic of this book. As Professor Ronel claims, sometimes grace appears unexpectedly, against the odds. It could appear as an envelope filled with cash, placed in the hands of a homeless, who just hopes for a few coins, and sometimes it can be a small and momentary act of grace. But whether small or big, the gift of grace is its ability to touch us, fill our hearts, and bring about the change which leads to something new, a new order that rises above the mundane routine of our lives.

What makes this book unique for me, what captivated me and struck me as both surprising and amazing, is the way it proposes to turn the path of grace and spirituality into a practical one, even providing an instruction manual to that very end. It wishes to teach us how to use tools in order to break free of harmful emotions, habits and feelings which limit us blocking our path to growth and change.

Grace and practicality may sound like opposites, much like spirituality vs. daily routine. This is what I believed before reading this book. We are used to thinking of grace as something exalted, something out of our reach most of the time, aside from rare and precious moments, and more importantly, something beyond our control, much like miracles or fate or luck. We go about our days busy with routine matters and material concerns, and when faced with challenges or hurdles, we react with feelings of difficulty, distress, pain, and powerlessness, hoping for grace to touch us and save us.

Yet, this book teaches us that it's highly possible to live in grace on a daily basis. Instead of hoping for it and longing for it, instead of dreaming about it, we can act right now as though it's already here, finding it first and foremost within ourselves. And this, the book tells us, is the bridge that can carry us over the troubled waters of feelings of powerlessness and material challenges, toward spirituality, toward good and love. Toward God as we, each and every one of us, understands Him.

This idea echoes the concept of positive criminology. It's an innovative criminological perspective developed, by Professor Ronel, which sounds like an oxymoron, but is based on the same perspective of recognizing the existence of human goodness and grace and their power to bring about change. It stresses man's ability to learn how to combine and use positive forces in order to bring about the decrease of crime and criminality.

How does one turn grace and spirituality practical? That's what this book lays out, step by step. Beginning with the Twelve Tools for change, together with other similar ones, also developed by Professor Ronel, such as understanding self-centeredness, lying at the root of powerlessness, and learning how to transcend it, the image of the serpent, its temptations and seduction ways, and how to break free of them; the behavioral spin, emotional begging, and emotional turbulence into which we are often drawn, and how to stop them.

All these are the swamp we are mired in. In order to successfully break out of it and grow, we need to first and foremost, recognize the obstacles, strive to break free of them, and at the same time look to continue to keep moving on up. This could be the essence of the saying in the Book of Psalms: "Turn from evil and do good." To grow spiritually, we need to identify the feelings and habits which hold us back on our way, and break free of them, focusing on striving toward the good and doing good.

This book is therefore, a guide to spirituality in the most practical, daily sense. Yet, it is no ordinary guide. Many guides, for practically every purpose, such as medical, psychological, and spiritual, in the form of books, booklets, and YouTube clips, are out there.

This guide though, is different. It merges spirituality and practicality, and as such, is a fascinating and exciting read. It combines personal and professional stories, metaphors and parables, structured plans, solutions and explanations, which guide the reader on his journey toward a spirituality filled way of life in his daily routine.

I wish you a pleasant read, which will help you find grace, and the bridge for inner change within yourselves.

Dr. Yafa Shir-Raz, Risks Communication Researcher

INTRODUCTION

Oftentimes we find ourselves trapped in repetitive behaviors, habits, thoughts, or emotional states which we don't want. In those repeat instances, we are usually unable to change our situation, and even when we do, our successes only work temporarily. We ultimately find ourselves in the same spot and in the same frustrating situation again and again hurting both us and others in our surroundings prominently.

Sometimes we aren't aware that something is constantly holding us back. We are hurting from its outcome but don't know why. And in those instances when we do realize what is going on and understand it, too often we cannot change the patterns that constrain us.

Some of these conditions are defined as addictions, such as, addiction to drugs, light or harmful, compulsive eating or self-destructive relationships. Other cases are not determines as addictions, but rather as "just" a habit which weighs on us, or emotions which force us into a familiar path of suffering. Other times we simply repeat mistakes despite their unsuccessful outcome.

Is this our fate, or can we break free?

This book suggests an in-depth description of a tried and tested method to break free of dependence on burdensome emotions and habits. This act of liberation from dependence on emotions, allows us to experience them fully, without being bound to certain patterns of action, being free of any particular emotion taking over our mind and experience. Breaking free of burdensome habits allows us to choose how to act as we see fit in any given situation, without finding ourselves compulsively repeating the same old harmful behaviors. It creates an actual promising way of life, with an increasing experience of choice, internal freedom and joy. It is a way based on the accumulated experience of decades, scientific-behavioral study, and a range of resources of knowledge, some of them new and others drawing on older traditions of culture, wisdom and spirit, the combination of which creates something new, suitable for us and our times.

This way, which offers spiritual development, includes behavioral and mental components, and is fundamentally holistic. It offers, enables, and encourages change. This change can be experienced on three levels in tandem: The behavioral change which occurs at the same time as the mental and spiritual one. Since this is a way which is primarily based on the actual experience of many people who practiced it, it is eminently practical and usable by almost anyone in their daily life. The practicality and utility of the way is also expressed in its simplicity. The way offers simple solutions for complicated life situations, and allows for a quick experience of relief and release, which gradually develops on all three levels.

A core part of the way of change, proposed here, is based on the twelve-step program, originating in the self-help group known as Alcoholics Anonymous, or AA. For many decades, the twelve-step program has helped many millions of people around the world, break free of a range of addictions on their various levels. It also helped people suffering from powerlessness, live a satisfying life, them and the people around them.

To The Twelve Step Program I added components of my own clinical experience, since the early nineties, as well as the experience of my colleagues, who learned the way from me in courses and workshops. I have also applied professional knowledge from the various behavioral sciences, and the wisdom of the many peoples of the world expressed by their different spiritual and religious writings. In my previous book, **The Twelve Tools: From Dependence to Independence Through Spiritual Change**[1], I described the way through methods of changed formulated, as twelve practical tools (briefly described below). This book expands on them and offers additional aspects for change.

I have called the overall way of change the GraceWay– a title which suggests a journey of a lifetime, for advancement along the path of change. The GraceWay is a framework to support processes of change, which and over time, are noticeable in those who walk its path. The very understanding that we are indeed on the path, allows us for both meaning and mission, which become ever more apparent as we advance and deal with the challenges we encounter along the way.

The meaning of the word grace is a good, charitable, or beneficial act for others, usually without seeking anything in return. This is how the word appears in the Bible, and is considered one of the attributes of God[2]. It reminds us of an experience of goodness, of giving, of something that transcends the usual order of things and goes beyond it[3].

When we encounter grace, when, for example someone offers it to us, we might experience transcendence, a feeling of rising above the way things usually are in our life. It seems as though, even for a moment, a new order has been created for us. Sometimes grace appears at a time, in a manner, and of a quality which surprises us with a goodness we could not have imagined. This is the holistic change the way offers , a change experienced as a gift of grace – touching us personally, refreshing, expanding something in our heart, enabling a new, surprising order in life, as though we've just hit restart and broken free of painful processes. Sometimes grace can be a small moment, but it contains goodness that breaks boundaries by its very nature, creating something new from which we can advance.

The act of grace is an act of connection, between contrasts, between the expected and the unexpected, and most importantly, between the earthly and the spiritual. The grace which the way is described here, guides us, serves for us, living in the material world, as a bridge through which we can live the spirit lying at the essence of all. Grace is a bridge which carries us beyond the experience of powerlessness, brought on by material life, toward what lies just beyond. In rare moments, grace removes the veil of lack of knowledge from us, and then at once, spirit, goodness, and love are revealed before us and in us. These are unforgettable moments which we strive for their return in the future.

The GraceWay offers us something practical. Instead of waiting for grace to come to us, striving for and expecting it and in meantime dreaming of it or imagine scenarios of it, we can simply live the grace, as though it is already here. In other words, we should act with the grace we wish to be ours. That's how it enters our lives, through grace. And as Tolstoy put it: "Do not deny yourself the grace given to you[4]."

How can we live grace? More on that below.

The first chapter of this book briefly presents the GraceWay's twelve tools, each of which enables a certain change, and together create a way of life which transcends dependence. The second chapter describes a common state of affairs among most people, a high degree of self-centeredness, becoming too occupied with ourselves. In all states of dependence on emotions and habits it is possible to identify high self-centeredness. The chapter describes that at length, offering methods for transcending self-centeredness breaking free of that painful dependence.

The third chapter, proposes an image for the force driving us to dependency, continuing the well-known story of the Garden of Eden: The image of the serpent, with its assisting forces within us and methods that can be used to subdue us. The chapter also suggests a way to break free of the serpent's suffocating embrace.

This book goes on to describe the painful process of behavioral spin, alongside emotional or thought-based spin, in which we lose control of ourselves and increasingly spiral downward to the point of risking a crash, and consequently serious harm to ourselves or others. The chapter suggests what we can do in this tangled situation.

The two short succeeding chapters describe forms of emotional subordination, from which we can break free. The first is the common but embarrassing state of "emotional begging", offering a way to avoid it. The other describes an emotional seesaw which hurls us from a sense of paralyzing powerlessness to one of false omnipotence. Additionally, it describes how to find balance beyond the experience of emotional subordination.

The following two chapters present a method for self-examination that allows us to break free of the barriers we have accumulated over the years, which prevent us from advancing on our way to change. The first describes the exposure of and the release from barriers most of us share, with the second describing a delicate and unique liberation way from barriers that we have carried with us from past traumatic experiences.

Later on, typical patterns of behavior are described, as well as a way of liberating ourselves from binding patterns of self-centeredness. The following chapter examines the deeper motivation which leads us to different actions in life, along with a suggestion for guiding us toward finding serenity, freedom and love. The next chapter connects the GraceWay to a method for rapid change originating in Hawaii - Ho'oponopono. The summary chapter then directs us to continued spiritual growth , on a journey which ends with the transcendence of all endings.

For decades, the GraceWay has been taught at group meetings, primarily to experienced professional therapists and students of therapeutic professions, and sometimes to a wider audience.

Subsequently, this book is written in the form of a workshop with a personal appeal to participants, and with exercises which demonstrate the way, and offer personal practice for the readers.

The book contains many personal stories which portray the various points. All, unless noted otherwise, are based on actual events I encountered, usually during therapy sessions, with obvious changes to protect the identity of the participants The narrative we share is what matters; the personal details are naturally less important. The names I chose for the protagonists are of course entirely made up. If someone nevertheless believes they can identify someone in one of the stories, it is likely because of the shared human element which leads us to experience similar things.

GraceWay is a spiritual way, one aiming toward God. To distinguish between it and religion, and to avoid coercion, which by its nature is contrary to the spirit, I chose to adopt the formulation of the twelve-step program: *God as we understand Him*. Everyone understands as they can, and as the Medieval Sufi sage Ibn Arabi put it: "God is revealed to Man in the color Man can see"[5]. Thus each of us can see God, albeit in different colors. As we advance along the way, we see how the color which we see God changes before our eyes, until we clearly see that all the colors are from and in God, and He Himself has no color.

My personal journey: How I came upon the GraceWay?

In the beginning of the eighties, I worked as a student at a central office of one of the big banks in Israel, a job that mostly involved evenings and night shifts. During one of the rare morning shift I worked, our department manager, a quiet and pleasant man whom I rarely met, talked with a colleague of his from the bank's central headquarters.

The conversation was right next to me, so I couldn't help but hear it and honestly, the content made me make an effort not miss anything. Surprisingly, they spoke of something that sounded to me like a spiritual or personal development method. They also mentioned the name of the way they spoke of, which had started to gain in popularity in Tel Aviv. When they finished and the lady went on her way, I turned to him with utter abruptness, confessed that I heard the conversation and asked for details. A few days later, I was invited to meet representatives of that way.

I was a young psychology student at the time, a respectively successful one, and had plans to continue my studies. I lived in a pleasant apartment with roommates in a central but quiet part of Tel Aviv, and due to the uncomfortable work hours, the job at the bank was very remunerative and I managed to both have fun and save up. Even romance was not lacking then.

But even though all was well, something was missing, something very basic, as though I was wearing a mask of goodness. But what was behind it? This I wished to discover. For some reason what I had ceased to satisfy me. In fact, despite all the good I ostensibly had, I felt a great emptiness, a sense of missing out on life, and everything I knew until then was not able to fill me up.

When I took more of what life offered me, much like everyone else around me, more fun, more of what was considered success, the emptiness increased. Was this all life had to offer? Was this all I had to offer life, the world, myself? Deep down I thought and hoped it could be otherwise, without knowing what that meant. Therefore I felt tremendous excitement when I heard of something different which was out there.

I went to that meeting with a friend who was also starting some vague search. We weren't so impressed. There was too great a gap between what was stated and that which was actually presented. But that was the beginning. I returned home knowing that whatever happened, I was going to soon find a change that speaks to me, a change I could live with.

What and how, where, when? I had no idea, but I didn't want to go on like this.

A few weeks later, at a boring class, where I dozed off a bit (I was working nights…), while sitting in the back row, a good friend next to me, who was also bored, surprised me with a question:

"Have you heard of Shlomo Kalo?"

"I think so, the one who translated books from the east?"

"Yes, he's a spiritual teacher."

"How can one learn from him?"

I surprised both of us with my last question, without asking for details, without any background, without even understanding the concept of a "spiritual teacher." Just an outburst of intuition, entirely ignoring the fact that we were interrupting the class.

"I know someone who is close to him, not everyone gets accepted!"

"Can you get me details?" I asked him

A few weeks later I found myself in the office of the late Shlomo Kalo (1928-2014), after working hours, at a clinic where he was director of the regional lab. The conversation was very unusual. In his precise manner of speech, without asking what I was looking for and why I came, he gave me a few exercises on the spiritual path, which to this day direct people to live the grace we wish to encounter. Without any background stories, I started on the path.

Katmandu. A few years later, in the mid-eighties, a time when I struggled with and was attracted to the way of the spirit. A backpacker's trip, heavy use of drugs considered light, empty leisure, natural life mistakes, and a way of life that flees itself. Complete subordination to confusing emotions and habits which offer false security and subsequent suffering.

Without being prepared, she was there, Gila, who became the most wonderful of women to me, with a heart broader than the universe, even though I didn't know then just how much. But wait, we know each other, no? We really did, and it only seemed that we hadn't seen each other for a few years, maybe since we were born, because we hadn't met yet, but we knew each other, and we both knew it, without many words. Again, intuition directed us in its way, playing with us. With the grace of God, we haven't separated since. "Can two walk together, unless they are agreed? [6]"

As if not to waste time, we overflowed with words to tell each other what we've been through since we remembered ourselves, like a couple of lovers who separated because of life circumstances and who met after years, and want to make up for every moment, telling and hearing every important event. When I told her of Shlomo Kalo and the D.A.T. path (tr. Always Know Yourself), her eyes sparkled. She, too, knew her way. Together, and each separately, we chose to return and cope with ourselves, and we have since been united on the path of grace and love.

At the beginning of the nineties. I was looking for a topic for my doctorate in criminology, focusing on rehabilitation from drug addiction. The name NA, Narcotics Anonymous, started to become known in Israel. I volunteered then at a rehab and methadone maintenance center in South Tel Aviv.

There, I witnessed an interesting phenomenon, patients who claimed they attended NA meetings were also "clean." Those who fell back and relapsed usually had grievances against NA. A few months later, I started to go to NA meetings in Tel Aviv, deepening my research.

I had purchased my "entry ticket" before, having used too many drugs, which also used me for their pleasure. Although I had put that behind me a few years earlier, thanks to the spiritual way I returned to, NA gave me something new, effectively demonstrating the human element which aims toward the spiritual, alongside simple routine practicality.

At NA, and especially its twelve-step program for change, I heard a language of spirit and change very much like the one I knew, but with a special adjustment for the painful, sometimes very painful, burdens of life. I learned a simple way of life, appropriate for almost anyone, even if they don't have any particular wish besides ending their suffering. A way which if one takes it, reveals a growing spiritual striving and living grace.

In the 2000s I became a full faculty member at Bar-Ilan University. Many research opportunities have opened up to me. Alongside studies on rehabilitation from addiction, as well as of criminal and victims of violence, I embarked on research of the spiritual aspects of change and rehabilitation, suggesting new fields of research such as positive criminology and spiritual criminology. The knowledge accumulated from this work added another aspect to the GraceWay taking shape.

The unique combination of the way I learned from Shlomo Kalo, known as the D.A.T. school, a way of honest effort, focus, and direct experience in the spirit without words, with the practicality of the twelve-step program, appropriate for almost everyone, guided me in my professional path.

I worked as a therapist, a clinical criminologist, where I applied the way of the spirit as it formed into the twelve tools and the GraceWay. At the same time I also advanced as a researcher and lecturer at the university, and tried to ensure that the spirit and spiritual path led there too, with the grace of God.

The GraceWay reflects what I learned after decades in academia and professional work. It reflects processes of change I saw in thousands of people, together with the human knowledge present in every place and time. Grace is one, after all, while only the places, times, cultures and people, change.

"Do not list your achievements or bemoan your stumbles.
Discover the God in your heart".

CHAPTER ONE

Twelve Tools for Change

Let's start with a moment of silence. We try to let go of everything – thoughts, emotions, memories, expectations. Just be. Quietly. When we but let go of ourselves and the world, silence takes on a life of its own – a lively, awake stillness, with its own unique sound, the voice of silence. Let's listen to it a little.

Self-change is a seemingly big task. Oftentimes, we seek to change something within ourselves after we've already suffered a lot of pain from it, and after it has exacted too high a cost from us. So high, in fact, that we prefer to change it rather than continue on with what we know. Unfortunately, sometimes the familiar is our safe, comfortable place, though not necessarily a beneficial one, which is why we put off thoughts of change and remain chained to emotions or habits.

Yet, when we start to change certain things, it could work out and we advance quickly. When this happens, we need no outside help. Great. But sometimes it works out differently. When that happens, it seems that despite the good intentions and deep understanding, we continue to repeat the same behaviors   which hurt both us and others. This is when change involving outside support or setting is required. Change which has a structured path which guides us in moments of confusion, which encourages us in moments of "material fatigue", and which protects us from the complacency of passing, superficial joy. This is the purpose of the GraceWay, which offers a change in life which is a destination – the grace – with the destination also being the path itself; we live the grace we aim and strive for, and thus achieve it.

To live and to be the grace we wish to encounter. is a goal which is appropriate both for situations in which we feel burdened or distressed or suffering which we seek to break free from, as well as those where we feel content in our life being ordinary and even excellent, but we nevertheless want something else. Sometimes we can name it, sometimes we cannot. We have a clear notion that underneath the visible forms of daily, routine life, with its joys and challenges, there is something else, which we seek to uncover.

By its very nature, this other thing exists. But for this or that reason it is still not a part of our life, which means some effort is required to reveal it. The GraceWay guides us toward it. The goal and the persistence in keeping to the path, are more important than the motivation that brought us to it, whether it started from suffering and the desire to break free of some burden, or came from a longing for something else.

The GraceWay offers tools of change, twelve in all. This number is not random, referring as it does to one of the sources of the path, the twelve-step program of AA and similar groups such as NA, OA, and others (see Appendix), which are correspondingly called twelve step groups. These groups offer their members a spiritual program for change as a way of life, appropriate for almost any individual in our modern world. It is especially appropriate for anyone who understands that they engage in repeat behaviors which harm them and others, which they cannot stop on their own, such as alcohol use, compulsive eating, a tendency to be dependent in relationships, or an inability to be regularly employed.

The twelve tools, learned from the wisdom of the step program and its members, and from the practical wisdom of other spiritual traditions, offer spirituality-based solutions for various daily situations, as well as a structured program for personal development. Some of the tools were adopted from the recovery of members in twelve step groups[8] . while others are an original articulation of the GraceWay. I expanded at length on the different tools and their use in the book Twelve Tools, where I discussed each and every one in detail, demonstrating their use and analyzing the meaning of each one in relation to changing oneself.

In general, the twelve tools offer us a program of change which is modular, but whose parts connect into a greater whole than the sum of its parts, to a daily way of life guided by spirituality. The tools offer different angles of action, ultimately aimed at the same overarching goal, to know the grace in our life. Each tool can be described as part of a hologram which contains the entire way within it, and the more tools are accumulated with their unique perspectives, the more the resolution of the hologram increases, with the picture of grace inside it becoming sharper and more focused.

After presenting the different tools, we focus on a number of aspects of change, which further increase the aforementioned hologram's resolution. All the aspects presented here appear in the twelve tools, but each aspect has its own unique emphasis. For instance, the first aspect, the description of self-centeredness, focuses on something which repeats itself from the get-go and most characterizes the path itself, the striving to transcend self-centeredness. This is the ambition of every spiritual path, the essence they all share. The twelve tools describe a path for breaking free of self-centeredness, each offering their characteristic application for this challenging possibility.

The second aspect, the image of the serpent, continues the self-centeredness issue, using the practical metaphor which helps us in daily exercises. Other aspects present specific situations in life, such as the behavioral spin, emotional begging or emotional turbulence. Some offer us continued progress, such as the continued growth aspect, or the purifying of the consciousness via the Ho'oponopono method, and there is also the aspect which offers an examination of our style of behavior in the world. An important aspect presented here is healing from a harmful experience, which will show how the path can help us grow, even from extreme situations in life and in the face of great challenges.

The Twelve tools

1. Abstinence
2. Just For Today
3. The Serenity Prayer
4. Gratitude
5. Distinguishing Facts
6. Being Positive
7. Finding in Ourselves
8. Truth Only
9. Choosing in Advance
10. Correcting Errors
11. Promoting Good
12. Living the Spirit

Tool 1 – Abstinence

The first tool, and the basis for any deep change, is **abstinence**. Abstinence, as the name suggests, means abstaining from a particular action or situation, which harms us or others. Some of these are destructive in themselves, such as the tendency toward criticism, and some are harmful because we cannot do or be them "just a little," such as the range of compulsive behaviors which personal experience has shown are "all or nothing" for us, with no middle ground.

Abstinence offers us the simple, direct instruction of: "nothing." Choosing "nothing" allows us to create and experience something else. This sounds very logical on its face, and it should ostensibly be easy for us to accept, but a slightly deeper look shows how we often try to change while trying to preserve something of that we wish to change, and that doesn't go so well. Or at all. The tool of abstinence points simply to the option we are avoiding, to entirely stop the particular behavior or situation and see what happens.

Abstinence can also work in the reverse, abstaining from non-doing something that needs doing, if we have an unhealthy habit of putting off desired tasks to the point of completely evading them, despite the pain and harm this causes. In this case, abstinence would be avoiding putting things off. In practice, it would mean carrying out the selected task, despite the strong tendency to run away from it.

Abstinence is a means and a process of change, rather than its end. It's a step we climb, so that we can continue to move on up. Every so often we use it in accordance with the needs of life and the moment when progress stops and a literal escalation is needed to continue with changes.

There are different kinds of abstinence. There are behaviors and situations we should stop right this minute, such as smoking , and never go back. There are behaviors which cannot be entirely stopped, such as eating, but part of which can be entirely stopped , such as snacking or midnight munchies.

Some behaviors and situations are worth stopping all together for a certain period in our lives, until we grow a bit stronger and can come back to it in a controlled manner. For instance, we can entirely avoid efforts to find a partner, if we have a tendency of being dependent in a relationship, in a harmful way to both the relationship and ourselves. While engaging in abstinence, we can allow other tools to direct us toward a deeper change, after which we can have another go at finding someone, this time differently.

Another aspect of abstinence refers to what we are abstaining from. We usually start with abstinence related to behavior. Abstaining from behavior usually creates a rapid change. For instance, a person deciding to abstain from arguments with his wife, immediately created a change in the atmosphere at home. We can go deeper and move on to mental abstinence. For instance, someone who expected to get rich quickly, leading to pressure in his work as a freelancer and tension which disrupted his normal functioning. He decided to abstain from such expectations, letting them go when they arise, which in turn led to relief and greater calm. In this kind of abstinence, the emphasis is on abstaining from attachment to expectations for a desired result, profits we seek, or fears we have about an unpleasant result.

When there is progress in the process of change, our capacity for abstinence advances as well, which enables reaching abstinence directly related
to the spiritual level: Abstinence from the desiring itself. If the person from
the above example was ready, we could have suggested he abstain from
the very desire to get rich. This abstinence involves spiritual development,
since it offers only one form of desire, the desire for the spirit, for God, as
we understand Him, eliminating all other things, such as getting rich or
transient pleasures.

Tool 2 – Just for today

The second tool is **just for today**, without which most of us will not succeed
in maintaining the abstinence we chose for ourselves. This tool guides us
to limit our effort only to today, and even just to this very moment. Just for
today reminds us of a simple fact of life, we exist and act only in the present,
and should therefore focus our efforts on the here and now.

We often get caught in memories of the past, expectations or fears of the
future, or fantasies about what could have been different in the past or in
an imagined future. Just for today guides us to live in reality. The past, as
much as we enjoy or feel pain in remembering it, is gone. The future has yet
to arrive, but we can still aim for a future that we desire in the present. The
future has a wide range of options, some of which can be imagined and some
which are surprising in their own way.

We can have some influence on these options simply by virtue of focusing
on the present on something we chose, which we think is right ,a kind of
abstinence. For instance, someone who started studying at the university
despite her fear of failure, which is based on her past disappointments. With
the help of just for today, she started studying while ignoring the question of
future success or failure as much as she could. The fear and apparently even
the expectation for failure continued to accompany her throughout her years
spent getting a degree, and even after she graduated cum laude and went on
for an MA program. But she learned how to function despite the fears and

negative expectations, just for today, and that was a big change.

In addition, just for today offers us the option for breaking down a large task into small, manageable parts. Sometimes we look at a large task, become terrified at its enormity, and give up. **Just for today** proposes that we look at one part at a time, and proceed with it. This focus allows us to better make use of our abilities.

Continuing the previous example, before she began her studies, the young woman's task was to register for college. Then a new task appeared, in which in order to be accepted she had to convince the faculty that they should give her a chance, despite a slightly problematic academic background. This was a focused task she also completed. During her studies, she learned to break down the various tasks into small, manageable units, just for today, and her success grew, alongside her ever-present fear of failure. If she had formed a plan that included long-term studies from the start, she probably would not have done the whole effort in the first place. Breaking down the task into smaller ones, allows us to rack up achievements, thus changing the story we tell ourselves.

Just for today refers to the way in which we adopt change, and how we work on it. The twelve tools offer us a daily self-check, with each tool covering the specific issue it points to. For instance, if we decided to follow a certain form of abstinence, we will look at how we did at the end of the day, and so on. Thus, with the aid of this daily self-examination, we can develop a deeper awareness and make progress in our efforts for change.

Tool 3 – The serenity prayer

The third tool is the **serenity prayer**. A famous and common prayer, which various "anonymous" support groups from AA onward, have adopted[9]. The GraceWay has also warmly adopted it, to the point of including it as one of its tools. The prayer asks: "God, grant me the serenity to accept the things I cannot change, the courage to change the things I can, and the wisdom to know the difference."

This is a prayer like any other, and as we will see below, the act of praying itself can be used as a tool for change. In addition, the unique form of the prayer offers us a way of looking at the world, which continues and expands the focus of just for today and serves as a plan for personal change.

The prayer begins with an appeal to God, as we understand Him. This very appeal is a declaration to ourselves that we are, in fact, not God. This would seem the most obvious thing in the world, but too often we tend to forget this fact, and as they say at AA[10], we "play God" in our lives or in the lives of others.

Sometimes this is expressed in our demands from others or the world, as "I deserve this", in which we don't really see other people and just "take it" as though it's all ours. "Taking it" does not necessarily mean something physical, it may also refer to things like demanding positive treatment and attention from others, or simply skipping the line, or cheating to get something we want. Sometimes "playing God" is expressed in our excessive striving for control, over other people, over events and situations, over ourselves, over almost everything. It's as though the keys to the universe and its fate were given to us together with divine knowledge.

The appeal to God tells us, regardless of our belief in Him, that we, the individual striving in this world to improve our condition, are not God. We can let go of that and loosen our grip.

The second part of the prayer offers us a simple distinction. To feel serenity, we must accept something, and if we are not serene, there must be something we are not accepting. For instance, we do not accept our past and try to flee from it, imagine it was different, and so on. Just for today focuses us on the present, and the serenity prayer expands this and suggests we accept the past, even if it wasn't pleasant, was painful or contained missed opportunities.

Similarly, there are many other things we don't accept, trying forcibly to change what cannot be changed, which prevents us from achieving peace. To make the distinction easier, we can say that we cannot change other people, or the world around us, or the future as well as the past, and the effort to forcibly change them only leads to more pain.

Obviously, all these can be influenced, but influence is fundamentally different from the desire to change, as it focuses on the right process rather than the right result. To influence things, we have to accept that we cannot change them, as they are external to us. As the prayer says, we cannot make them into something they are not. In addition, there are things we cannot change about ourselves, despite our strong desire and excessive focus on them, such as our appearance, our family background, and even our traits and tendencies. Paradoxically, their calm acceptance opens the path to personal change.

The third part of the prayer offers us an additional distinction: Change requires courage. Especially when it hurts, we continue with the painful old things because we lack the strength, desire, or belief to change. Courage is needed in order to decide to change, despite all the doubts, hesitations, and dilemmas, and despite the attraction of the known and familiar past.

While examining ourselves honestly, we will discover that there is always – yes, always – something we can change, and this is how we react to a given situation. Even if the options for changing our behavior are limited, and even when there is some trait or tendency that we cannot change, we can always change how we react to them, starting right now.

For instance, if we have a tendency to compulsively check if the door's locked after we properly locked it, we can avoid this checking, despite the internal demand to do so. The trait will remain, maybe even the pressure and anxiety, but our response will change, and that's already a lot. After a while, the pressure and anxiety might also decrease and we will heed the internal command to check if the door's locked less, but still return in tense moments in our life. The pressure, the anxiety, and the internal impulse are not in our control, but our response to them certainly is.

Other times, our different response is simply changing the story we tell ourselves, changing how we interpret the world in which we operate, without changing reality itself. We can exchange bitterness and self-pity over our bitter fate in the past, with acceptance of the challenge, deciding to grow from it. We can do the same, for example, with thinking about our parents who we feel neglected us, adopting a new perspective of acceptance and looking at what they did give us.

The summary part of the serenity prayer offers us a distinction between two things we tend to mix together, and ties it to wisdom. A distinction between what can and can't be changed, between what is proper and appropriate for us and what might be attractive, but inappropriate, or a distinction between what's the main thing we should focus on, as opposed to the marginal things we can let go, and so on. The ability to distinguish increases the more we work according to the plan offered by the prayer: Letting go and accepting what cannot be changed and courageously changing what we can at any given time.

The use of the serenity prayer, as a tool for change, can vary. Sometimes all that is needed is to repeat it and thus replace a negative and disturbing thought, or a pressuring emotional response, with the positive message of prayer. There are times when the prayer reminds us of its distinction and allows us to change our reaction in real time. Remembering the prayer helps us change the story we tell ourselves, and replace the excuses of "Why not to change" with "How can I change?" In addition, we are advised at the end of each day, to examine ourselves: Where have we tried to change that which we couldn't change? Where did we let go and calmly accept? Where did we not change what could be changed, and where did we succeed in courageously changing? By so doing we will serenely grow, just for today.

Tool 4 – Gratitude

Gratitude is the fourth tool, which also represents a worldview that develops during changes. Gratitude comes in the face of an experience of a specific or general, existential sense of lack which most of us feel. Let's look at ourselves on a typical day, with our typical meetings with others. Let's try and view the moments when we tried to get something from someone, positive feedback, appreciation, affection, or some benefit. Let's also see other situations, where we try to receive something from the world, or are angry when something doesn't work out like we wanted, or fear that something will harm us or that we will lose something.

All of these are situations of lack. We lack something and we are angry. Seeking to feel satisfied by the world or other people, or fear that lack in the future. We experience a certain lack in the present, or a sense that something of ours has been taken away from us, or will be taken from us, and react accordingly. Let's note that lack is always subjective. We experience it depending on our stage in life, while others certainly experience it in different ways. Lack has to do with the story we tell ourselves about ourselves, the world, and other people. But we forget this simple fact; we treat this lack as though it were absolute and objective, and react accordingly with an emotional response, a behavioral response and usually both.

We can see just how much our story of lack harmed and still harms our various relationships, daily functioning, and even our ability to adhere to the principles we believe in, as well as how much this story of lack has to do with an experience of internal compulsion and behaviors driven by painful dependency. Being in the subjective state of lack, is as if we are forced into a particular reaction, behavior, or a series of behaviors, meant to make up for it. Life with a story of lack creates an experience of dissatisfaction which forces an emotional, behavioral, or cognitive reaction. But this is not a necessary experience. Per the distinction offered by the serenity prayer, since the experience of lack is our response to the world, it is always changeable. One of the tried and tested ways to change it, is gratitude.

Gratitude is the search for and the creation of the experience of fullness, experiences in which "I have." We find and experience the pleasant feeling of gratitude or gratefulness when we feel "We have," when we receive something. Since this is also a subjective experience, we can use this tool to create it. When we identify an experience of lack within ourselves, we have the option of immediately searching for something we are grateful for, and give thanks for it in our hearts. Thus, we shape the story we tell ourselves about the world, others, and us.

At the end of every day, we end our self-examination by noting at least three things for which we are grateful. In addition to the pleasant experience of feeling complete and satisfied at the end of our self-examination, this everyday practice of gratitude will deepen our absorption of it, which will become easier to find gratitude even in times of distress. Over time, gratitude becomes an internal experience which emerges even spontaneously, then we experience grace for which we can also feel grateful.

While practicing gratitude, we usually think of something good that happened to us, or was given to us. It's great for a start, because this is a change in tack – we no longer take something good that happened to us for granted – yet we remain dependent on something external we have received. Over time, gratitude can become an experience which stands on its own, independent of anything external – we are grateful by our very existence, and gladly so, not because we remembered something we received. This is spontaneous gratitude, which becomes a worldview and a way of life.

Accordingly, the "addressee" of gratitude changes during the process. In the beginning, gratitude is directed toward those we believe did us a favor or kindness. Sometimes gratitude is directed toward ourselves, for something we succeeded in doing. Over time, gratitude is directed toward God, as we understand Him, which strengthens the humility developing within us. We are grateful to God, asking for nothing in return for this wonderful experience. The very sense of gratitude, the ability to be satisfied in almost any situation, is the most rewarding result.

Tool 5 – Distinguishing facts

As we progress in describing these tools, we can see that there is a gap between the factual reality in which we live, and the story we tell ourselves. In effect, we live our story, which includes a subjective reality and our interpretation of it. We react to our story about the world, not the world itself. Almost all of us do, sometimes more and sometimes even more. But the greater the gap between our story about reality and the facts revealed to outside observers, the greater the potential for our clashing with others and the world, for misunderstandings, mistakes, errors in communication, harm to relationships and greater suffering.

Every tool tries in its own way to close that gap, and the tool of **distinguishing facts** does so directly, allowing us to recognize the plain facts as much as possible, with fewer masks and subjective interpretations. The tool offers us to examine the main areas of our life where there might be a burdensome gap between our story and the facts of reality. With that examination and identification comes the ability to change and act in a way which is in line with the facts.

The first such field is the distinction between pain and suffering. Pain exists in the world and within ourselves alongside pleasure and happiness. Pain is inevitable. It is a natural experience, part of the human fabric. Pain is a feeling, physical or emotional, in response to an external or internal stimulus (say, a blow or hunger or loss), with almost always a painful stimulus in our surroundings. Suffering, by contrast, is our interpretation of reality. It is usually an interpretation of pain which came from a clear cause, and sometimes an interpretation of pain whose cause is unknown, or even without any initial painful stimulus.

Suffering is our story about reality, painful or not. Pain cannot be entirely prevented, despite our natural and understandable desire to be free of it. Pain can and should be relieved, we can and should reduce or minimize it and even prevent it partially or temporarily, but it will probably still appear at one stage or another, and at some level of intensity, as it is an inseparable part of human existence.

As opposed to the inevitable pain, suffering is our own "masterwork", which we can strive to do away with. And until we enjoy the wonderful grace of suffering's disappearance, we can work to reduce, minimize, relieve, and most of all ignore it. Because we "feed" suffering by paying attention to it, the moment we "starve" it, its place in our lives will shrink.

Paradoxically, the desire to remove and eliminate pain, a logical and natural desire, is in fact one of the biggest contributors to suffering. The opposite is also true, and the more we accept the fact of pain, and continue on our way to do what needs to be done to relieve and most importantly not make a big deal of it, our suffering will lessen. The very distinction between pain and suffering is a welcome change which brings about an increasing ability to ignore suffering until the day of grace in which it will disappear entirely, even though pain, even very strong and acute, will still be a possibility.

The gap between our story and the facts of reality are clearly seen in our emotions and thoughts. Due to a range of factors, past habits, strong influences, inborn traits, karma[11], fate, and even biological structure, every one of us has a specific emotional system that reacts to the world, as well as a specific thought system, and both react to each other, thought to emotion and emotion to thought, with both often reinforcing one another.

Emotion can derive from a prior thought, or can similarly create an almost nonstop stream of thoughts. In any event, the more we become mired in our thoughts or emotions about reality, the more we move from reality itself. In moments of pain, emotion and thought will tend to invoke typical interpretations of a particular stimulus, usually, interpretations which increase suffering, and in moments of pleasure and satisfaction, that stimulus will produce different emotional and thought-based interpretations.

In the spirit of the serenity prayer, the very acceptance of the fact that our emotions and thoughts are in fact a colorful story about a reality which seems to be different, leads to change. As we progress, we understand that there is one fact which is not our changing story: the fact that we feel and think. This is the human structure of our consciousness, with thoughts and emotions forming and running it.

The content of the emotions and thoughts themselves is fickle, ever-changing, and dependent on many factors, known and unknown to us, and is not necessarily related to the reality to which we are responding. Put simply, the fact that I was angry at someone says very little about that someone and their behavior, and more about my reaction. Although my anger is trying to convince me that it's all their fault. The anger is my creation, working together with many factors. The distinguishing facts tool teaches us this fact and offers us a daily examination of the emotions and thoughts that manage us, so we can learn to recognize the facts.

Another field this tool offers is the distinction between what is ours and what is the emotion, thought, or behavior of someone else. It turns out, while examining ourselves that we tend to confuse between what is ours and emotions, actions, situations, or the opinions of someone else. Thus, if someone speaks to us in anger, we automatically react to that anger, perhaps becoming angry ourselves, and thus turn his anger and behavior into ours. Someone else tells us their bad opinion of us, and we react as though our entire life depends on changing their opinion. Distinguishing facts, the knowledge that any behavior, emotion, or response to someone is theirs, allows us to take responsibility and ownership of our response, freeing us from an automatic reaction. Many possible ways to respond then open up before us, which are ours, including defending ourselves if need be.

Tool 6 – Being positive

Life is often challenging. It leads us to struggles which seem more than we can handle. We want to act in a certain way, but feel an inability to do so, which paralyzes us. Our mind is filled with pessimism, lack of faith in ourselves, and negative emotions or thoughts which overwhelm us. Thoughts of lack, accompanied by an appropriate emotion, reinforce each other, and become a self-fulfilling prophecy. When this happens, thoughts of lack, "I don't have," "It won't work," and so on, seem to be the reality itself. But this is of course a distortion of reality, whatever it is, and is indeed a negative story we tell ourselves.

It is a story we can and should stop, replacing it with a positive story, as made possible by the **being positive** tool. This tool teaches us how to strive to fill our mind with the positive, while dealing as little as possible with the negative, even if the negative tempts us with some dubious and momentary satisfaction. The tool is meant to ensure that in every situation, no matter how burdensome and stressful, it will be both possible and worthwhile to find something positive from which to grow. When we delve deeper into this tool, it offers us something else, a mind free of any interest, without any story. It is probably the most positive mind we can strive for, one which is hardly present when not needed, and which appears in positive form only when necessary.

The being positive tool can be joined with another tool, such as the distinguishing facts tool. When a negative emotion takes over, we can tell ourselves that it's just an emotion, perhaps painful, but passing, rather than a fact. Instead, we can opt to practice gratitude, which fills our mind with the positive. We can regularly practice abstinence from the negative message presently in our mind, and look at how our day went at the end of each one, and so on.

One of our most common negative mental messages is complaints. Almost all of us, with impressive frequency, tend to complain about many things in the world, as well as about ourselves. A complaint contains dubious momentary pleasure, but it tends to perpetuate negative thoughts. When dealing with something negative like a complaint, the negative focus clings to our mind and takes over. Therefore, the being positive tool proposes that we steer away from complaints, even in our hearts. It seems impossible at first, but once we get used to it – great relief results. Over time, we learn how to give others suggestions on how to improve without complaining about them, discovering that it's easier for us to positively influence them this way, in addition to the beneficial influence on us.

Instead of complaining, or any other pessimistic thought involving lack, the tool suggests we repeat a particular positive sentence in our mind: "I have, and I need nothing from them." "I have" – this is a fact, as from the very fact that we exist and we already have - something, anything. We have existence, and we do not need it from anyone. This is spiritual existence, which goes beyond the limits of the physical body, and is not dependent on others. We have God, as basic knowledge, as an absolute fact, and we are therefore not dependent or in need, whatever happens in a changing world. Everything passes, anyway, including the temporary lack. All except the eternal, the divine. Therefore we have it, and it does not depend on others as such.

Similarly, the sentence "Be the grace we want to encounter" is a positive message which reminds us, like the serenity prayer, that we can choose our response at any time, for instance, to try for a moment to be and live the grace which we yearn for. No matter what happens, we aim for the grace and live with it, just for today, and so also reveal it, even in moments of distress. The world and its inhabitants can take almost anything from us that is in or belongs to the world, except for us and the ability to be, despite it all, the grace which we aim for.

Part of being positive is to choose the influences we are exposed to, or our teachers for life. The being positive tool offers a number of aids to continue and choose the positive story we tell ourselves. To start with, we should of course move away as much as possible, from negative influences – people or situations which push us away from the grace we are aiming for. Instead, we should seek out the places and symbols which had a positive influence on us. These will help us continue in the direction we wish, with the process of change which we can remember in moments of distress, letting them fill our mind with their positive influence. Similarly, we can remember positive people in our lives, if we can actually get close to them, great, and if not, we can reach them in our mind, through the story we tell ourselves, and grant them an important place in it.

Tool 7 - Finding in ourselves

The tools presented so far, showed us an important fact which becomes clearer the more we progress: We are strongly influenced and even controlled by the outside world, through our attitude toward it and the story we tell ourselves about it, as well as our own desires from this world. It seems that everything in our mind, emotion, passion, sense, or even thought, have a reference point outside ourselves and reflect the influence of the outside onto us. This includes people, relationships and things in the world (such as property), and at this stage on our path, even God. Something which is outside us and serves to stimulate an internal process. We react to this external object, tell ourselves a story about it, and are stimulated by it. Sometimes even our attitude toward ourselves is almost like we were from the outside world, such as when we make ourselves into an object of anger, blame, arrogance or complacency.

The tool of **finding in ourselves** guides us to find something internal, free of outside influence. What is it? When we begin our examination, we discover, sometimes as a very pleasant surprise, that there are many such options, all of which direct us to an internal anchor. For instance, a strong intuition which can direct us if we listen to it. Another, deeper thing we can use is self-awareness, which is not the story we tell ourselves, but rather the observer, narrator, and listener to the story. In other words, awareness which is not specific mental content, but rather that which views all the contents changing in the mind, those more pleasant and less so, and which is always separate from them. These contents, the different stories and our reactions to encounters with the world, are always changing. Their nature is change. But basic awareness, the being of the internal self, is always there. Even before we were born and after we have departed here on our path. Even when there is no content in the mind, such as during a deep sleep, there is always a sense of continuum, more precisely, the knowledge of a continuum, to which we awaken.

The GraceWay and especially the tool of finding in ourselves guides us to learn that continuum toward that self-awareness. The internal awareness which for us is infinite, connects us to the deepest experience of "I have," which is why remembering it brings the most basic positivity for us. The world cannot harm it, and we can only occasionally forget it. And then we remember, sometimes with the aid of this tool.

Despite the existence of an internal anchoring point, which is pure awareness, free of changing circumstances and only aware of them, we sometimes move away from it to a point where we cannot find it or get close to it on our own. In these cases, the tool of finding in ourselves offers us something else, vital, which is the ability to find the internal strength to ask for help from the right person. Asking for help in moments of trouble and distress, or even openly sharing our troubles with others, are actions of self-reliance, as we are no longer interested in continuing to suffer our burdens, and subsequent actions are called for to cope with the same, and instead enlist the aid of someone who can help us achieve this change. An honest request for help breaks down the wall of isolation which distress creates, as well as the pride that tends to accompany it, and brings us closer to our shared humanity. The beneficial influence of someone positive is wonderful, and it is sometimes which enables us to find the change and stick to it.

Tool 8 - Truth only

Along our winding road, we see more and more how easy it is to deceive us, and how much we confuse facts and illusions of our mind. The various tools direct us, at increasing levels of resolution, toward something which is always present, beyond our self-deceptions. That thing is nothing less than the truth.

What is truth?

In our daily life, we cannot know what truth is, since we live the story we tell ourselves about ourselves and about the world. In moments of distress, our story makes itself felt even more strongly, while the truth is even less visible to our eyes and our mind. Hence a strange view develops and passionately argues in the postmodern world, according to which there is no single truth, only " each one and their truth," meaning each one and their story, which is their subjective reality.

This view presents itself as though it is an objective truth, as though the fact that there is no objective truth is itself is an absolutely objective fact, an obvious internal contradiction. The way of the spirit, by definition, refers to the one, unchanging truth as the basic reality which can be exposed and revealed, despite our limited ability to know it. The tool of **truth only** offers us an attractively simple option: To speak and act only truthfully, which will bring us closer to the truth and free us from the deceptions and illusions of the mind. To encounter the truth we strive for, the tool suggests we live with it and cling to it as much as possible, despite the many stories we tell ourselves.

How do we do that? We try as much as we consciously can, to speak truth, only truth, and also act truthfully. We will avoid making false displays and not consciously deceive or cheat people. We will not fudge the truth. We will remain true to our word, keep our promises, try and be precise in our actions and words, softly, gently, happily. And if we don't succeed? It's not the end of the world. We'll fix it, admit our deception or mistake, and try to succeed again tomorrow.

A daily examination of ourselves will strengthen our ability to calibrate the true scale for weighing our decision-making processes, and also develop our sensitivity to the truth. The more we become used to the truth the more we will discover that we are enjoying the internal freedom and tranquility that comes with it. In addition, the world's ability to deceive us recedes, as it relies on our various self-deceptions to aid it.

When we adhere to truth unconditionally, as a categorical decision, our resolution will be challenged by the trickery of life, which will surprise us as much as possible to get us to dilute our decision. Painful as it is, that trickery actually helps us, the more we meet its challenge and learn that we can stand ever more firmly in the face of the deceptions of life, the more we realize just how great a gift it is, that which we can give to ourselves at every moment.

Tool 9 - Choosing in advance

The GraceWay guides us to live in a state of increasing internal freedom, independent of the circumstances of life. This internal freedom is expressed in our choice, when faithful to the path and decisions we have taken. Choice that takes reality into consideration but is still free of dependence or dictates, or the influence of changeable pains or pleasures. It is a spontaneous choice freed of the mechanism of an automatic response to any given stimulus.

The tool of **choosing in advance** helps us sharpen and develop our ability to make choices. To reach that point, the tool offers us a habit which we can and should practice every day, drawing up a short work plan for the following day as part of our daily self-examination. Such a plan, simple, soft, flexible, adapted for predictable and not so predictable circumstances, serves as a fence with resting posts for us to lean on, at stages in our life with strong side winds which are trying to divert us from our path. The fence is the plan we have jotted down for the next day, and the posts are the advance preparations we have made for those challenging moments we expect .

For instance, a man comes twice a week to pick up his son from his divorced wife, the mother of the child, was almost always short-tempered, finding himself swept up in a petty argument with her. To prevent this, he preplanned these days and included a number of interim moments. For example, when he was in the car on the way, he cleansed his mind with a brief meditating exercise, reminding himself of the wish not to end up in another fight, and only then he goes to pick up the kid. The debates and fights stopped almost immediately.

Similarly, we can choose paths of action in advance, deciding that whatever happens, we're sticking to the plan as much as possible. This will help us advance with tasks we tended to put off, and keep us moving in the direction we wish to go. A plan of action established ahead of time, allows us to break free of automatic responses to changing internal and external stimuli, without losing ourselves to one of the mental deceptions which harm our freedom to choose.

In addition to the daily plan of action, it's a good idea every so often to stop the general flow of our life and ask ourselves: Where it is going? Are we living the life we wish to live? When and how are we expressing the grace we wish to encounter, and when are we less successful at it? Such an examination will help us define possible and desirable goals, as well as a periodic plan of action for achieving them.

Another aspect of the tool is its proposal that even this very moment be chosen. I described the plan of action as a fence with resting posts. But a fence also has openings where unexpected influences might penetrate. If we made a decision to adhere to certain rules of behavior, those defined by other tools – such as truth only or abstinence from certain behaviors, we also have the ability to choose in advance at any challenging moment, with its surprising influences. The aim is to create a mindset for ourselves which examines and knows every small step we take, and can guide it – softly and gently – toward where we wish to be. It is choosing this moment in advance, this present step for life, making use of the just for today tool and honing it to a spontaneous "just for now" tool, which lives the changing circumstances but does not let them divert us from our path. This free spontaneity, which maintains a high degree of awareness and alertness without getting swept up, expresses the serenity prayer – accepting the changing moment and changing our response to it, in accordance with the tools and the path they pave for us.

Tool 10 - Correcting errors

The more we practice the different tools and try to apply the principles of the GraceWay in our lives, the more we develop a new, deep consciousness with a new set of priorities, with spirit at the top of the list. The aim to be the grace we wish to encounter, including insisting on truth, as well as taking notice of the facts and the ability to find within the be positive, becomes a goal toward which we yearn and a strength which drive us, gradually, with greater power than anything else affecting us. Our perspective and vantage point - together with our proportions regarding life, also reflect this developing yearning, which leads us to change our interpretation of the world. We are more aware of what delays and even blocks us and are ready to work to break free of both.

This is what the **correcting errors** tool is for, offering us a new perspective on our actions in terms of correct and incorrect, as well as a new response to our relationship with others and the world. The tool's emphasis is that when we operate based on self-centeredness, past habits, or internal compulsion, there is a chance that something in our actions will harm others or the world, use them for our benefit, or simply ignore their benefit and wellbeing, which is worth fixing. Self-correction is vital so that we can be and live grace. Correcting our mistakes with ourselves is made possible by the other tools, and this one places more of an emphasis on correcting things vis-à-vis others and the world.

We can say in general that there is hardly any spiritual path which does not take note of the need to correct mistakes, especially between us and others, or not offer means of doing so. The steps program, for instance, stresses this in steps eight, nine, and ten[12].

Correcting errors is relatively simple, after getting over shame, pride, or other personal and social obstacles. First, after soul searching or based on sensitivity to the response of the others we hurt, we identify the error itself. If need be, we will ask for help from others to identify the error and what needs to be done to fix it. Second, the error type will guide the manner of correction – we are trying here to fix and return things to where they were before, and even improving them as much as possible.

We can say as a general rule that when we break something, we try and put it back together or recreate it to the best of our ability. In other words, we will try to patch up relations we have damaged, apologize and do what needs to be done so it doesn't repeat itself.

During the process of correction, we will do our best not to examine others and look at the mistakes they made to us. Obviously, we will not allow someone to continue to harm us, but the focus needs to be on fixing our side, not theirs.

The ability to correct errors is a virtue containing sparks of internal freedom. Gradually, with a great deal of patience, we will discover that we are making fewer errors based on past habits, and that we are even more sensitive than ever in identifying any kind of error, even the smallest one, to the point that we can identify an error or harm we do in its very beginning. The day will come when we will be able to identify almost all of them before they start, or when they're really small, and when we don't – we'll keep fixing things.

Tool 11 - Promoting good

A key statement of the GraceWay is that the very fact that we act with grace means we will encounter it. But how do we act with grace? We will know the answer when we remember those cases in which someone else acted toward us in a way that was beneficial. Generally, if we don't have a lot of internal noise, others' good behavior toward us resonates strongly[13]. Our good behavior toward others also resonates within us, and this is the purpose of the tool of **promoting good**. The more our behavior is free of any desire for reward, benefit, or appreciation, or a sense of need or compulsion, when it becomes giving for its own sake, whose sole purpose is to promote good, that's when it penetrates deep inside us.

Good behavior that's free of any expectation of a result, which does not think highly of itself, but which is done naturally and simply, increases good in the world and brings about change within us. The change begins with the very ability to engage in good, pure conduct, and when it deepens even more inside us, it creates joy and a sense of internal freedom. The good we gave someone else comes back to us in a big way, without us asking for it, and the love that awakened within us becomes a possible reality, stronger than the troubles and travails which were or will be. Pain exists in the world and appears every so often, but the strengthening of love through our beneficial behavior, prevents it from becoming suffering.

The tool of promoting good offers us a beacon for benefitting which is being in the world and what's important to us. This intentionality guides us to action, to do the work of increasing good. The focus and action guide and strengthen each other. The tool therefore proposes that we systematically introduce behaviors in our life which promote good, such as regularly volunteering for those who need help. The more we seek out opportunities to increase good, both in our daily life when the opportunity presents itself and in volunteering work, the more the idea will penetrate and become our way of life. A life of grace, which is definitely possible.

There is one reservation worth noting: none of this means allowing others to hurt us. Over time, when being good becomes a way of life, we will dis-cover that this is infectious and that others exposed to this good inflict less harm, at least on us. This is not a promise, because we're not expecting results, after all, but sometimes the grace that does not depend on us spreads through us to others, to everyone's benefit.

Tool 12 - Living the spirit

Applying the tools creates change, sometimes as a revolution and sometimes as gradual evolution. The weak points and weaknesses in general succeed in fooling us or controlling our lives less and less, while the simple spiritual points of truth, love, grace, and freedom are present in moments of choice. The significance of all this is that spirituality has become a way of life, as the **living the spirit** tool suggests. This tool summarizes all the other tools, offering us a clear intentionality at every moment – toward the spirit. Even pain and pleasure can be a reflection of the spirit. Living this way ends the artificial break between matter and spirit. The material of the world is the means we have to live the spirit, and the various tools are our signposts for advancing and operating within a world in which we direct ourselves toward the spirit.

This tool offers us exercises that help us deepen our awareness of living the spirit. The first is contemplation or meditation, meaning a time every day solely devoted to contemplation, with no other activity. This time is generally allocated to the early morning hours when we wake up, waking up earlier especially for this, and also do this in the afternoon. During this time, we sit straight but comfortably, with our eyes slightly or entirely opened, while we focus our mind on the topic of contemplation (a mantra like), which can be in the form of "absolute purity" as proposed by Shlomo Kalo[14].

We will set this time slot in advance, using a timer. Thus, freed momen-tarily from the troubles, joys, and worries of the world, and from any story we have about it, we will try and focus our mind on the subject of contem-plation, clearing it of anything else. Over time, we will gain the ability to live with an ever clearer mind, which will accompany us joyfully through different moments of our life which will bring us closer to live the grace.

Another exercise is prayer. It's possible to introduce prayer in our lives, such as before eating or immediately after waking up. The prayer formula should fit what we want. Prayer is to God, as we understand Him; it is personal and is not dependent on any religious ceremony or tradition. Prayer clears and purifies the mind and creates a mental connection with God, to the point that we will merit living the divine for a moment during prayer. Regular practice of this creates habit and skills, and over time prayer can be at our disposal in different life moments, capable of helping us deal with the various challenges of life's temptations – old habits, strong influences, pain and troubles which still try to trick the mind and take it over. Prayer, and contemplation, help us choose to live the spirit. Gradually, spirit and grace become a reality which we can transcend to our own.

***

The twelve tools offer us a plan for life and help continue on the Grace-Way. Their implementation should be flexible, soft, and adapted to life, "in the spirit of a loving God" as they say in the twelve-step program[15]. Daily practice with these tools supports every process of change and makes a difference. Later on, we will look at other aspects of the way which can help us adopt the tools in our life, and most of all live the spirit and grace, as we would like to.

"Seek the will freed of all will; the longing and the yearning, which rise above all longing and yearning[16]."

CHAPTER TWO

Self-Centeredness: The Root of Powerlessness

Let's begin with a moment of quiet, loosening our whole body into the quiet.

Now let's use our mind to go over every part of our body and where we feel tension, we'll loosen up, gently. We will sink comfortably into our sitting position, letting it all go into the delicate silence that fills our mind.

There's a fundamental term in the twelve-step program, that's shared by most, if not all, spiritual traditions and that is "self-centeredness[17]." This term is fundamental to the GraceWay, describing a way of being, which is important to know and identify in order to be able to transcend it. Being the root of various states of powerlessness and indeed of most of the behavioral and emotional disorders, it's significant.

When we transcend self-centeredness, we live and act through grace and experience it in a way that works for both our benefit and those around us. All the spiritual traditions offer different ways to identify self-centeredness, with the aim of breaking its grip on us.

What is self-centeredness?

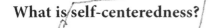

Is self-centeredness just another way of saying egotism or selfishness? The answer is both yes and no. Yes – egotism, in the common meaning of the term, is a prominent form of self-centeredness. When the ego is in the center, a person is certainly focused on oneself. But self-centeredness is a broader term, including situations which do not seem to involve selfishness.

For instance, someone who has a tendency to please others, seems to be the opposite of selfishness. Yet, it involves a high level of self-centeredness, as the person is focused on a positive result or the fear of a negative response toward him. If someone collapses into themselves out of anxiety or depression, they are also very self-centered, but are not behaving in a way we would consider selfish.

Self-centeredness includes a wealth of different situations with differing degrees of selfishness, with something they all share: We are largely focused on ourselves, either in a way that we experience as positive – e.g., our success or power, profit or pleasure – or in a way we experience as negative – e.g., fear, failure, distress, suffering, or anger, and everything in between. The content is secondary to the process which is at the focus – not "what," but "how."

Below, we will speak of self-centeredness as though it has a life and ambitions of its own. We should note that this is only a figure of speech for demonstration purposes; there is no such entity as "self-centeredness," nor is it a personality trait. The expression refers to a process, our changing situation at different moments.

Aside from a few chosen individuals, almost all of us are focused on ourselves to one degree or another. Despite this universality, there are things we can do. The basic claim of the GraceWay is that self-centeredness is actually the root of all our and others' suffering, and that even if things are good for us now, self-centeredness is potentially destructive. In any event, self-centeredness is a barrier on our path to progress through the GraceWay. This view is shared by all traditions focused on the spirit. Most well-known writers on spiritual traditions speak of self-centeredness and especially on how to transcend it – the essence of the spiritual path, each path and its unique approach. The life stories of people who walked or are still walking on the spiritual path describe a stubborn fight against self-centeredness with an increasing ability to identify and transcend it in "real time[18]." Paths which only claim to be spiritual, tend to compromise on self-centeredness and even strengthen it at certain moments. By contrast, a true spiritual path does not compromise on self-centeredness, and guides us onto a journey which leads from self-centeredness to spiritual realization. We can illustrate this statement with a simple formula, per which a person's perceived value is inversely proportional to his self-centeredness[19]:

$$\text{Human Value} = 1 \: / \: \text{self-centeredness}$$

Per this formula, a person's perceived value is greater the lower their self-centeredness, and vice versa. In moments where we decrease our self-centeredness to the point nearing[20] zero, we strive – mathematically and practically – toward the divine. That's where the grace lies. By contrast, in moments of increasing self-centeredness, our perceived value always declines. If we wish to encounter grace, the way to do so is to give up on self-centeredness as much as possible, or at least transcend it to the point of its disappearance for more and more moments.

How can we do that? This is what the GraceWay focuses on, as do other paths. It's what the twelve-step programs are all about. A critical stage in transcending self-centeredness is getting to know and identify it. Being acquainted with its appearances and tricks allows us to identify it even when it tries to camouflage itself. Then we are able to make a choice: stick with it, as we have until now, or transcend it, thus becoming – even for a moment – the grace we wish to encounter. It's encouraging to know that this is a possible choice for us at any moment, including this one right now.

A range of self-centeredness

All known behavioral or personality disorders contain an element of intense self-centeredness. A high level of self-centeredness is a universal human condition, present in circumstances and people entirely different from one another, who face different challenges of one kind or another.

It's relatively easy to see the self-centeredness among those who tend toward criminality or violence, or addicts. In every behavior which openly harms or endangers others or the society, indeed in all behaviors in which someone tries to dominate others, get some benefit out of them, fight them to remove a threat, or the like, we will see a visibly prominent level of self-centeredness. There are people among us for whom this is their way of life or primary trait. They seem to have a tendency toward a particularly high level of self-centeredness.

An elevated self-centeredness can also be found in people who were harmed to the point of trauma and are mired in what is known as a "victim identity[21]" or post-traumatic stress disorder, or among those who tend to collapse into states of depression, anxiety and the like. For some of them, self-centeredness will also be marked by acts of self-harm or harm to others.

There are people whose self-centeredness is usually pretty average but sometimes, in circumstances unique to them, a high degree of self-centeredness bursts forth and dominates them, leading them to engage in unusual behaviors. In extreme situations, such self-centeredness can happen to almost anyone. *judging less*

Self-centeredness is how we exist in the world. Its frequency and intensity can change depending on the circumstances. For instance, someone on their journey of self-awareness and gradually succeeds in transcending self-centeredness, but when the self-centeredness returns and dominates, its power is as intense as a terrifying storm. Someone else could be less successful in transcending self-centeredness, but still doesn't fall into a deep abyss of destructive self-centeredness.

How, then, can we measure the intensity of self-centeredness?

*prayer – bring them everyth I don't
that to you want for your life this.
Let go of Resent → Acceptance*

The answer is that we don't measure it. We assess, and sometimes we are off in our assessment. How do we make assessments? Mostly from the way a person behaves and less from the content of their behavior. For instance, we can clean the house with happiness and a sense of fun, or we can do so indifferently and even under protest. The same behavior can thus be done in different ways and with different levels of self-centeredness. With a bit of honesty and a lot of practice, we can properly assess our self-centeredness. The process of honesty is fairly circular – the more we manage to transcend states of self-centeredness through practice, the more we can see it and understand our need to transcend it.

Diagnosing self-centeredness is different than diagnosing based on symptoms or well-known personality structures. What we propose here is simplicity in self-assessment which can help us both avoid excessive self-analysis and understand what we should do, with the aim being to learn in order to change. Based on this examination, we can identify our own range of self-centeredness in reference to our motives, choices and actions, at different moments and in different life situations . We thus have a ceiling representing our exalted moments, when we are relatively distant and freed from the burden of self-centeredness, and almost entirely live the grace which we want. But we also have a floor representing the moments when we didn't want to or failed to find grace within us, when self-centeredness ran our mind and our life. This is the range of choice which everyone has, as described by Rabbi Eliyahu Dessler[22] – between high and low self-centeredness.

The Bhagavad-Gita similarly describes a low to high range of self-centeredness[23], a description typical of most spiritual traditions. A study which formed the basis for Jewish criminology, for instance, presents a pyramid-shaped model of progress, which is also based on the movement from high self-centeredness, represented by the base of the pyramid, to its reduction up to transcending it, represented by approaching the pyramid's peak[24].

Between these two extremes we mostly have average states of self-centeredness in our daily routine. Within this range, we can identify our

Not Need them to be a certain way
[Personal investment]

"weak areas," areas of life in which our self-centeredness is relatively high. We can also identify "wellbeing areas," situations and areas in life where we transcend self-centeredness. This self-examination helps us see the need to transcend self-centeredness as a default state, and know how to avoid it in those situations in which we typically experience an increased level of self-centeredness. On this basis we can try to improve and grow toward grace, leaving behind our self-centeredness.

One expression of a high level of self-centeredness in our lives is a state of powerlessness. In these situations, we find ourselves acting as though some force greater than ourselves, has taken hold of us and is now directing our actions. Powerlessness is usually marked by our emotional experience – there is an emotion which has overwhelmed us and acts as a force greater than ourselves. Even our thoughts can do the same in a state of powerlessness, taking over our mind and leaving us unable to stop or break free.

Powerlessness can be a regular, powerful part of our lives, in cases where we have a prominent, repeat dependency, a behavior we repeat compulsively, or a thought that will not leave us. But a state of powerlessness can also occur, for various reasons, at a bad time. In such a case, including as a response to something outside us, there is a prominent foundation of self-centeredness, which we will expand on below. If we identify states of powerlessness of varying kinds within ourselves, we can also identify self-centeredness. Naturally and simply, moving beyond the latter also takes us beyond the former, then we experience it as liberation.

Similarly, continual transcending self-centeredness allows for liberation from most – and perhaps all – known behavioral and personality disorders, which also express states of powerlessness. At least at the moment of transcending, these disturbances are not relevant to our existence or functioning in the world, and we rise above them. A similar argument was made by AA members regarding alcoholism[25]. Other Anonymous groups make this argument, related to the specific problem they focus on[26]. Here, I made the argument as a generalization regarding the essence of the different disorders, all of which contain a prominent element of self-centeredness. This is why the twelve-step program was defined from its initiation, as a journey of self-liberation, moving closer to God as we understand Him, and the GraceWay entirely adopts this definition.

Sounds simplistic? Yes, it is pretty simplistic, or better still, simple. But this is not a flaw – on the contrary.

In the philosophy of science, simplicity is something to strive for[27]. A saying, apparently mistakenly attributed to Leonardo da Vinci, argues that "Simplicity is the ultimate sophistication[28]." The GraceWay also strives for simplicity, indeed it is part of its charm. Despite this, it's not that simple to break free of self-centeredness, and it does not happen without a painful struggle. Although we need to transcend self-centeredness in order to break free of the pain and distress of various behavioral and personality disorders and bad habits, it's relatively rare to see people who really accomplish this and find grace while in a state of distress.

There are great barriers which prevent us from breaking free of self-centeredness, chains which bind us to it. It means to effectively fight ourselves, even cutting into our own body. Personality and behavioral disorders, for instance, express a high level of self-centeredness which also bind us to it, and is another aspect of powerlessness. We therefore need an external means to help us break free from the vicious cycle, such as the spiritual exercise offered by the GraceWay and the twelve steps. The simple practicality of the tools ignores the definitions of personality or behavioral disorders, and allows us to transcend self-centeredness even when we are mired in it.

Once again: Every one of us, in every situation, has some level of choice with which we can transcend self-centeredness; we usually do not act on it, allowing the self-centeredness to dominate us and choose for us, even convincing us that our choice was our own, freely made. It is in this broad context that the Indian thinker Kirpal Singh wrote: "The call comes to the many; but few choose to be chosen[29]." Unfortunately, for the many self-centeredness makes the choice. How does it happen to us?

The development of self-centeredness

Congratulations – a baby's been born, and there is much joy. The soul in the baby's body chose to inhabit it in accordance with its fate, a new mind is created which is almost entirely self-centered. It might at first somewhat recall where it came from, but this new mind quickly forgets the soul that is the basis of its existence, and it is as if everything has started anew. Extreme self-centeredness is a necessity; the born baby has no way to survive in the world if it is not sensitive to its every need and does not express these needs as loudly as possible. Since it is still physically limited and lacks the skills to encounter the needs of the world and life, it sees the world through the immediate gratification of its various needs, which is excellent. Its world is also viewed through pain and threat, which is also an approach appropriate for its development stage.

If the baby is fortunate, its parents are focused on it and sensitive to its needs, protecting it from threats and pain. It has many moments of satisfaction and can grow up into a safe experience in the world. In moments of satisfaction and security, it's easy for the baby to forget itself entirely, and then self-centeredness, meant to help its survival, ostensibly disappears. This is part of the baby's charm.

The born baby is in a state of survival in which self-centeredness is a vital means for ensuring existence. Self-centeredness is thus linked to survival. When it seems that our existence is in danger, self-centeredness is high, and in states of high self-centeredness, we experience a survivalist need. It does not matter what led to what; high self-centeredness and a perceived great need for survival go hand in hand from infancy. If all conditions in early childhood are appropriate, there is no reason we do not gradually transcend this perpetual sense of need for survival and self-centeredness. But if something goes wrong, as it often does, we end up stuck in survival mode into adolescence and maturity. Most of us have some sense of an existential-survival level challenge, conscious or not, expressed as a self-centeredness challenge.

The more the baby grows to become a child, teenager, and adult, so does the ability to survive in the world, grow stronger – if growing conditions are sufficiently good, of course. A characteristic of proper growth is a better ability to take responsibility for oneself and effectively also a greater ability to choose. For instance, the child learns to choose their own clothes (at first, also ones which are less appropriate for the weather…), can dress themselves, and ultimately go off to school and then to college by themselves. They decide, as adults, what to do for a living. If at this stage they are still not independent to make their own choices – then something is unusual and out of place. Proper growth is marked by the increase in our freedom to choose, and a reduction of the perceived survival mode with its accompanying self-centeredness.

An extent of choice

The process of maturity exposes us to two contrary options: The first is growth in our ability to be in the world safely along with a growth in our possibilities and ability to choose. The second is remaining in a state of high self-centeredness and survival mode, where it feels as if our options are narrowing, and we are operating out of a sense of necessity and powerlessness.

Survival mode is an experience of "existential anxiety" or necessity, disabling freedom of choice and leading to high self-centeredness. In survival mode, we believe that the world - people, events, even animals – might invade us, harm us, take from us or seemingly swallow us whole. It also seems to us that we have few resources to survive in the face of the challenges of the world and time. In such a state, in which we experience the danger of losing control over what's happening to us and over our lives, we have no choice but to take back control, and all means are considered appropriate to that end.

Alongside survival mode, there is another, equivalent state of self-centeredness – one of physical or emotional gratification or the desire for it. The baby does not just survive, it also grows and develops through its experiences of satisfaction. Its desire for satisfaction is more complex than threats to survival, as it creates the illusion of choice. We ostensibly choose how we achieve gratification and oftentimes it is achieved through the expanding of self-centeredness, to the point of a symbolic "consuming" of others, seen as a means for gratification only.

Such a consuming is prominent in a competitive world in which people do whatever they can to get ahead of others, advancing at the expense of the others' loss. Wherever one person's gain is another person's loss, or is achieved through the use and exploitation of another, a kind of consuming takes place, in which self-centeredness grows and expands. Ostensibly, the spread of self-centeredness strengthens the experience of safety, reducing the sense of danger, giving us the illusion of freedom of choice and action. But the very need for gratification "screams" from within us, forcing itself on us to the point of being choice less, and powerless. Accordingly, we end up perceiving threats to satisfaction as being the same as threats to survival.

Ultimately, survival mode or the possibility of gratification are the same thing – a high level of self-centeredness. This is the essence of high self-centeredness – threat alongside temptation, pain and suffering alongside pleasure and satisfaction. These aren't the usual situations in life, where we can examine possibilities, take survival risks, or defer this or that gratification. When self-centeredness explodes in intensity for one reason or another – when we perceive something to be survival-related or fiercely desire some satisfaction we perceive to be existential – we are driven by the situation which creates imagined necessity. This sense of necessity is false, a habit of reaction developed due to disruptions in our proper development, or to our initial conditions in the world. Our challenge is to grow into grace despite the challenges we experienced, and the habits we developed. This leads to correction, improved karma, advancement of the soul, or however you wish to call it. What matters for our purpose, is that every habit can be changed.

In states of high self-centeredness – and almost all of us still have them – we are easily influenced by any outside stimulus, and believe our response as necessary. In these situations, we are driven believing we lack any choice.

These are states of powerlessness. Sometimes the situation is pleasant and sometimes not so much, but the principle is the same. For instance, when we smell something tasty, our mouth begins to water and we feel hungry even though there is no physiological need to eat at that moment. We are being activated by an outside stimulus, which seems like a real necessity ("I really want it, I couldn't say 'no'"…), and there's high self-centeredness, marked by the burning need for satisfaction. Similarly, when someone acts in a way that angered us, we perceive the situation as a threat, and our furious response looks to remove that threat, a survival-driven response of self-centeredness, which is the only choice we could think of.

The opposite direction is when we transcend ourselves toward God, as we understand Him. Then the world cannot tilt us with the stimuli it offers us, and our freedom of choice becomes complete. In those moments and situations, we have full confidence in God, and the path to him is a bridge beyond any powerlessness – and we react accordingly. The reactions are more moderate and measured, despite the encounter with the necessity of survival, and they are certainly not driven by high self-centeredness.

A basic point for understanding our development is that the more we transcend self-centeredness, so does our capability for choosing to become greater. By contrast, when we are "stuck" in self-centeredness inappropriate for our development potential, our freedom of choice is damaged, leaving us in a deterministic, survival-driven world, whether consciously or not. These are the state of powerlessness which the steps program describes so well. It is between these two extremes that we live and move. We do have the option of directing this movement so we can move closer to focus on God and an increased freedom of choice.

A story of self-centeredness

Is a state of high self-centeredness, where we move between the desire for quick satisfaction on the one hand, and an experience of existential threat on the other, effectively expressing the Id as described by Freud[30]? Is self-centeredness that Id, that basic, primal core of our personality, which is driven by urges and instinct? There are certain parallels – for instance, instinctive, urge-driven action is deterministic, and high self-centeredness is experienced as such. The content is similar, but self-centeredness refers to a broader definition.

Every part of the personality described by Freud, expresses this or that level of self-centeredness – the Id, the rigid "superego," and the ego which tries to mediate between the two. The ego, the center of the conscious personality, is the expression of self-centeredness in everyday situations.

Generally, conventional psychology treats various processes of self-centeredness as the norm, and for some reason ignores the wonderful possibility of entirely transcending from it into the spiritual world. There are of course exceptions, including important mainstream figures such as William James, Carl Jung, Abraham Maslow, Viktor Frankl, and others, who clearly refer to the spiritual dimension[31]. There are also others, especially from the nineties, who address the spiritual dimension of people[32], but everything referring to the psychology of the ego and its internal dynamic expresses the psychology of self-centeredness.

As mentioned earlier self-centeredness is our way of being in the world. This means that it influences every aspect of our life and leaves its mark on it – thought, emotion, desire, and worldview. We effectively live our life being self-centered depending on its degree and intensity. We are "absorbed" within ourselves, in our interests, in our longings, desires and lusts, needs, fears and worries, our disappointments and more.

When we are that absorbed within ourselves, we see, hear, and experience others through our own filter, which sometimes hides more than it allows us to see. We tell ourselves the story of our life as it is controlled by self-centeredness and influenced by its power and appearances, and the degree of our identification with it in general as well as at any given moment. We perceive the world as it views us in accordance with the degree of self-centeredness, thus shaping our story. Thus, we move about the world, focused on ourselves, telling ourselves the story reflected by the self-centeredness, live it, continue to tell it based on the experience we encounter, which is influenced by the way we tell the story, and so on.

Even when we are in ordinary life situations and are not mired deep in the depths of self-centeredness, it still finds expression within us, sometimes powerfully. For instance, self-centeredness is expressed in our self-importance. We treat ourselves very seriously, and expect the same from others. This self-importance is expressed in our emotions, opinions, beliefs, and satisfaction, even when we are not in survival mode. Usually what we are going through is preeminent in our experience, for the simple reason that it is happening to us, and it is ours. "Every man is considered a relative to himself," says the Talmud[33].

Thus, it's possible to view situations where we try to convince others that we are right and debate with them whose view is marginal in our eyes. Although we don't think anything of their opinion, our self-centeredness is targeted toward convincing others to think like us or at least respect our thoughts, which are the right ones. Similarly, we crave respect from others and do a lot to get it – even if we find that deep down, these are people whose respect we really don't care for. But in "real time," we behave in such a way for them to look at us, sing our praises, discuss us, refer to us, as though our fate depends on it, a clear display of powerlessness.

There are cases where self-centeredness leads us to become domineering, manipulative, or worse, so long as our view wins out. For instance, there are those who join organizations promoting peace and goodwill, who in the name of what they think is their just ideology are prepared to fight, smear, and even outright harm any who think differently. The goals may be exalted, but due to self-centeredness the means are far less so, and even harmful to others.

An interesting aspect of self-centeredness in daily life is our demands of others. This can be emotional – demanding respect or attention (as we mentioned above and will expand on below). It can be a demand for a certain behavior toward us. It can also be a demand for thought – specifically for them to agree with us all the time. Such demands are marked by our direct expectations or requirements of others, or could also be manipulative demands made indirectly. For instance, someone who is speaking a lot and slowly, repeating themselves over and over with the self-importance of someone who enjoys being listened to, and who effectively demands it by taking up so much of everyone's time. This demanding approach is also revealed when it does not achieve the desired reaction from others, leading to our responding with offense, anger, withdrawal, or any other dramatic way which expresses our disappointment in not getting what we have expected.

These are everyday situations which don't involve a particularly high degree of self-centeredness. We use the world depending on the caprices of our self-centeredness and the possibilities created by the situation. Self-centeredness is pretty creative in identifying these possibilities, usually without us knowing. Not all of them can be described here, but if we understand the principle, we can identify it in situations that are new to us.

As part of our story of self-centeredness, we are certain that other people are acting based on motives similar to our own. If we are in a deterministic, survival mode, we interpret others as being in a similar state – for instance, we see them as self-interested parties threatening us or seeking to exploit us, and react accordingly. Remember the arguments we use as an excuse in these moments: "The whole world's a jungle," "If we're not the predator, we're the prey"?

When we are mired in the depths of self-centeredness – the other, even a close other, can be perceived as a bitter enemy who wishes us ill. Let's think, for instance, about a couple who supposedly love each other. But then one is struck by a high degree of self-centeredness and is momentarily certain that their spouse is against them wishes to harm them. . Indeed, they cannot see their spouse as being an independent person that can have entirely different motives than their own.

The influence of the intensity of our self-centeredness on how we perceive social situations was demonstrated in a study which found that the level of a person's moral judgment – representing a particular aspect of their level of self-centeredness – influences how they understand the moral judgment of others. People usually understand motives representing moral judgment at their level or slightly higher, but are less understanding of motives which represent moral judgment that is significantly higher than their own[34]. Our reason and ability to understand are limited by our ability to transcend self-centeredness, which reflect our range of self-centeredness.

Transcending self-centeredness

Self-centeredness is thus, the state of being of all human beings as such, aside from those few unique individuals considered saints of one form or another. It's fair to ask: since this is common by practically everyone, and since this is apparently natural, what's so bad about it? Eventually, it's a matter of personal choice, so long as no-one is hurt. But the question is actually different, and goes beyond the issue of good and bad – how do we wish to live our life? Are we comfortable with the idea of being dominated by self-centeredness lacking all grace? To be tossed about into delicate situations of powerlessness?

The view of all genuine spiritual traditions – not those which simply pretend to be spiritual - is that self-centeredness is a painful handicap which hinders our spiritual progress, and we should do everything we can to transcend it. Indeed, they have a simple, common saying as to what constitutes moral behavior: Observing values and simple rules of behavior ("abstinence" – the first tool) aimed at transcending self-centeredness is a basic component in spiritual development.

We obviously need to stress that this means that everyone maintains their own morality without forcing it on others, coercion that demonstrates high self-centeredness. As we said, our moral judgment represents a certain aspect of our self-centeredness, and cognitive-behavioral psychology made a number of interesting and relevant discoveries in this context.

The first is that there is a developmental process, shared by different people in different cultures, which starts with the high self-centeredness of the baby. While acquiring cognitive and other skills, the maturing child can understand the world and human situations in such a way as to gradually reduce their self-centeredness, as noted above.

The second is that there are known stages in the development process. A person who starts with high self-centeredness, and who primarily fears pain and is interested in gratification, undergoes a certain expansion of his own experience to a social sense (self-centeredness of our affiliated group), continues through a readiness to let go of self-centeredness in the face of an external law, and continues on through an understanding of moral principles, which seem to us proper and human and contain reduced self-centeredness, all the way to a complete transcending self-centeredness toward God or a Higher Power which represents pure morality[35].

The third is that a similar process, with differing stages, occurs in a range of similar subjects that have been studied: Moral judgment, developing the ability to forgive, developing empathy, developing altruistic behavior, and even the development of faith[36]. It's also possible that development in one field is tied to development in another, for our ability to transcend self-centeredness is what develops and gradually appears in all areas of life.

What happens when someone who highly transcends their self-centeredness, encounters someone highly self-centered? For instance, when someone gives of themselves to a person who is self-centered in a way that seems altruistic? Does such exposure help the person receiving this goodness also transcend his self-centeredness? We looked at this question in a study conducted with distressed youth, who generally represent relatively high self-centeredness[37], and who were exposed to the good-heartedness of others who volunteered to help them[38, 39].

We observed that the higher the self-centeredness of the youth, the less they noticed that someone was volunteering to help them and who cared for them. There were cases where they really "didn't see" the volunteers, despite their efforts. Similarly, when these distressed youth were given the opportunity to volunteer for others, there were those who felt freer and positively experienced the ability to transcend self-centeredness, even if only a little. But there were others whose self-centeredness was so strong, that even doing good for others made no impression on them.

Our conclusion was that self-centeredness was a conceptual barrier preventing them from seeing something outside their self-centered focus. They seemed to be mired in such a demanding survival mode, a powerlessness so deep, that prevented them from directing attention to something unrelated to that need to survive. Accordingly, it seemed to them that everyone in the world is the same, and they could not see anything else. On the other hand, there were cases where the experience of good was so strong that it broke through the youths' self-centeredness barrier.

We witnessed a power struggle between self-centeredness and exposure to goodness, the ability to perceive goodness and its corresponding conduct. On the one hand, when our self-centeredness is high, it hampers our ability to see good behavior directed toward us. We may benefit from it, but we take it for granted, as though we were entitled to it. We do not feel any gratitude or consider it to be beyond the world order familiar to self-centeredness[40]. But if the giving we receive is strong and continues over time, something in that wall of self-centeredness starts to crack, and then we can see the goodness directed toward us and even be thankful for it[41].

At some stage, such an exposure to goodness can lead to us somewhat reducing our high level of identification with self-centeredness, as we saw a number of times in studies we conducted[42]. This led us to the concept of "perceived altruism," seeing behavior as altruistic by the recipient of the good. We found that this perception could bring about a positive impact upon its beneficiaries. In addition, in moments of relatively high self-centeredness, when we give to others without asking for a return, our own giving can lead to the beginning of a reduction in self-centeredness. Based on these insights from various studies, I defined the concept of positive criminology a number of years ago, a perspective in criminology which studies and activates positive influences which can reduce prominent behavioral disorders and the self-centeredness underlying them[43].

Of all the different breakdowns of human situations, the one relevant here is that between the giving power and the taking power, described with great precision by Rabbi Eliyahu Dessler[44]. The taking power expresses the self-centeredness that wishes to take more and more for itself, to the point that it seems to want to consume the whole world and the satisfactions that it offers, fighting against any real or imaginary threat.

The giving power is the opposite state – it is the aspiration toward love, expressed in the joy of giving to others. A giving lacking any interest or asking for something in return, not even a request for a hidden reward (as opposed to giving in order to appease, for instance). If there is a reward for the giving – great; and if not – also great. Love expresses the peak of transcending self-centeredness, and therefore goes hand in hand with free choice. We have a simple and clear movement – with self-centeredness expressed in the desire to take and a deterministic experience, conscious or not – at one end, and the option of love and free choice, on the other.

To simplify things even more, we add another basic element – the aspiration toward God, as we understand Him. Outgrowing self-centeredness means growing to focus on God. It is a growth by love and into love, since one way to understand God is that God is love, as various spiritual writings have said[45]. In God we find complete freedom of choice, even freed from being ruled by the need to survive.

We have the possibility for a developmental journey which starts with high self-centeredness, that should lessen with our growth and which aims toward the possibility of completely transcending it toward God, as each one of us understands Him. Completely transcending means the end of suffering and more – it is like being reborn into a reality of self-contained happiness, freedom of choice and a giving love.

It sounds great – but what of spiritual men who harmed others? Or when horrible injustices were and are done in the name of religious paths and groups? For instance, teachers considered to be spiritual who were found to have raped and exploited women who believed in them?

These tragic cases do not contradict what I said. On the contrary. They very much demonstrate the power of self-centeredness, which succeeds to produce great injustices in the name of faith and beautiful values, and even God, in order to express a self-centeredness which effectively denies God, no matter how loudly it protests to the contrary.

People who struggle with their self-centeredness and reach a religious or spiritual path and follow its principles, are still bound by the forces of self-centeredness. Sometimes it bursts forth suddenly and sweeps them into an extreme, unforeseen situation. I knew a man who practiced a spiritual path and stuck to it while holding fast in the face of many trials and fighting himself uncompromisingly, until the day he had a particularly destructive outburst of self-centeredness.

Was it a surprise? A little, but even before that, one could detect signs of self-centeredness in him underneath the ostensible progress in behavior. As I said before, it's not the behavior, but how it's done. The "how," not the "what." For him, his behavioral exercises, meant to help him progress and grow, were rigid and domineering, pointing to a destructive level of self-centeredness.

Could the outburst have been prevented? It's possible, if we can see the self-centeredness preparing itself and gently use the various tools in our possession to neutralize its power. In any event, it's highly desirable to avoid generalizing about a spiritual path based on these examples, which show us just how complex we are.

Living the grace we wish to encounter, means living the Divine, as we understand it, while still being ourselves. This is the goal of the soul's journey in this life – to know itself as one with God which is love[46]. The essence of the soul is the self, which lies beyond any self-centeredness. In Hinduism, this is called **atman**, which is one with Brahman, the divinity[47, 48].

To reach the point where this knowledge can be lived, a journey of moving away from self-centeredness, which hides the soul from itself, is needed. The body and the mind are supposed to serve the soul on its journey, to let the soul be their guide. We can compare the body to a carriage hitched to horses with the mind as the driver, and both the horses and the driver ignoring the owner of the carriage – the soul – which alone is supposed to direct the journey.

The journey is for the owner, not the horses or the driver, but they enjoy a degree of autonomy and refuse to accept the soul's authority. A challenging internal struggle is taking place as the carriage is in motion, but in the end, when it comes, the soul gains mastery, as this is the sole possibility and the truth. The soul is our human essence which is equally divine, and transcending self-centeredness allows our essence to reveal itself.

To focus on and move closer to that place beyond self-centeredness, and fix ourselves to move ever closer, we have many methods, including the tools of the GraceWay. The beauty of the GraceWay in my eyes is its simple focus. Therefore, we will practice self-inquiry of our self-centeredness – where does it express itself daily? We will examine ourselves every evening and also try to identify states and processes of self-centeredness during the day, and when we identify them – we will transcend them with the help of whichever tool we find appropriate. That's what the tools are there for. When we identify self-centeredness, we'll decide that we don't identify with it. The moment we call it "self-centeredness," we identify with it less. We'll look at it from the side as we let go of it and its temptations – aware of it, but not identifying with it. The more we cease to identify with the self-centeredness, the more we avoid thinking that self-centeredness and we are one and the same, the more we can transcend it. The rest – is in the hands of God, as we understand Him.

"Have you tried to rise above yourself? – To remove feelings, thoughts, images? To try and be like an infinite space, an eternity without boundaries? If you succeed in this – you will earn a great and delighted surprise[49]."

CHAPTER THREE

Leaving the Serpent's Temptations

Let's take a long moment of silence and delve deep into it. Contemplating on our breath, we let the quite rise by itself within with the breathing cycle which we watch quietly.

Years ago, when I was still involved a bit in NA, I had the chance to participate in a series of workshops hosted by Rachel, a clean addict fully acquainted with the twelve-step program, who studied it in depth, and took part in program workshops, especially in the US. She was also a social worker with experience in working with addicts. One of the concepts I learned from her was the struggle with the "serpent."

This image of the serpent symbolizes the tempting power which rises in our mind and makes us commit to the same mistakes and engage in the same painful habits, despite all our nice resolutions and sincere desire to change. Rachel's concept of the serpent spread to other NA members in Israel, where it was further developed and expanded upon.

I adopted the concept fairly quickly to my twelve-step program and the developing GraceWay, and became acquainted with the advantages it offers. The picturesque simplicity of the image of the serpent sharply and quickly expresses the idea that we do not identify with what is happening to us – it's not us, it's the serpent. But this does not mean casting off responsibility – the serpent is in us and may drive us to act, which is why we must "take care" of it, as we will soon see.

The image of the serpent presents a focused challenge of preventing the serpent from taking over the show, and under no circumstances does it allow "It's not me, it's the serpent" to serve as an excuse. In this chapter, we become acquainted with the image of the serpent and its various components, focusing mostly on what can be done when it takes over our mind, so we can reduce the harm to us and others as much as possible.

A few years after this workshop, when I was already an experienced professional in the field of addictions, I hosted an experiential workshop about the twelve-step program for a welfare unit team dealing with people addicted to drugs and alcohol. I presented them with the image of the serpent, and the term was readily accepted.

In the follow-up meeting, conducted a few weeks later, two therapists told me they chose the serpent as the work topic with patients. As part of group therapy, they hosted an art workshop in which participants drew the serpent and its traits. These participants were usually fairly passive in the group therapy, but the image of the serpent, with its colorful vitality, roused them to activity. The unmediated expression in painting, appropriate for the language of imagery, demonstrated things better than words could. A few weeks afterward, the image was still the subject of group work, and patients could describe how it improved their struggle to recovery.

The serpent is the symbol of everything that wants to bring us down, or leave us stuck in the present state without change, without growth, and certainly without spiritual development.

The serpent drives us down into states of powerlessness. It is like the chief commander of self-centeredness, working within our mind causing us emotional distress and discomfort. It places traps of temptation before us, which we easily fall into in a state of hedonistic happiness, which tends to end less joyfully. At certain moments, it stops us from acting and in others it directs us to act in accordance with strengthening self-centeredness.

The image of the serpent whispering poisonous things to us, is a continuation of its Biblical image from the story of the Garden of Eden. There the serpent takes on the role of the seducer, offering Eve - and through her,

Adam – an offer that cannot be refused "And you will be like God[50]."

Self-centeredness does not need to hear more than that – to be like God? Let's go! That's how the downhill tumble begins, from the hidden desire to be like God and the illusion it gives to be almost like Him, even if for a moment, while we identify with our limited body and mind.

The serpent also fills a role in our reaction – that of self-blame, depression, and despair – as in both cases, it controls us. We'll talk about the movement between these states below, but for now let's delve deep into the image of the serpent. We will present the serpent as a living creature present in our mind, with its own will, ability to act, voice, and most importantly – malicious intent.

The serpent is a poisonous creature, whose bite can be lethal. The poison of the serpent of the mind is lies, deceit, fraud, deception, exaggeration, distortion, absurd appearances, and other states that drive us away from the simple truth. The intuition, untainted by the serpent's poison, knows there is such a truth, despite the common claim today that truth is relative, or that everyone has their own truth, and the like. The claim of relativity best represents the serpent and expresses its poison – it disguises itself as something real and poisons our mind to the point that we believe there is no absolute truth but at the same time perceive this claim to be absolutely true... Truth exists and only our ability to know it so long as we are self-centered is relative and limited.

Usually we know when we are lying, deceiving, faking, pretending, and being evasive about the simple truth. Sometimes the lie is done consciously and intentionally, sometimes there is some uncertainty or a pang of conscience, and sometimes there is a process of self-deception that convinces us why we should lie at a particular moment, and that perhaps it's not entirely a lie, and so on. There are also situations where we are not aware of our lie, and this lack of awareness is a poisonous act of the serpent.

Sometimes we can identify and even stop the serpent's poison from the start, but this becomes harder to change the more it increases. We are weakened by the serpent's poison, which gets stronger and celebrates at our expense.

When we are poisoned by the serpent most of the GraceWay tools can help us. For instance, the "distinguishing facts" tool or the "truth only" tool both neutralize the poison's power. So long as we use them regularly, we have a protective shield against the poison, which will prevent it from penetrating our "blood vessels." But every so often, almost all of us loosen our hold on the tools and everything they represent, or forget them, and then the poison penetrates and corrupts everything it can with its lies.

Why would we loosen our grip on the tools and allow the serpent to poison us? That act of loosening our grip is also a sign of the serpent's successful work on our mind, with the help of hidden methods and agents.

Hidden agents

The serpent, although a poisonous and malicious animal, is also very polite. It cannot spread in a mind which is unequivocally uninterested in its good services. Usually, the serpent identifies some crack we left open in our mind, peeks in politely and asks if it can come in. Even if we are not openly interested in its help, it still shows us some of its amazing skills. Like a merchant at a bazaar, inviting us to enter their shop. Even when we say we aren't interested and aren't buying, it invites and tempts us– don't buy anything, just come in, look around, maybe have some hot sweet chai to drink? And the moment we entered – the store's goods are spread before us in all their glory, and without understanding what happened, we left with lots of bags and a lighter wallet.

The serpent peeks at us and offers us something, very useful for that particular moment, tempting, and if we hesitate, consider, weight the options, it identifies an invitation in this response, which means it's already in. Our hesitance is its hidden agent, waiting for us to open the door from the inside.

There are a few such hidden agents, serving as a fifth column in our minds: **hesitance**, which clings to the serpent's tempting offer and opens the door for it; **doubt,** which succeeds in repressing and silencing all our powers of resistance, brings us to despair with a feeling of having no strength, and removes any opposition with a message of "there's no point" and "no meaning" and certainly "no truth." When doubt appears in the mind - for instance, doubt in grace and the path to it – it's easy for the serpent to suggest ostensibly practical solutions.

An additional hidden agent of the serpent is **self-pity**, experienced as a painful situation which must be solved, and then it seems that the serpent has one to offer – ostensibly. The moment self-pity starts its barrage, the situation becomes intolerable and requires action, and the path for the serpent is now clear, the gate is open, and we are even waiting for it and asking for its help.

Whenever we identify the serpent in our mind, it's clear that we play at least a small part in all this – we either actively invited it, or allowed it to enter and grow inside us. Sometimes we are tempted to invite the serpent temporarily or solely on a case by case basis, and just enjoy a small favor as if to say: "Solve this one thing for me and then leave, kind serpent."

But such a restricted invitation is not possible. Even when it seems to benefit us momentarily, the serpent is no good for us. When it's inside, it runs the show, runs our mind and behavior –not for our own good.

The serpent's gates

The serpent uses a number of typical gates through which it penetrates our mind and injects its powers into it, which increase and multiply the more space it occupies. We will hereafter describe three main gates, which are porous during most of our life and controlled by the serpent's powers.

The first has to do with our power in the world, the second to property, and the third to hedonism and the desire for gratification, especially physical gratification. Oftentimes, the serpent attacks two or even three gates at once, and sometimes when one gate opens, a second will open soon enough.

Let's start with the gate of power, through which all the issues related to our conception of our power in the world enter, including our power of control and our self and social respect.

The assumption of the serpent, the commander-in-chief of the self-centeredness forces, is that we want the experience of power, control, and honor more and more. The serpent therefore does one of the two: It either shows us a threat to that power, control, or honor of ours, which leaves us no choice but to open the gates for its forces to protect us against the outside threat, which we think to be existential, or it shows us that we can "improve our position" of power, control, or honor – and who wouldn't want that?

This is obviously a subjective perspective, and has no relation to our actual power, control, or respect in the world. Even if we have ostensibly been privileged in our life, the serpent can easily make us feel that we don't have enough, that we are truly in danger due to a lack of power, and we should therefore want to secure more, and fast. Most of us can identify times when we enter into power, control, or honor struggles, even, or sometimes especially, with someone close or dear to us, such as between parents and children or intimate partners.

Let us imagine a situation where a father asks a child to do something, and they answer, "In a bit", because they're in the middle of a game. The father gets angry and tells the kid to do it now, "Because I said so." He feels his parental authority is in danger, and begins to fight for it. The fact that it was certainly possible to wait, as the child suggested, is irrelevant to him in this tense situation, as the question now is "who's in charge" – not whether and when the child will do what they were asked.

But who are the sides of this power struggle? The father and his young child? It's easy to assume that such power struggle within the family is common. There are similar struggles in other relationships, in which it seems that someone is threatening to take away our authority, our control, our power or our honor, and we have no choice but to use more of it.

We then appeal with a clear invitation to the serpent: "Welcome, serpent, you are invited to destroy our relationship." That is, after all, what the serpent does – when it enters our mind, it activates destructive means –fights, anger, violence, hostility, which only ensure its continued control.

Sometimes, because of life circumstances and personal history, the serpent succeeds in making us think that we have no power, control or respect, and we don't deserve it and certainly won't gain any – a state of self-despair and despair of oneself. This experience of lack of power is typical, for instance, of those who were harmed in their past by abusive of violent people , usually repeated or extreme violence such as sexual assault.

In a situation where a person surrenders in advance to any power strug-gle, giving up and even appeasing others, flattering them and giving them a sense of power, it would ostensibly seem that the serpent avoided bringing in forces through the gate of power. Eventually, the flatterer or submissive person maintains what little power they have, by giving up in advance, thus cutting their losses and sometimes even "earning" power through identifi-cation with the ostensibly "stronger" party to whom they are so submissive. Through appeasement, these people try to ensure control for themselves and secure quiet and security.

AA gave this a name: "reverse pride[51]." Ostensibly there is no pride here, but in practice this is not true modesty, only a "suffocated" desire for power and honor, driven probably by a past experience of harm. This harm then created a weak point for the serpent to enter unhindered that person's mind through the gate. When it penetrates, even without dragging that person into a power struggle, it can leave them stuck in a harmful relationship, making them repeatedly enter into relationships that are unhealthy for them, prevent them from standing up for their basic rights, and other such destructive results.

The second gate loved of the serpent, which is easy for it to enter, is the gate of property and possessions. The serpent uses the same principle to enter this gate as the previous one: Sometimes it makes us think that there is some threat to our property or our money, that we are in danger of losing it and have no choice but to use its good advice and help to do things like steal, cheat or swindle.

Sometimes it sends us to work more and more as though we face a real threat, when our actual financial situation does not justify that feeling of danger. Other times, it causes us terrible anxiety over our financial situation, that makes us bitter, stressed, fight with our family over money, and more. There are times when the serpent suggests we expand the assets and possessions we have, based on the assumption that we want more and more, and that all we need is the serpent to show us how we can get it.

A common such case is people who evade paying taxes. One example I heard from many people, is that they came to a therapy session and the therapist (this includes a range of therapists from different fields) suggested two payment rates for their service – a higher one with a receipt and a cheaper one without it, thus cheating the tax authority and tempting patients to take part in the fraud.

I assume we've all run into something like this – therapists, mechanics, handymen, or other service providers who would love to not have to give a receipt when they're done. If we ask them, we'll hear a range of colorful explanations, as criminology shows consistently[52], whose message is "why we had to lie" or "why it's very desirable for us to cheat." After the gate has opened to deceit and the serpent does what it wishes to do with our minds, this behavior will very easily repeat itself, in a behavioral spin we'll come back to later[53].

Like reverse pride, we can identify opposite situations at the gate of possessiveness, in which we ostensibly refuse any sort of possessiveness or material objects, to the point of an extremely thrifty and even miserable lifestyle. These are also the works of the serpent, who makes us focus on matters of property, albeit from the opposite direction of the desire to want ever more things. Here, the compulsive flight from property, which seems to deny the idea of possessiveness, is in effect a reverse possessiveness, an excessive dealing in property which has taken over our mind, thus revealing the serpent. For instance, a person who lives an ideologically thrifty life and deals in petty accounting for many hours, even though he could let loose a bit with his actual financial situation.

Oftentimes, there are flanking maneuvers which the serpent conducts to enter two gates at once: For instance, we take pride in our property to feel a sense of social honor, personal honor or control – things like showing off designer brands and the like. Possessions are the metric for personal power and the need for more power directs us to pursue even more of them, and the serpent celebrates, satisfied for its dual achievements ensuring a strong hold on our mind.

Take a young man from a fairly affluent family, but which he believed is not affluent enough. His friends were richer, or so he thought. So as not to feel himself of less worth, he became the generous one of his group and every so often invited everyone to dine at his expense. But it really wasn't at his expense – he found a particular system of fraud where he paid in stolen money. Everything was seemingly good, as he knew that the truth was less pleasant than appearances, and the desire for power wasn't really being gratified, on the contrary. Every so often he experienced a deterioration of his feelings about the social celebration. In time, the deceit was revealed, he was caught and even felt a degree of relief.

This is the relief we get when the serpent disappears momentarily. But it usually comes back, with new proposals. The self-centeredness is still here, hiding on the side of the road and a little ashamed, and this shame might also come from the serpent, the kind of reverse pride we discussed above.

The third gate, through which the serpent sends in its loyal forces, is hedonism. This is expressed in many ways, such as the striving and longing for the pleasant and the comfortable, the desire to do the minimum and enjoy the maximum, and of course, the desire for immediate sensual gratification as powerful as possible.

The same serpentine principle is in effect for all expressions: The desire for more and more gratification and pleasure vs. the fear and threat that someone will take it away from us. We cannot ignore the hedonistic social cultural background in which we live. In our world, there is an emphasis on immediate gratification, the maximizing of personal profit with minimum effort, and fleeing from any pain or struggle which does not pay off. Indeed, in almost every period in history, there was a social message of hedonism. Nevertheless, there is always an alternative teaching. The ancient as well as new spiritual sources continuously direct us to personally struggle with our hedonism, with this mighty gate of the serpent.

The moment our personal serpent starts working in us, the background and direct cause for our preoccupation with hedonistic desires don't matter. Blaming society is just another excuse, provided by the serpent, to flee responsibility, a kind of self-pity which as a I said, is one of the serpent's hidden agents.

The serpent can also work in the opposite direction at the gate of hedonism, directing us toward extreme asceticism and avoidance of anything that seems to be pleasant. Both established religions and their esoteric offshoots, allow for extreme asceticism toward bodily pleasures. People run so far away from them, and so strongly oppose them, that they are effectively obsessively occupied with them, and the serpent ends up having a party in our mind. We see this in the extreme flight from anything resembling femininity, for instance. This is where the gate of power and control can be found, leading to the repression of women by covering them up from head to toe in any weather while men can walk around dressed as they wish.

The excess occupation with asceticism is also expressed in the Talmud's saying that "the voice of a woman is nakedness[54]," without getting into various interpretations and meanings and sticking to the plain meaning of what various people often quote in order to coerce people religiously. It seems that nakedness is present in the mind of those who wish to flee it, and the more they try to flee it through external and coercive forces, the more it surges in their mind, which is another, almost amusing, trick of the serpent, which leads to much pain and suffering.

Different bite methods

The serpent "bites" into our mind. Sometimes this bite is sudden, surprising, intense, poisoning us at once and leading to a rapid deterioration, without our being able to control it. One moment everything was OK, and the next it all became chaotic and even dangerous. Such a bite can mortally wound us. These are usually situations where we were complacent and made one wrong choice, a choice which agreed to a sudden temptation of the serpent, which appeared with a destructive power we could not imagine beforehand – or perhaps did not wish to imagine.

A tragic example is a drug addict prisoner in recovery, who was making good progress at the therapeutic community within the prison. Thanks to his impressive progress he was released on leave and met with his former partner, a woman as addicted to drugs as he was. A meeting, which went against both the advice he was given and his own logic, since their relations were destructive for both. A short time after that encounter, still on leave, he overdosed and died . Tragic and dramatic. It can be quick and destructive for us too even in less dramatic moments. For the serpent – a massive success in the blink of an eye that catches us off guard and complacent.

Another method the serpent uses to bite, seems light and almost un-noticed, with the poison spreading slowly until it brings about the desired destruction. For instance, a fairly common situation in which we made the decision to totally abstain from eating anything sweet. We got the results we wanted and are happy with both the decision and the path.

In time, the serpent offers us something sweet, just once, in a special event. Debating for a while, we ultimately agree to the offer, tasting one small bite of something sweet and pleasant, and that's it. Nothing special happens afterwards, and we go back to abstinence without binging.

After a few days, the thought arises that we actually don't need to avoid the sweet stuff completely. We're in control of ourselves, and if we indulge a little bit, it'll be alright. We take a little bite again, and indeed, everything is still OK. Then again, and it's still OK, and again, and again, and again, and the serpent is inside big time, with abstinence a thing of the past. Slowly, but surely, the serpent dulled our alertness and gradually led us to lose control over sweet things, despite our successful abstinence. It managed to dominate us with a patient, slow approach, almost without our noticing.

Another path the serpent brings us down hard is when it gradually wraps itself around us and slowly lets itself into our mind, but this time without any resulting behavior. We can't really notice it, because we haven't done anything under its influence, but gradually our mind is entirely wrapped around the serpent, until it is ready to make the final twist that threatens to strangle, swallow, or bite us while we are powerless against it.

For instance – and this is not something I heard, but rather a possible story comprised of a number of them – a married man loyal to his wife, who heard from a friend about a pleasure trip abroad. The idea was entirely foreign to him, didn't appeal to him at all. But the idea had already entered his mind. The seed began sprouting. The man took care to water it and cultivate it without being aware that his mind was being wrapped by the serpent.

He started to fantasize about the trip, became interested in possible destinations - in short, he prepared himself, even though he consciously did not actually want it. As time passed his mind was already so flooded with the idea, which has now become a dark forest of passions and desires and not just a small sprout. Later on a more help from the serpent, the time came when he chose the same action he summarily rejected in the beginning. The collapse of his marriage comes next; sometimes this can be fixed and sometimes not. I met a couple which experienced something similar at the very start of their relationship, and they're still together, twenty years later, but the betrayal of one of them still hung between them and exacted a price from time to time.

Other serpentine methods

The aim of the serpent is to take over our mind. It poisons us with the acid of lies, sends hidden agents to make us invite it, and marches its forces through our mental gates. The serpent has a number of effective methods to accomplish this mission. These sometimes seem beneficial or vital for us – but the ultimate result is usually the opposite. Sometimes we understand the undesirable result to be the result of the serpent's actions, leaving us an opening for welcome change, and sometimes the serpent convinces us that it's all because of the world or other people, which leads to continually unpleasant results, to the point that life forces us to change something. There are people who never managed to understand that the serpent is always harmful for us, and that its goal is to embed destructive poison in our minds, which is why it should be avoided as much as possible.

One of the serpent's methods is making plans which include expectations about the world and what it can have in store for us. Expectations are one of our strongest thought distortions, causing us to confuse facts of reality with the expectant imagination. Thus, they cause us to become disappointed with reality, fight it and the people around us to try and bring about the imaginary facts we ostensibly deserve.

For instance, someone expected her partner to invite her for a vacation over the weekend. There could be some justification for this and there could not be. It didn't really matter, since the moment the expectation began to play in her mind, she was already enjoying her dream vacation. Being convinced she deserves that vacation and leisure, any change was perceived as a direct harm to what's hers. It's easy to imagine what happened when it turned out that for one reason or another, justified or not, her partner never made the arrangements.

For the serpent – this was a nice victory with desirable results, such as disappointment, emotional pain, unnecessary suffering, and sometimes even the destruction of a relationship. How nice... therefore, to avoid such an entanglement, it is both possible and desirable to attribute all expectations to the serpent, an attribution which makes sense of the mess. Every expectation is the traces of the serpent, regardless of whether the expectation is justified or not, logical, reasonable, or anything else. If disappointment follows expectation, as is generally the case with expectations, we know it is a trick of the serpent.

In a case where the expectation was temporarily realized and we got the desired result, the serpent will be quick to propose a repeat expectation, or even a bigger one, which means disappointment will come sooner or later thanks to its actions. It's easy for the serpent in both the expectations and disappoint stage, to propose additional courses of action which benefit it, but less so for us, according to the particular gate we opened for it.

For instance, someone expects his friends to show gratitude for something he did – the gate of honor and power opens – the gratitude he received didn't meet his expectations, so he feels disappointment, insult, and is sure he is being mocked, leading him to react with force to "correct" his situation. He quarrels with his friends and the serpent has a ball.

To avoid such results, we can create a generalization per which every plan which contains an element of expectation, binds us to an outcome which we believe is desirable, thus allowing the serpent to take over. With this understanding, it's relatively easy to stop the serpent when it is just beginning to propose some form of expectation to us.

Another tried and tested approach for the serpent to take over our mind is the complication of relationships, especially close ones such as couples, parent-child , siblings or relationships within the broader family, as well as between friends or in the workplace.

For instance, Meirav – a nice women in her late twenties, then single and living alone – has a good friend, and they share personal information with each other. They would meet a lot and talk almost every day. Recently, her friend started a new romantic relationship, and naturally "disappeared a bit" on Meirav. Meirav did understand this ostensible distancing, but still felt hurt. She noticed that she was initiating meetings and phone conversations now, which made her feel offended so stop initiating altogether.

They now met relatively rarely, and after a while Meirav "opened up" to her friend, who wasn't even aware of all that. It was all a story which Meirav told herself, a nice story which the serpent cooked up for her, which may have been related to the facts, but which certainly distorted them.

Meirav, driven by the serpent, was hurt by her friend's insensitivity, and her friend was hurt by her offense, and the gap became even wider. This break is a typical celebration for the serpent, containing a growing complication of a relationship with mutual expectations, offense, lack of communication and misunderstandings, offending behavior and finally a break and sadness.

The closer and more meaningful the relationship, the greater the potential for the serpent to complicate it and take over. We can primarily see this complication among couples, who begin so nicely and excitedly and then reach peaks of complication, offense, illogical and incomprehensible harm. There are many reasons for it, and all can be combined into one cause which allows for focused treatment – the serpent, which serves self-centeredness. When there is ostensible profit – self-centeredness enjoys itself in an egotistical sense. When there is loss and complication and pain, self-centeredness perpetuates itself through the suffering and the survival mode we entered into, leading to another increase in self-centeredness and the sufferer becomes occupied with themselves even more.

The serpent complicates anything it can, not just relationships. Any complication we have in our life or in our mind allows the serpent to offer magical solutions. The complication can be external – all sorts of facts in the world and in life which tend to become complex, but there is always an internal element of our own involved – our response to the facts, our over-analyzing of them, excessive occupation with various issues. Overthinking is also a complication created by the serpent, which it can use to guide us wherever it wants and cause us to act in a destructive manner.

An interesting approach of the serpent is via feelings of guilt – self-blame. Even when it seems that blaming ourselves is taking responsibility – we are examining our behavior against a moral yardstick in order to correct matters – becoming mired in feelings of guilt actually expresses a decline to self-centeredness, and our mind is filled with that negative occupation.

Positive or negative preoccupation with ourselves is actually the same thing – excessive preoccupation with our own concerns. Self-blame can lead this inward focus to reach new heights. To adopt self-blame or despair as a result of ostensible failure, is to be driven by the actions of the serpent. When we measure ourselves against a criterion wishing to amend our behavior while the serpent has no other courses of action in our mind, self-blame is the only one it has left. It offers rigidity within our self-examination and even exaggerates the criterion we chose, to ensure that we locate some painful failure which would drive us into despairing self-blame, allowing the serpent to celebrate within our tortured mind.

We can assume the serpent has other methods, which are pretty creative, always reinventing itself whenever it wants to enter our mind. When we sincerely follow the spiritual path, the serpent's hold on our mind weakens as does our hold on it, leading the serpent to become ever more creative in the methods it invents so it can strengthen its hold on our mind. If we understand that notion, that the serpent effectively serves self-centeredness, and aims to take over our mind and make us forget matters of spirit and grace, we will then succeed in identifying it in unexpected situations and get to know the creative methods it invented specially for us.

But we want to break free of it, not just identify it. So...how?

Breaking Free of the Serpent

After our detailed description of the serpent, with all its methods, entry gates, and hidden agents, along with its poisonous bite, it would seem to be pretty complicated to break free of it . In practice, such freedom seems impossible. We cannot get rid of the serpent once and for all as we would like, and it almost always returns in one form or another. But, and this is an important "but," there's always something we can do with it and even to break free from it for a moment or in a given situation.

All we need is to entirely stop or avoid "feeding" the serpent with our attention. Let me repeat this simple instruction: All we need to do in order to break free of the serpent at any given moment, is to avoid feeding or empowering it with our attention. Just let go of it. Ignore its tempting proposals, its threats or scare and terror tactics, and forgo the profit it ostensibly offers us or grants us. Complete disregard, as though it didn't exist.

It is then that the great wonder happens – we can lose interest in the serpent while also be disinterested whether it's still in our mind or not. If this disregard is honest and decisive, it has no choice but to disappear, and our powerlessness will go with it. The serpent is the product of our attention, a projection of our self-centeredness, which uses certain facts to increase its control over us.

Without our attention, without our holding onto the serpent or the facts it shows us, there is no serpent. No attention – no serpent.

So, why did I go on at length about it? So we know how we pay it attention, which in turn is how it works within our mind. We can break free of it at once, for a moment, just for today, and all that is needed is a quick and whole-hearted decision.

Why does such liberation not take place? It turns out that it's hard for us to be so decisive and it even feels pitiful to entirely starve the serpent of our attention. We continue to feed it even when the bitter consequences of its bite are entirely apparent, a marker of our powerlessness over it. But when we expose it and its agents and methods, it's easier to make this decision.

This is why awareness of the serpent is almost all that's needed to break free of it. Identify it, be aware of its influence, and then one small and meaningful step – let go of it. Entirely and completely. It's not possible to just give it up a little, or feed it only partially or temporarily. If we give the serpent our attention – even a little – it will run rampant within our mind. Entirely deny it attention – and this wonder happens – there is no serpent. It works as simply as it sounds.

Simplicity is an important principle when it comes to fighting the serpent. It is a basic principle of all the tools and throughout the GraceWay. The truth is simple and is expressed through simplicity[55]. There's something humble in simplicity, something unpretentious. It clings to the facts and preserves the truth, and when we seek it, the serpent's ability to cling to us declines. We should seek simplicity in every situation, as a basic principle of action, thus increasing the odds of making life difficult for the serpent.

We can add another simple "trick" to the principle of simplicity: Reverse psychology. When the serpent tries to take over our mind or succeeds in doing so, it proposes certain contents and insights which are supposed to get us to "dance" to its tune. Sometimes its control of our mind is so strong that we have hardly any ability to notice anything and certainly not to choose. In such a situation, we can use the trick of "reverse psychology," an action which due to its unexpected paradox, sometimes succeeds in suddenly changing the balance of power in the mind.

Let's take an imaginary scenario based on many actual cases I've encountered. Say someone expected his wife to prepare something for him - doesn't matter what. For her own reasons, she didn't do it. He goes on a rampage driven by anger, frustration, disappointment and self-pity. The serpent, which succeeded in taking over his mind, can continue and further complicate matters for both of them, so swift action is needed.

The "reverse psychology" trick offers a formula which describes what can be done immediately, without deep analysis or thought: You expected your wife to prepare something for you and she didn't, so prepare it for her or do it for yourself. Both options represent a simple action which is the reverse of what you wanted. All at once, we detach a certain pattern of action and thought, and act in the other direction. Expectation to receive is an expression of the power of taking[56], which seeks to take as much as possible from this world in favor of our self-centeredness. The disappointment creates frustration and tension.

The reverse action is as the term suggests – reversing the course from taking to giving. We give up on the power to take in favor of the power to give, a renunciation which both derives from love and strengthens it. The complete process is: Expectation – disappointment – tension and frustration – "reverse psychology" – renunciation – giving – love and joy.

It's worth it, isn't it? The "reverse psychology" principle turns a desire to fight to a desire to reconcile, a false action to an action based on truth, and more. The serpent is usually caught unprepared for this response, and the satisfactory results are surprising in their rapidity.

Gabi and his wife were going through an ongoing, violent conflict– hers was verbal, his physical. Gabi started to practice the GraceWay and chose to let go of the violent response. One day, his wife came to him with a complaint, she was unhappy with his calm response, and continued to hurl colorful curses at him. She knew his weak points and pressed on them. In the past, this would make him fiercely frustrated to the point of outbursts. But this time, he responded in the exact opposite manner, with a quiet which surprised her when he told her: "I love you even when you curse." That's it. She, for her part, burst out crying and apologized.

In fighting with the serpent, or trying to break free of self-centeredness, there are two concepts which can help us: The first is "loosening our grip," in other word, detachment, and the second is "non-identification." Both are reminiscent of Buddhism, and are also fairly central in other spiritual paths.

Loosening our grip offers us a unique kind of release. What are we gripping and are attached to? It's easier to answer in the negative: What aren't we holding onto? The pleasant, the comfortable, the pleasurable, expectations, as well as emotions, pain, or suffering, self-pity, our being offended, or our ideas, reason, self-image (positive and negative). In short, what aren't we attached to; indeed, ultimately we hold onto ourselves and our story about everything.

When we loosen our grip – even for a moment – that release is like letting go of a rope that someone is forcibly holding at the other end: The rope is free and the one holding it – the serpent – drops to the ground. For the serpent to be able to hold the rope of our mind, it needs us to grip it with the same amount of strength[57]. The rope is the story we tell ourselves, which the serpent tells us to hold onto.

Loosening our grip brings an immediate result. Loosening can be done at varying levels of depth. There is loosening which is about holding on at any given moment – we identify what we're holding onto now, let go, and the serpent drops down and temporarily vanishes from our mind. There is also a deeper and more continuous loosening, letting go of our fixed hold on something. Abstinence, for instance, is a deep and drastic continuous loosening, where we entirely let go of a strong holding onto some significant habit. The deepest loosening is a thorough detachment, that is, the letting go of our grip on images of self-centeredness. A complete transcending of self-centeredness means truly letting go of it, as it says in Psalms: "Be still, and know that I am God[58]."

The second concept, which is quite close to the first, is non-identification. Part of our holding onto something amounts to identifying with our suffering, emotion, drive, thought, or image. What aren't we, in fact, identifying with? ... Through the many details we identify with, we identify with the story we tell ourselves. We shape a story and act the hero, and sometimes – like the anti-hero.

Non-identification, which continues the release, means stopping to identify with ourselves, and it starts when we attribute our thoughts, emotions, and all the rest, to the serpent. If all this is the serpent – then it's not us. We can even stop identifying with suffering or pain – we tell ourselves that someone's in pain, and it happens to be us, without making a big deal of it. We feel the pain of course, even very intensively, but we don't get carried away.

We can see that non-identification includes a reduction in self-impor-tance. Why make a big deal of myself if I'm not so important and not the hero of the story? The "distinguishing facts" tool expresses non-identifi-cation in a focused manner, helping us not to identify with the suffering, emotion, or thought, or with our interpretation of the world or the situation or the experience that someone hurt us. The deepest possible non-identifi-cation is non-identification vis-à-vis self- centeredness, and breaking free of the serpent is a very focused and direct way of moving in that direction. Non-identification contains large doses of relief and joy. It is a whole way of life, which becomes stronger the more we progress in it. When we begin with not identifying, the alternative – returning to deep identification – is no longer tempting.

Galit and Elad were in a good place in their life together. So good, in fact, that they decided to celebrate it. It had been many months since his vio-lence behavior toward her ended, on all levels, and she went back to feeling safe near him. The strong love which they claimed they once shared also returned, and even stood firm in the face of a few trials brought on by life.

They therefore felt the need to celebrate the change. Elad borrowed a car from a friend and promised to bring it back a few hours later. They arranged for him to pick her up from home at a certain time. When he arrived home at the allotted time, Galit was not ready – she was sitting on the reclining chair absorbed in reading a book.

Elad was frustrated. He felt rage rising in him, like in the past. He thought she's mocking him and not appreciating the effort he made to get a car and come pick her up on time for the happy occasion. He started to criticize her, she responded, the tones got higher, and ... Suddenly, apropos of nothing, he stopped everything, told her "just a minute," went to the door, opened it dramatically and gave an order: "Outside, now." He closed the door and softly laughed . So did she. They laughed together. Without words, she understood that he expelled the serpent. The serpent did indeed disappear, and they had a wonderful evening.

It's not easy to accept something so simple, that the serpent is a function of ourselves, of our attention, of the story with which we convince ourselves, which is an expression of our self-centeredness. It's not easy for us to accept that in the moment of truth, when the serpent bombards our mind with its proposals, all we need to do is remove it with non-violent resistance[59]: Just stop cooperating with it by completely disregarding it. Applying the tools of the GraceWay helps us achieve a greater ability to act in this way. After we absorbed them, it becomes simpler for us to avoid cooperating with the serpent.

Let me stress again that abstaining from cooperating with the serpent is an excellent solution for a given moment of need, pressure or desire. The serpent will surely return later. We cannot fully free ourselves of it, just as we cannot fully break free of self-centeredness on our own, only with the grace of God.

There are people – outstanding, unique people – who succeeded in breaking free or detaching themselves from self-centeredness, the serpent, or anything else of that sort. These are the great spiritual teachers who were privileged with complete liberation with the grace of God. Until we get there, we will continue our persistent efforts to identify the serpent in our mind and our lives, and when we do – we'll simply ignore it.

The identification of the serpent at the moment of truth is not always easy, and sometimes we notice it only after it managed to make itself comfortably at home in our mind. Sometimes we identify it after a long time , when we've already experienced the destructive consequences. No matter, this is the nature of our struggle with ourselves. We can continue onward without making a big deal out of it - the serpent loves making a big deal of everything, after all – but simply, as soon as we spot it, let go of it entirely.

To learn our lesson, we will write a "serpent diary" at the end of each day, checking and noting when the serpent tried its luck into our mind today. When did it succeed? What happened? When did we manage to identify it and let go of it? What happened?

Let's enter into a state of complete silence and let go of everything. We'll examine ourselves from the side and search: Where was the serpent in our mind today? Even right now.

Let's examine its hidden agents: self-pity, doubt, hesitance – How did they try to work on us today?

Let's see the lie – the Serpent's poison – the deception and the fraud – where were they today in our life? What happened to them?

Let's look at the serpent's gates: the gate of honor, power, and control; the gate of money and possessiveness; the gate of dominating pleasures – when and how did these gates invite the serpent today?

We will look at the serpent's methods: expectations, guilt feelings, complication of relationships, and so on – Where did they work on us today?

Let's let the serpent go entirely.

We'll let go of any attention to it and let it dissipate in the world of imagination it came from.

"A person's weakness: To know what to do but not doing[60]."

CHAPTER FOUR

Exiting the Behavioral Spin

Let's start with a moment of silence. Everything we had before in our mind is dissipating and disappearing. We leave it on its way. We focus on the body which becomes looser, and let go of it, as well. We stay for a brief moment in the silence that has no end.

Among the most common forms of powerlessness taking over our mind and behavior, we can identify unique situations in which our behavior, emotion or thoughts seem to "become independent" or take on a momentum of their own, evolving into a state of behavioral spin, as well as equivalent situations of emotional, mental, and social spin. Below I describe the development of spin situations and look at what can be done to break free of these processes.

Let's look at an extreme example from the Bible which can be used to learn more about simpler cases, which we encounter almost every day. Remember the story about David and Bathsheba[61]? A juicy story, rich with captivating drama: It has a burst of passion, death, a war of heroism, a brave prophet which stands against a king, repentance and forgiveness and ongoing love.

Let's look at part of that story, which ripens toward one of the dramatic climaxes of the plot. According to the Biblical story, the king goes up on the roof of the palace to enjoy a nice evening breeze. So far, so innocent. There's no hint of what's about to happen. I note this, in order to understand the changes in the plot to learn something about ourselves and in general.

From the roof of the palace, the king notices Bathsheba who is bathing.

Her beautiful nakedness is now exposed to him. This moment of discovering Bathsheba is one of the most important parts of the story, though not yet a climax. It's still possible to take a number of paths. For instance, avoid peeking at the nakedness of the woman and thus avoid awakening his lust for her because it might turn out that she is married, which indeed turned out to be the case, which is a violation of "Thou shall not covet[62]."[63]

There are certainly additional options, but the king chose the one which led to the dark drama which developed: He was interested in Bathsheba and invited her to his palace. We could say that the moment he noticed her naked, enjoyed her exposed body and felt himself lusting for her, is the moment that the die was cast which ended his previous, pleasant innocence. One event followed another, the king's ability to stop increasingly declined until things got out of control and ended in something extreme – murder.

A similar process, which starts with stepping over the line dividing innocence and its deliberate loss, is something which I have already called "behavioral spin." In the context of the story of David and Bathsheba, which ended in murder, the behavioral spin is unique and more focused – "criminal spin" – but it also has characteristics which can be found in any behavioral spin, including non-criminal ones.

If we look at ourselves honestly, we'll discover that we are all in a spin on a daily basis, sometimes strongly and sometimes gently. Therefore we should know how to identify signs of being in a spin.

Spin on the king's road

After the king invited Bathsheba to spend the night with him, another possible point of stepping off the spin was shut. The moment they were together, with her a married woman forbidden by the laws of the time and place, the die was cast. A serious crime had been committed.

Mysterious are the ways of fate and God, and the story which could have ended with the crime of adultery became more complicated. Bathsheba became pregnant by the king. Since her husband, Uriah the Hittite, was far away on the front, a brave soldier in the service of the king, the behavioral spin, which had already gained momentum and has become criminal with the adultery, could become public knowledge.

The king chose an ostensible inventive solution, that continued the spin. He invited her husband to return from the battlefield in the hope that Uriah the Hittite would be with his wife, the pregnancy would be considered his, and everything would work out. We can see that this is the solution of the serpent, a false survival tool using devious means. The story demonstrates how after entering a particular gate, the serpent spreads, grows, accumulates power and momentum and complicates matters, even for someone as unique as King David.

According to the Biblical story, Uriah the Hittite, who was faithful to the king, refused to be with his wife while his comrades were away fighting. Since he could not reveal why it was important that he spend the night with Bathsheba, the king tried a different trick: Uriah was invited to the palace, where he was plied with wine and got drunk, in the hope that his nice principles would be worn down and washed away. Another trick of the serpent offering ostensible solutions.

As it turned out Uriah the Hittite was immune to these serpentine inventions and refused to go home and be with Bathsheba. So only one choice seemed to remain – to get rid of him. The king ordered Yoav, the military commander, to send Uriah to the front, where he was very likely to get killed. This is the ultimate solution of the serpent – an outburst of violence, to the point of murder. This time it succeeded. Uriah the Hittite was killed in a needless skirmish, planned specially for his death, while a others were also killed fighting alongside him. Now the king was able to take Bathsheba as his wife, and everything ostensibly worked out. The serpent succeeded.

Almost. The behavioral spin reaches a climax which is almost always followed by a crash and becoming "sober", which can then open a new window of opportunities.

The Biblical story is that of the way of God with its grace. After Nathan the Prophet, God's messenger, confronted the king about what he did, the king, who was a model man of faith, admitted his tragic mistake, regretted his actions, asked forgiveness, and bore the consequences.

The response of the king is another climax of the story, this time positive, with the choice of God's solution rather than the serpent's one. In the end, the son born to them (not from the first pregnancy, where the child died a week after birth) was King Solomon, who merited bringing about the greatest prosperity of the kingdom. Despite King David's sin, we mention the days of David and Solomon as a period of greatness for the Jewish People.

This dramatic story shows that even King David was a struggling human being who could err, which does not detract from his heroic image. The story teaches us about human struggle and shows us what could happen when we enter into a spin of self-centeredness, but it also teaches us of the possibility of stopping, changing direction, and fixing things through confession, regret, and complete repentance.

The king represents a case of falling, but also the possibility of getting back up afterward and even rising. We can all adopt the hope from this story, even when we can only control ourselves, and our story is less dramatic.

A spin of losing control

Behavioral spin is a process of losing self-control over behavior due to being increasingly swept up, while control weakens. The process might begin in a controlled manner, out of conscious choice, but then something happens and the process gains momentum, snowballing, as if taking on a life of its own, and we have less and less control of the situation, consciously or not, until the spin reaches a climax which could be destructive.

A common example is our response to food. Know anyone who ever managed to stay on any sort of diet, even a limited one, just as an experiment? It's a rhetorical question: It's simpler to ask who hasn't stayed on a diet? Maybe we called it something else, maybe we just decided to limit our food choices for some reason.

Usually, staying on a diet is pleasant and simple until the serpent appears, playing a nice game with our mind. It happens when we encounter some food which isn't part of our diet. Gently, the serpent lifts its head and directs our attention to that dish, our appetite grows, and the serpent starts to explain to us why we should have, even just a little, just a taste.

For instance, someone is on a particular diet, and her colleague's birthday is being celebrated at work, along with a cake she made. The cake smells wonderful and looks amazing, but it's off-limits because of the diet. An internal dialogue starts, a conversation with the serpent. Convincing arguments are made as to why she needs to have a little bite: It's her birthday and she should join in her colleague's celebration, just a small bite wouldn't hurt, the cake was made specially for the occasion and if she doesn't have a taste, her colleague might be hurt, it's not good to stand out, the diet is too harsh and inappropriate for her, anyway, and it's not healthy to be extreme.

If none of these excuses convince, there are always other ones. If she starts to listen to them, an excuse will eventually come along which succeeds in bringing her to have a bite of the cake. If she only take a small bite – then there is no spin. But oftentimes, we just have a small bite of a "forbidden fruit", and found ourselves having more, then another forbidden fruit and soon enough, there was cake, there was a diet, and both are gone.

This is the behavioral spin – when we start something that pushes us over and brings us to places we neither chose nor wish to be in. The spin describes a process in which we experience powerlessness driven by loss of self-control. At first we aren't aware of the powerlessness, but then it takes over our mind and pushes us to a behavioral climax which we experience in full. Sometimes the spin is so strong that we only understand after it ends that we were in a spin, lost control and were powerless.

Familiar with the "flywheel effect[64]?" The flywheel is a heavy mechanical component, which turns and maintains a high level of rotational kinetic energy and keeps things in motion. It usually takes a lot of energy to drive it, but when it moves fast, stopping it becomes a challenge. Behavioral spin describes a similar situation, in which a behavior forms which may require energy to get it started, but which easily becomes stronger once in motion, building on its own momentum, which is hard to stop.

Similarly, the spin can be compared to sliding down a slippery slope. It's still possible to turn away from the slope to another, safer path before entering. Sometimes there's even a small fence before the slope with a "Danger!" sign, to warn us and make it hard to enter this dangerous area. But when we pass that sign and that fence and are already on the slope, we start to slide down. At first the decline is slow, but the more it continues, the more it speeds up, powerlessness increases, and it all usually ends in a crash. Similarly, the behavioral spin usually ends in some form of collapse.

Here's an example. Joe established an import business with his wife. They were a loving couple with two small children, the business succeeded, and the family was happy. Due to work demands, Joe would go abroad every so often. Usually, it was strictly business and he came home as soon as he could to the family he loved. In one of the trips which took a little longer, he happened to meet a woman. They were strongly attracted to each other and eventually spent the night together. This was the first time he experienced something like this since his marriage.

On the one hand, it was wonderful. On the other hand, he woke up with feelings of guilt and remorse. He had never thought about cheating on his wife, and now he has done it. He came back home shaking on the inside, ashamed, and afraid he would be found out and the family would suffer. To his relief, no-one discovered what he did. It was as if nothing had happened. He was relieved. On his next trip abroad, he again found himself with a woman, this time for fee, but his guilty feelings were weaker. He started to look forward to this pleasure from trip to trip, either paid or from a chance encounter, and the business began to turn to an excuse for his trips.

Outwardly, the family knew nothing and was still loving, so outwardly all was well. But then a new thought popped in his mind: Why wait until he went abroad? He could have fun at home, too. At the time, the business had expanded and a second branch opened up in the north of the country. He discovered that it's possible to pencil in a short and pleasant bit of fun into his many trips to the distant branch, with no-one the wiser. He had an excuse for himself– these are not real relationships or betrayals, just paid sex, with women engaging in prostitution under this or that heading ("massages," for instance) or casual sexual encounters. It was merely physical satisfaction, which certainly doesn't bother anyone.

But naturally enough, as the betrayal spin continued, other things happened, and Joe became impatient at home, became emotionally distant from his wife and his kids, and would just wait for his "forbidden" pleasures, whose frequency only increased. As time passed Joe met a woman he really liked. They had a brief affair. He became even more distant from his wife, getting tangled up in lies upon lies to justify his disappearances. A short affair and then another, and Joe met another woman, this time with whom he had a more serious relationship.

The more it went on, the more his relationship with his wife deteriorated. When she ultimately discovered his infidelity, it was almost a relief for both of them. But the family nevertheless fell apart in a painful divorce process. The joint business was broken up, in a painful process of financial collapse.

States of spin

There are a number of typical states of behavioral spin worth knowing. Behavioral spin can develop very slowly while gradually picking up speed, as in Joe's case, and following our example of the flywheel. Spin can also develop relatively quickly, as in the Biblical story of King David. Like on the slippery slope, once we enter it, deterioration and decline cannot be prevented. Spin can also be sudden, like a sudden fall, such as the first time Joe cheated on his wife abroad. It had a quick climax ending in an emotional crash. But then the behavioral spin continued to develop, gradually as we saw above.

Behavioral spin can also be acute, even once-in-a-lifetime, but it can also be chronic, an ongoing spin. In Joe's case, the first time of cheating on his wife was a case of acute spin. It happens that we are sometimes swept into something, can't stop and usually don't want to stop, end up sucked in entirely, reach a climax. Then sometimes the spin fades on its own but sometimes it ends with a crash.

We can compare this to a fight which someone was dragged into, despite their nature, which gets out of control. We can also think of some deception someone didmp, which also isn't like them, which may have worked for them and may have ended in collapse, and again – it ends there.

An acute spin can be very painful and even lethal, but it's limited in duration. It does develop a life of its own and a degree of durability, but it ends relatively quickly, and we can only hope that the results are not tragic.

The spin can also become chronic, a form of typical behavior or even a way of life. There isn't necessarily a climax in a chronic spin, unlike in acute cases, but there is a perseverance in the way of life captured in the spin. For people who fell into a life of crime, we can see a chronic criminal spin. We can also see how ongoing violence can become a chronic form of response.

For instance, a couple that has violence in their relationship will contain typical patterns which create an unhealthy balance which sometimes reaches climaxes of violence followed by a brief relaxation which also fades with time. In cases where one of the partners is the aggressor and the other the victim, each side enters into a typical, chronic spin, one into a violent spin and the other into a victimization spin. Together they enter into a mutual chronic spin, with one fueling and preserving the spin of the other.

In any case, chronic spin is a state in which we are in a regular pattern of behavior where we feel trapped and powerless. It has an increasing cost – not just emotional but also an ever complicated and even "stuck" life.

Let's think of someone who doesn't like his place of work, but fears change because the workplace is good and the conditions are excellent. He usually comes to work frustrated, does what he does with either open or hidden unwillingness, and carries out what he needs to, inefficiently. He returns home tired, without any interest in anything, collapsing in front of the television with a beer or a joint. Sometimes he goes out with friends, but usually doesn't have the energy. He certainly has no strength or desire for a relationship. Life is stuck, and this stuck has an inertia which perpetuates itself. This is the spin of stuck-ness, and I have met many who are in the thick of it.

Another example involves various forms of addiction, including normative ones like addiction to relationships, all of which contain a component of chronic behavioral spin, which is sometimes marked by a consistent behavior with a growing cost.

Chronic spin can also express itself differently, as a regular repetition of acute spins, with states of calm between them. Outbursts of behavioral spin including loss of control to the point of a climax and a temporary crash, repeating itself in a regular way.

We can observe similar chronic spin with people swept up into temporary relationships that aren't really a fit, and of course in the cases of criminal careers or a tendency toward violence. There are forms of addiction involving this form of chronic spin – e.g., alcoholics who drinks only on the weekends. During the week, they work and function normally, while "disappearing" on the weekend into drinking to the point of losing their senses, only to wake up in the beginning of next week for another round. This pattern of drinking is common among normative drinkers.

A similar and perhaps even a more common pattern is compulsive eaters. Many people fall into binging on food, followed by an emotional crash, clinging to their diet and then binging again, and so on in an endless cycle.

To make things more complicated, behavioral spin can also be a collective affair. Let us remember how many times we found ourselves acting according to the norms of the group in such a way as to lead to a spin and loss of control, even if we would not have acted this way if we were alone?

Once again, eating is an excellent example – social eating is fairly common and oftentimes becomes a binge easier than it would if we ate alone. This sort of gluttony happens when the group has someone who leads it or when these are the norms of the group. Take the case of a celebratory family meal, where people eat far more than they usually do, with family members prompting each other to eat more.

We see the social influence involved in criminal spin in all cases of collective criminality. For instance, youth who get organized into gangs leading to more criminality than if they all acted alone[65].

There is also a modern phenomenon of small groups of men who travel abroad for the experience of paid sex, usually to developing countries where prices are lower. The clean title for this is "sex tourism." In practice, it's a phenomenon involving rape and open sexual exploitation – the women have no choice. This is a case of collective behavioral spin, who choose to ignore the meaning and consequences of their behavior. It's easier to ignore it when they're together in a group.

A similar process happens when we are more tempted to "go wild" in a certain company in ways we wouldn't normally do, and this easy minded behavior is the beginning of collective behavioral spin.

Very similarly we can identify a cognitive or emotional spins. We can have small thoughts which become big to the point of taking over our mind. The same goes for being drifted by any emotion into an emotional spin. As in the case of behavioral spin, cognitive or emotional spin has a clear and stable direction and a gradually increasing intensity, or a chronically high intensity. Usually in cases of behavioral spin, emotions and thoughts enter into their own at the same time. Cognitive or emotional spin can lead to behavioral spin, and sometimes we can't tell which led to which. So far, I've described mostly behavioral spin, since it's easier to observe. It has external consequences, which both we and others can spot. But cognitive or emotional spin can also be equally painful, and sometimes even more so, as the Talmud says: "Sinful thoughts are harder than sin[66]."

Spin motifs

Every spin contains a visibly increasing component of self-centeredness. Acute spin is an outburst of high self-centeredness, while chronic spin expresses continuous decline into a state of high self-centeredness. A Collective behavioral spin involves an outburst of self-centeredness among a group of people, and is socially contagious.

Moving beyond self-centeredness is no less contagious. When we are exposed to a group of people acting in a way that transcends self-centeredness, we sometimes find ourselves acting similarly, and then we encounter the grace we act on in each other. Sometimes even this good influence is maintained for a long time after the collective encounter, and can be absorbed into our lives.

The power of social influence and its direction depend on the power struggles within the group we are in: Are there more people in the group who tend to enter into a spin with high self-centeredness, or more people who seek to transcend self-centeredness? Which of these has more power?

As part of self-centeredness, behavioral spin has two characteristic motifs. The first is "I can" and the second is "I must." The first motif – "I can" – refers to our allowing ourselves to engage in the behavior diving into behavioral spin. At a particular moment, we think it's OK to start or continue a certain behavior, even though it might be problematic. In the case of Joe, even though he did not consider himself as wanting to cheat on his wife, there was one time when, in a decision made in the moment, he allowed himself to be swept up pursuing a woman he was attracted to. Acute behavioral spin then gets into gear, self-centeredness increases with urges and lust, and the promise of gratification, with the results I already described.

The "I can" motif has another meaning – in addition to being permitted to act, I also have the ability to carry out this act. I have the needed strength, skills, and conditions. Joe, for instance, experienced himself as someone who can initiate a relationship with the attractive woman abroad. Before that, he wasn't sure of his ability, but then he proved his ostensible manhood. To the same degree, the men who travel together to buy sexual satisfaction abroad, feel an amazing capability for ostensible manhood, expressed in their ability to buy the services of poor, socially weak women, who have no choice but to do what the men wish them to.

Self-centeredness likes this false sense of increasing personal ability very much, even though it oftentimes serves as cover for the lack thereof. The serpent convinces us that we have power in a way that increases our dubious sense of self-respect and our feeling of control over the situation. Indeed, a false sense of self-control is the beginning of losing control. Behavioral spin is a process in which we lose control of our behavior, which gains a life of its own and preserves itself, while we have a decreasing ability to stop it. It starts with the illusion of control and the sense of "I can," and leads to an internal necessity and an inability to stop.

That's where the second motif comes in – "I must." Behavioral spin includes the sense of necessity, sometimes from the start, as a drive to behave out of a feeling of need. Other times, this feeling of necessity develops during the spin. In both cases, the necessity is such that we have no choice but to continue the behavior we started, and even double down on it.

Take someone who tells a little lie, what he thinks is a "little white lie," for his own benefit. He feels that he can, and he lies, just a little. But something goes wrong, and the lie is discovered. Now he must, ostensibly, add another, bigger lie, and another on top of that, and maybe even cheat, deceive and so on.

What began as something innocent, the sort of lie which is unfortunately fairly common and socially acceptable, turned into a whole complication and tangling of relationships, out of a sense of necessity and the need to ostensibly salvage something. Obviously if the lie is discovered, there is a painful crash, though sometimes there is a crash even when it isn't. In terms of the path, the first lie was already a crash of grace.

When a spin involves a fight or violence, it's easy to see the "I must" motif – we feel a necessity to "stand up for ourselves," "get our point across" or simply tell someone something painful. And when they answer, we feel that we cannot let them have the last word, leading to a spin of fighting. A spin of "just" piercing and biting debate is unfortunately too common, even among people who are usually not violent. Self-centeredness is hurt or threatened fairly easily, leading to a "I must" respond, a reaction to save ourselves. In a state of chronic behavioral spin, the motif of "I must" leads us to repeat an unhealthy pattern of behavior, sometimes almost addictive.

The two motifs tend to cooperate with and strengthen one another. "I must" can drive to action, and then "I can" allows for completing it, or vice versa. When the spin becomes stronger approaching its climax – both are usually in full force in a state of powerlessness.

Alongside these two, there are other mental states typical of spin. For instance, a state of narrowing and restricting perception. While in the midst of the spin, we focus on one course of action, with thought and emotion becoming more focused on it, to the point of being unable to feel or think otherwise. Let's imagine a lover's quarrel: They feel the need to say something, can say something unpleasant to their spouse, who answers of course, and then need to respond becomes stronger.

The more the fight continues, the possibility of responding differently weakens. It's as though a magnetic force in the fight is pulling us into it, focusing more and more on it, while being somewhat blind to any other option. Our thoughts become more focused on how we're misunderstood, mistreated, and it's time to stand up for ourselves, and other internal dialogues that strengthen the spin.

Emotion also reacts accordingly, caught up in a whirlwind of offense, anger, and/or fear, becoming stronger in its pull. The spin is a state of unhealthy focus, and a narrowing of our range of options, to the point that they disappear, leaving us with one relevant option– spinning out of control, powerless. In the story of King David and Bathsheba, the more the acute spin advanced, the more there was a duty to continue the destructive course of action, with all the other options which could have stopped it, disappearing.

Alongside the destructive focus of the spin, we can also see a narrowing of our ability to empathize at the same time, with nothing to talk about in terms of love or grace. Since self-centeredness increases at the rate of the spin, we are mired within it, have no room for others, and cannot feel empathy toward them, understand them, or see their side.

Someone who quarrels with his partner, for instance, saying hurtful things during that argument, if he "sees" her for a moment and feels her pain, he will likely not be able to continue to hurt her. Maybe even the contrary. Continuing to cause more pain requires being shut off. In any case, to continue and exploit someone else, requires insensitivity to the point of losing all empathy, such as the spin of business fraud or tempting someone for personal self-gratification.

When loss of empathy happens with couples who love each other – the result is painful for both. Going back to the men who travel to use women for sexual gratification in exchange for money, their harmful exploitation expresses a spin uninterested or incapable of viewing women as human beings, only as sexual objects who can be used for money, even if they are forced into it. Such a view might continue and even become stronger when they return home.

Another thing that characterizes the spin, is lack of self-awareness. The more the spin advances, the more our own awareness weakens. More and more, we live the script we construct for ourselves, as described above, and are less and less conscious of the consequences of our actions. We identify with our emotional state and thoughts, and experience a lack of choice and loss of control, being sure it is our choice, without knowing that we'd lost control of ourselves and the events living in a powerless condition.

Sometimes we become aware of what's happened when it's too late, and our ability to stop is low. Let's take someone sliding down a slope, after ignoring the warning sign, jumping over the fence. At first, he enjoys the speed and his amazing ability to slide, not aware that he is spinning out of control. Then there comes a time when he wants to slow down or change direction, but it's already too late.

Similarly, harsh words bring about results and actions which become painful. The experience of control and ability – "I can" – disappears in many cases, leaving only "I must," to the point of despair with the crash inevitable. I met a couple whose relationship had deteriorated. Both turned to counseling. Both heard good advice how to stop the spin. Both chose individually to continue the spin, unaware of acting within it, to the point of increasing losing control lacking any choice. The spin led to a petty and long divorce trial, which was an ongoing crisis of collapse. Can this be prevented? It seems so, but apparently not. In the end, the spin was stronger than them.

Stopping the spin

What can be done about behavioral spin? In the thick of it, not much. This is our powerlessness. Spin has a life and momentum of its own, and it knows how to preserve itself thanks to our self-centeredness, aided by the serpent. Still, there are things that can be done.

Initially, we have to identify the situation as being in a spin. Sometimes we'll be able to understand our being in a powerless spin, sometimes we'll be able to identify it through the consequences of our actions, and sometimes with the help of someone else, who will reflect it back to us. It doesn't matter how we realize it, as long as we do.

When we identify ourselves as being in a spin state, that's the time to quit everything, and I mean everything, because anything we do could deepen the hole we're digging. The moment we identify the spin, "just for today," or "just for this moment," we set aside everything we can, rest a bit, try and ask for an outside perspective from a trusted person. We should cling to positive symbols of change, look at ourselves from the outside, pray, pray more – for instance, the serenity prayer – and go inside ourselves, deep down, as the spin usually acts outward, and can be stopped with an inward look.

We'll find inside what we always find, deep and hidden, but possible – quiet, calm, live non-doing, the light of love. We'll choose this moment, and it alone, and succeed in enjoying a respite from the spin. We can use that break to continue to elude the state of spin with any tool that works for us at that moment.

For instance, the "distinguishing facts" tool can help us quit a state of emotional or thought-based spin. The "correcting errors" tool can help stop the spin from spreading. The correction creates movement in the opposite direction of the spin, and allows escape from the slope. The "truth only" tool brings us back to solid ground.

Additionally, the tools of positive action, "gratitude," "being positive," "finding in ourselves," and "promoting good" create a defensive wall against entering into a new behavioral spin. When we regularly introduce the principle of "living the spirit" into our lives, it distances us from the slippery slope of the spin. So long as we apply it in life, we will avoid entering into a spin, and even if it happens, it will be relatively weak and possible to easily identify and stop .

> *Let's take a quick moment of silence. We'll delve into it, quietly. We'll look at ourselves from the outside and seek out behavioral, emotional, or cognitive spin that happened to us recently. We'll examine how it started. If we find it repeats itself, we'll examine whether we are in a kind of chronic spin. We will examine its various motifs from the outside, such as "I can and "I must." We will see how self-centeredness becomes stronger and spins out of our control, or almost out of our control. If it's already over, we'll learn what led to its end and how.*
>
> *Let's return to the quiet.*

Such an examination can be done every day, at the end of the day. Through it, we will develop an awareness of the spin's tendencies, using any tool that helps us change direction.

"Your nature is divine nature, which no-one can best, not even you[67]."

CHAPTER FIVE

Identifying Emotional Begging

Let's enter into a brief moment of silence. Silence is usually the best medicine. It's also the appropriate answer, almost for anything. When it's really silent, and not just an internal noise that's only ostensibly silent. The silence is also infectious and becomes even stronger when we gather together in silence. We'll go a little deeper, into a few moments of silence. Listening to everything beyond the noise and the sounds we hear now. To a silence in which the sounds rise and recede.

At a workshop I gave way back in the nineties, I described behaviors relating to emotional powerlessness. One of the participants, a social worker and therapist, gave it an amazing and accurate definition: "emotional begging." I warmly embraced this definition, and it has since helped many people to identify their own painful compulsive motif and break free of it.

Emotional begging happens when we are preoccupied with others' responses to us, trying to find a positive reaction. We make an effort to get that desired positive response and are willing to do a lot for it – please, flatter, bribe with our own positive responses, and other inventions.

It is a common and well-known situation, and a painful one. Emotional begging to get emotional "handout" – attention, respect, a good word, affection, a supporting touch, warmth, and more – is boundless and insatiable.

Sometimes emotional begging is just the desire to let others know we are worth a lot, as we emphasize some impressive family connection, profession, class, education, degree, affiliation, or social acquaintance with someone as though it's important – or indeed, anything else.

There are times when we only throw out vague hints, as if engaged in seduction, so that the other side latches on to them and asks clarifying questions, creating a process of light euphoria due to the increasing attention and respect we momentarily get from them. Unfortunately, when we receive such emotional handout, it has only a temporary effect as well as a price, at times a fairly heavy one.

Sometimes the price will double – both the cost of the emotional handout itself and the personal cost one continues to pay when the pleasant warmth of the handout dissipates, leaving behind a taste either bitter or bland, with a painful emptiness and a sense of inauthenticity. There might even be a triple cost, as emotional begging something becomes quasi-addictive, a hungry inner creature whose demands only grow the more you feed it.

Emotional begging is an expression of a strange condition. We experience ourselves as though we are in a state of emotional want, and someone else seems to have what we need to become fulfilled. Therefore, we ostensibly have an emotional need for the response of others and make the effort to get it, sometimes demanding it.

Emotional begging is an expression of an emotional dependence on someone else, who has what we think we lack. But if the other person gives us what we think we lack, the attention we seek, the emotional "hole" still remains, and we find ourselves once again seeking attention. Maybe from someone else, maybe in different circumstances, maybe with a higher degree of urgency.

Emotional begging is a marker of dependence, based on a lack which the person tries, but cannot, resolve. Sometimes it expresses a fear of social rejection, as though rejection is the greatest threat of all. Collecting emotional handouts is a kind of an insurance policy against rejection, but one which expires very quickly and requires an added "premium" to keep going.

While in the midst of the process of collecting emotional handouts, we attribute great power and importance to the other person, seemingly unconsciously, in a way that stands out given our own sense of powerlessness. The action of emotional begging effectively perpetuates the situation which leads to it – the more we operate on its basis, the more we experience ourselves as lacking something, the need for being externally filled increases, as does the emotional begging.

Other times it seems that we experience our own power and are full of ourselves, with others serving as an encouraging soundboard of that pleasant experience of strength, as though they are a means for us to get social approval. A state of ostensible emotional fullness seeking out a social soundboard is also a state of emotional begging, as underneath that experience of conscious fullness lies an unconscious experience of want, which directs us to accept support from others. After we peel away the sense of self-satisfaction, bloated by self-importance, and remain with the action of receiving support from others in itself, the emotional begging that drives us, becomes readily apparent.

There are many examples of emotional begging. A young woman who couldn't say "no" to anyone, for fear of "What will they think of me?" For instance, she met with someone who spent the whole meeting talking about himself and his affairs without listening to her or noticing her, but she could not get up and leave, hoping that if she stayed empathetic toward him, he might pay her attention.

Another example occurred in a conversation I had with someone, in which I noticed a strange habit of his: Every couple of sentences we exchanged, he would continue a word I had started to say, whose ending was obvious, and would end it for me. He seemed to be finishing my words to give me the impression that he understands and agrees with me. I asked him about it. He hadn't even noticed this prominent tendency of his, but then he became aware of it. It turned out that he wasn't finishing my words due to thinking about me, but based on a thought requiring a high degree of self-centeredness – that I address him positively, as a man quick on his feet and his understanding. This is emotional begging in action –collecting the positive attention from me.

Another common example is a woman who is considered pretty, who dresses in a way that emphasizes her gentle femininity, and tells others that she doesn't look good. The usual response is to flatter her appearance, then she rejects the compliment, but is ready to do almost anything to hear it again and again. The process is even more complex, as sometimes she refuses to believe the compliments and has negative thoughts about herself. She does enjoy a respite when she hears a compliment, but that lasts only until she has a negative thought which tells her how she isn't good enough. The need to hear something positive from others increases as her negative feelings do. This is self-centeredness in action, and another trick of the serpent trying to control us.

Emotional begging may seem strange, distant, and even a little amusing, but it isn't. It is usually close by, common, and most importantly – painful. What can we do when we encounter emotional begging by someone? Say, someone who sounds as if they're begging for a kind word? Usually, there isn't much we can do. Still, if someone consults with us or asks us for help, and we identify a tendency of theirs to emotionally beg for a compliment, let us remember that a compliment will usually not help. Even showing a person their skills and talents rarely helps, because we are effectively perpetuating that person's reliance on something outside of them – in this case, ourselves.

It's definitely possible, if relevant to the nature of the relationship as well as appropriate in terms of time, place, and those present, to talk with that person about self-change, raising awareness of their emotional begging and letting them choose what to do with it.

The twelve tools can help in such a case. They can offer abstinence from expressing the behaviors of emotional begging, direct people to the "finding in ourselves" tool, and the like. For instance, I asked the permission of the person who completed my sentences to tell him something personal, after which I reflected back what I heard, and we analyzed it based on an outside perspective. My response was well received, and he thanked me and said it was meaningful and that he would try to avoid completing sentences – but then immediately went back to finishing my words and sentences, because it was still too much for him not to do so.

> *Let's stop and take a brief moment of silence. We'll let go of the thoughts and emotions that arose in our mind, and stay for a moment in the deep silence that is always in the background. During the pleasant silence, we'll examine the range of interactions we had today with various people and search for emotional begging within them – where did we want an experience of positive feedback from someone else? If it didn't happen today – then maybe yesterday? And the day before? What did we do to get desired positive attention? What would we be willing to do? Let's look at ourselves from the outside, with as little judgment as possible, just seeing, remembering, and continuing.*

It's easy to see that emotional begging, as I said before, is very common. It is also very socially accepted. After all, it's natural that we would want to receive nice feedback from others; what's wrong with that? To understand our appropriate attitude toward the emotional begging we discovered within ourselves, let us delve again into the meaning of emotional begging. Someone feels they are lacking something, which leads to emotional begging, during which they have a great dependence on others, sometimes with increased pleasing or with insatiable demands.

Emotional begging deceives us and makes us think that we need a good word or positive attention. It also makes us dependent on others, sometimes a particular individual and sometimes anyone, who becomes important to us in that moment when we want to receive something from them. Emotional begging, in all its forms, strengthens dependence and the feeling of bitter disappointment since no emotional handout really satisfies us.

In addition, emotional begging is one of the serpent's methods to strengthen our self-centeredness. The more the habit of begging for emotional handouts becomes stronger and even dominates us, the more the serpent celebrates along with the self-centeredness now controlling us.

So, what do we do about our emotional begging?

First of all – awareness. At the end of every day, we note down the behavioral expressions of emotional begging we noticed today. Slowly but surely, an awareness is formed and sets in, which eventually appears during the events themselves, as we see ourselves from the outside at the moment our hand is stretched out in expectation, and our mouth is singing pleading songs for emotional handouts.

In addition to developing awareness, we practice abstinence from any activity based on emotional begging. How do we identify such actions? An action in which we give to others, and wait for desired attention or treatment is an action of emotional trading or begging, as opposed to an action done because it is right for us and others, with minimal expectation for any outcome.

For instance, speech that is seemingly flattering or looks like sucking up, which someone adopts in order to get positive attention as appreciation or acceptance, is an example of emotional begging. Gentle speech that does not relate to the emotional reaction of the ideas we raise –is an example of a situation that doesn't involve emotional begging.

Emotional begging has to do with what motivates us, rather than the specific content of our talk or behavior at a given moment, which each of us knows better than anyone – did I act out of emotional begging today? Do I have a repeating tendency to fall into emotional begging? What tool of the GraceWay have I used to break free of it?

Emotional begging can seem pleasant, desirable, satisfying, positive, legitimate, and what not – but like any means of self-centeredness, its promises are not real. Even if we get the emotional handout for free, it has no grace, and clinging to it means a price of increased self-centeredness. On the other hand, it's worth stressing the hope – there is life after emotional begging, and it is better. When we practice using the tools and live the grace we wish to, our self-centeredness goes silent for a moment and the serpent falls asleep, leading to the emotional begging being blown away in the wind. Instead of its emptiness, a grace is revealed which fills by itself, the gift of a Supreme Power. The choice? It's in our hands.

"Cling to God alone and do not depend on an object or person[68]."

CHAPTER SIX

The Emotional Seesaw –
Between Impotence and Omnipotence

Let's begin, as usual, with a brief moment of silence. We'll delve deep into it. Only silence, which comes from within, and the voices we hear outside are in it, but do not hide it. We succeed in hearing even the ticking of the clock and perhaps the barking of a dog from afar, and outside of all this there is also silence, a quiet different from everything. We'll feel how our forehead is entirely relaxed and our eyes pleasantly closed.

Let's stay like this, eyes closed, within the silence, and recall an emotion we had when something went really well for us, when we got something we wanted, or when we had some wonderful experience, and afterward, we felt on Cloud Nine. It could be something that happened when we were alone or with other people. It can be an emotion accompanying some gratification – physical pleasure, emotional satisfaction or intellectual.

What fun, right? Let's momentarily relive the fame we had. What happened to the silence, do we still hear it? Less? Definitely. The feeling of gratification and fame have brought the noise. A joyful noise, but noisy. We'll leave the pleasant memories, and return to the silence. Listen to it. Delve into it again.

Let's focus our mind on a moment of our deep disappointment or failure,. We can bring up an expectation of gratification which turned out to be cold, a task we failed in, an icy social response we received, or lack of appreciation or slack, a moment we were entirely ignored, or anything similar. The opposite of earlier. The memories arise. They cannot be avoided. Less fun now? What happened to the silence? We'll return to the silence, as much as possible.

There's a way to find silence quickly – we'll focus our mind on the palms of our hands. Just them. Without looking at them. Solely through our mind, we will examine each palm, for instance, how it's laid? We'll note whether each hand is comfortable. We'll relax them by becoming aware of them. There's no need to do anything special for this relaxation. We just need to want it, think about it, and let our imagination lead. The rest happens by itself. The relaxation reaches our shoulders. We'll let it flow. Once again, we'll enter into quietness.

Let's continue to play within the silence, and recall a particular fantasy of success. We'll choose something imaginary which occasionally came up or still comes up in our mind. Some imaginary event we would love to happen. Almost all of us fantasize. Some are very pleasant and some less so, sometimes really unpleasant. We also have recurring fantasies, scripts that repeat themselves in our mind.

Let's choose one that's pleasant, where we are the successful stars who gets something like fame, gratification, conquest, recognition, success, honor. Anything. Without being ashamed, almost all of us have such things, and also without worrying; we need not tell a soul.

We'll choose such a fantasy for ourselves, but instead of becoming devoted to its pleasantness, let's do something else with it. We'll examine ourselves from the outside, as though we were someone else, who sees us and is aware of our fantasy. We have a wondrous ability to read thoughts and emotions, seeing the pleasant fantasy as though it was someone else's. What does it look like from the outside? We'll stay there another moment.

Let's move now to another, unpleasant fantasy; a negative experience, an image of a burning failure or even a disaster. Something that didn't actually happen, but is a nightmare scenario that arises in our mind along with anxiety and negative expectations.

Once again, we'll look at ourselves from the outside, as if reading someone else's fantasy. We'll look, form an impression, and then leave and return to silence.

Let's focus on breathing. We'll become aware for a moment of the air that comes in through our nostrils, to its path to the lungs, imagining how the oxygen continues to the blood, reaches the heart and then spreads throughout the body with each heartbeat. There is no longer a fantasy in our mind, just silence.

If we wish, we can later share our fantasies with someone. Exposing such fantasies requires bravery, but when we share with someone, that sharing can release us from them. Why break free of them? I hope this will become clear immediately.

What we've done here was practice of two extreme situations which we sometimes veer between like a pendulum and sometimes sink into one of them. When we recognize and name them, this sharp movement calms down a bit. With little more awareness and effort, we can let go of it almost entirely, as we will see here.

When we experience extreme emotional situations, they can take over our mind and harm us. According to the spiritual path well expressed by Buddhism[69], what takes over our mind limits our free and full choice and actually harms our self-fulfillment at any given moment. It's natural and common that something takes over our mind every so often – this is an inseparable part of being a human being developing in the world – but there is a no less natural option of reducing that harm to our freedom of choice.

Awareness is an important means of liberation. This time, we'll take note of the movement between two conditions we can call "impotence" and "omnipotence." I will present these as extreme cases for the sake of clarity, but they are clearly very common in their less extreme forms. Our daily lives are full of mixtures of the two.

Impotence is a false state in which we experience ourselves as ostensibly having no strength or ability to deal with something, with a distorted self-conception and a negative expectation of failure. Sometimes this negative expectation leads to avoiding trying to do something, in other times it becomes a self-fulfilling prophecy that precedes failure, and at times it disappears the moment we start to do what's needed. It's easy to imagine impotence when focusing on extreme cases, but we also have plenty of "small" experiences of impotence in our daily lives, cases in which our belief in ourselves is low, in which our mind contains negative thoughts trying to convince us of our inability to carry out what we wish to do. Sometimes this feeling of lowliness appears after we failed by some definition, and sometimes it's a feeling that appears without any direct connection to some external event.

Omnipotence is the false experience of being all-powerful. It is a state in which we "play God." Ostensibly, everything is possible for us; we need but wish it and it will come true, all will do as we want, and everything will succeed. Omnipotence is also an ostensibly extreme state, but it is very common in intermediate forms. We can recall those moments when we are "full of ourselves" because of some good news, a task we succeeded at, some particularly good feedback, or exciting satisfaction we experienced. There are moments of emotional elation and the feeling of being on Cloud Nine, which can lead us to exaggerated actions and also undesirable decisions whose consequences we'd have to deal with afterwards. Success puts us in a state of fantasy, but we acted as though it was reality.

Omnipotence can also come at a time we feel angry or have a violent outburst, ending up out of balance viewing the situation in a distorted light, usually ignoring the other person involved. We are swept up in our emotions and behavior, momentarily losing perspective of reality, easily spinning out of control and acting in such a way that we will later regret.

Sometimes the other person seems threatening, driving us to act in order to remove the threat, while we are actually the aggressor, driven by a fantasy of omnipotence, probably based in an experience of impotence and existential threat. In moments of omnipotence, both those with a positive emotional sweep and those full of anger, we are drenched in an experience of power and personal ability, seeing reality not entirely soberly, and effectively run with that distortion.

In both states, impotence and omnipotence, the experience is an internal one, with a focus on the external results. These states represent a fantasy of results, not necessarily based on what really happened or is happening.

What do we mean by that?

Here's an example: A student with an important test coming up naturally fears failure and worries that he doesn't know the material or might forget it all. Thus far, the failure is internal. In his internal dialogue, the impotence is presented as leading to a stinging failure in the exam, which is the greatest threat, the failure in serving some function in the world.

The script could continue – maybe he won't graduate, and maybe he won't find a proper job, and who will want to stay with him without his ability to provide? And so on and so forth, an internal experience of worthlessness and inability to deal with the responsibilities of life, which is ostensibly in the outside world and in the negative consequences set to happen, even though this is still imaginary, one possibility among many.

The experience of omnipotence can work the same way: Let's say the student, still before his test, is sure of his ability to answer all the questions correctly, as it's "nothing" to him. Until now, as before, this was an internal process which "colored" the facts in his imagination which now seem external – the student imagines the moment of success, getting the highest grade in the class, maybe even to being invited by the Dean to a ceremony where he is awarded the excellence award he deserves, then gets an amazing job fitting his high capabilities, and worthy women compete for his affection, and so on. The story of amazing success, representing a fantasy in which the feeling of success takes shape according to the yardstick we invent – financial success, honors we receive, amazing pleasure and so on.

In both states – impotence and omnipotence – we deal too much in expectations of certain results or remembering specific events. Even when we remember past moments in our lives, as we practiced before, we still cling to the external, which creates a subsequent emotional movement within us. This process of remembering is never precise with the details, instead adapting itself to our emotional need and escalating our emotional movement. Memory is a fantasy of the past. So long as the emotional movement is light, the process is natural with no need to delve into it too much. But the emotional meaning of the experience of omnipotence or impotence might be more extreme and painfully domineering.

When we identify, ourselves or by others, a tendency to sink into a pleasant emotional omnipotence that gets whatever it wants, we can assume that it is also based on an experience of inability, of helplessness or unpleasant impotence. Sometimes the experience is of existential emptiness along with a lack of confidence of our place in the world, which emptiness is compensated by the fantasy.

It's important to distinguish between a fantasy of impotence or omnipotence and creative imagination. We have imaginations which are not "locked onto" an external result or gratification, and which do not deal only with us and our place in the world. Imagination is a creative tool which is another source of knowledge, especially when it is freed of self-centeredness. Creative imagination can bring good to the world, marked by some action, some creation, research, writing or other work. The fantasy of impotence or omnipotence abuses the power of creative imagination and strengthens the hold of self-centeredness on us and we on it.

Similarly, we should also distinguish between hope and the fantasy of omnipotence. Hope is not compulsive, there is no spinning out of control or locking onto a particular result.

What's so bad about that? After all, fantasies usually relaxes us, like the calm after having a good drink. We can ask ourselves whether being mired in fantasy is good for us? If so, why? Is its influence what we want for ourselves and life?

First of all, fantasies are addictive, leading us to spin out of control. It's easy to identify the addiction to the fantasy of omnipotence, which is pleasant, caresses our self-centeredness and serves it to deepen its control over us. We desire more and more of it, and it appears even when we have no time for it, but also lack the power, interest, or ability to be rid of it. Sometimes we become mired in it at the expense of life itself.

Even violent omnipotence can be addictive in its own harmful way, and we tend to become mired in that, too. For a brief moment, it removes the experience of lacking power and confidence in ourselves, providing us with the ostensibly pleasant feeling of power , despite the unpleasant content.

Strangely enough, the fantasy of impotence is also experienced as addictive, despite it's clearly being unpleasant, painful, and harmful. We could become mired in it, at the expense of life itself, and it affects our functioning. It's as if we have no ability to resist and remove it, even if it's unpleasant to the point of being a bad long trip , frequently repeat itself , or appear occasionally. In all its forms it takes over our mind and affects our emotions, thoughts and behaviors.

In addition, the awakening from the fantasy of omnipotence usually occurs to a reality which strikes us as relatively banal, painful, empty or threatening. The greater our fantasy of success, fun, or power, the smaller our experience of reality – banal, unsatisfying, threatening, painful, or just boring and bland. A large part of the pain comes from the very awakening from the great fantasy. We don't really choose omnipotence, it's more like it "chooses" us, and takes over, becoming more and more unpleasant, driving us to spin out of control.

Fantasies also often involve a process of desensitization. When we fantasize, the reality in which we live becomes unsatisfactory, driving us to want more. Even our actual moments of success in the real world do not align with the power of the fantasy. Eventually there are people who become addicted to fantasy and prefer it to reality. Some choose to continue with the fantasy and flee reality, even if it's some realization of the fantasy.

We see this clearly with sex addicts. Some of them prefer to watch porn and satisfy themselves, rather than have relations with a loving partner, or prefer to only have random encounters, preferably on a one-time basis, which serve as a fake fantasy or a show. In fantasy, everything seems shinier than reality, but it is one-dimensional without the depth and the variety of reality and without experiencing real challenges. The people we fantasize about are like objects magnifying our experience of omnipotence, and their existence depends on fulfilling the function we assign them.

Reality is of course different. People have their own life, desires and responses. We can influence the results, but not control them which can be threatening and burdensome. The more we become mired in and used to the fantasy, reality can become that much more of a bother. I've met sex addicts who dream and fantasize most of the day about wild sexual relations, watching hardcore porn and identifying with the dominating figure they are watching – but when their regular partner wished to have relations with them, sex seemed less attractive to them. That partner might once have symbolized their pinnacle of erotic ambitions. But that was some time ago, and now they are avoiding it, preferring to stick with the fantasies. Human reality strikes them as less exciting than imaginary fantasy.

On a side note – there are therapists who recommend that sex addicts who avoid relations with their regular partner have erotic fantasies while doing so, or watch porn together. Such a recommendation is akin to trying to put out a fire with a flammable liquid, or give the serpent and the addiction its favorite food. This recommendation neither benefits nor respects the other partner.

What happens when a fantasy of omnipotence can be realized? It's certainly possible that someone will fantasize about an achievement and attain it. And then all sorts of things can happen. One very common possibility is that the fantasy, now realized, only increases that person's sense of dissatisfaction in life, in turn increasing their sense of impotence.

If we look at the fantasy of greatness, we see it almost never suffices with the memory of any past success. Memory, since it focuses on a past experience, does not satisfy the need for an experience of greatness in the present. The need for omnipotence is a hunger incapable of being satisfied. The appetite naturally grows, as, in the words of Francois Rabelais, "appetite comes with eating[70]." Impotence, the hunger underlying omnipotence, is not satisfied by the "food" of the experience of success. The more extreme the experience of success and satisfaction is, the more it tends to melt and disappear into an experience of impotence, as though it was corrosive acid.

Since the previous fantasy is no longer enough, the need emerges for a new, more extreme one. If someone tries to realize fantasies, they effectively choose the path of increasing lack of satisfaction. This is the paradox of a painful reality tied to the spinning of fantasies out of control, leading to escalation, with life itself becoming more and more one-dimensional.

A prominent example of a painful fantasy spinning out of control is intimate romantic relationships. Oftentimes in the beginning, when the two fall in love, everything is experienced positively. The other partner seems more than perfect. Life is a fantasy come true. We feel a flowing omnipotence, as though the world itself is smiling on us. After the first stage, they get used to it and the partner becomes a given. The excitement declines. Maybe they're still convinced they're in love, but they also become a little bored.

They enjoy the habit and security of couple-hood, but also miss the excitement they once had. They miss that old fantasy, when all was new and fresh. The reality once desired has become the norm and can no longer satisfy the desire for omnipotence. Sometimes couples reach the point of cheating on each other and primarily betraying themselves, seeking out new thrills, trying to realize the experience of omnipotence. These cases usually won't work. The distress will return, big time, along with the emptiness and banality of the experience of impotence.

All these are states of high self-centeredness and the movement between them. Omnipotence is an experience of self-centeredness in which our ego experiences itself spreading out and conquering the world. Every conquest creates a desire for more for the ego. The ego is no longer willing to accept any stopping of its expansion, and therefore uses extreme measures to continue to spread out. The omnipotent ego is unwilling to tolerate what it considers as an intrusion into its territory, and reacts – sometimes violently – with self-centeredness increasing further in a growing spin out of control. Something similar happens in the state of impotence, but in the opposite direction: The ego collapses into itself and disappears into an experience of emptiness extremely self-centered. Here, too, there is a spinning into self-collapse, no longer willing to tolerate anything in its path. These states are two forms of the same self-centeredness, with an increase of one, guaranteeing the increase of the other, with painful movement between them. **So, what can be done?**

As the GraceWay proposes, what we can do is **let go** of the self-centeredness and **transcend** it, slowly, gradually, with the "spirit of the loving God." This transcendence begins with a paradox – **accepting** ourselves as we are. Acceptance begins with admitting to ourselves that we do indeed have moments of impotence as well as omnipotence, like a tendency that arises and tries to trap us in the sticky web of self-centeredness.

When we accept our tendency, we no longer have the need to fight it or act within it, as though it was reality itself. Instead of going back and trying to realize a fantasy, or become mired once again within the self-pity of impotence, we can let go and transcend ourselves. For instance, we can record the fantasies we had during the day, or the moments of impotence and omnipotence, when the day is over. The very act of recording directs us to look at things from the outside, from a non-identifying perspective, itself creating a change.

Each one of the twelve tools can be applied, and the movement between these two poles usually weakens. Instead of solving impotence – we let go of it, thus breaking free of omnipotence, as well. Without the exciting peaks and valleys, we can instead encounter reality as it is, and live in it, with grace.

Let's take another moment of deep silence. Into that silence, we'll introduce self-examination: We'll seek out an appearance of the experience of impotence which we've recently had, or one which seems to repeat itself in a manner typical to us. We'll momentarily let its memory arise full force in our mind. We'll observe ourselves from the outside, seeing ourselves in the fullness of the impotence experience, and will also see how it dissipates in its own way.

Let's return to the deep silence, introducing a moment of an experience of omnipotence we recently had, or one which repeats itself in a manner typical of us. We'll momentarily let the memory arise in full force in our mind. We'll observe ourselves from the outside, seeing ourselves in the fullness of the omnipotence experience, and will see how it dissipates in its own way.

Let's return to the deep silence – deep, without any memory or time, just silence.

"We must distinguish between yearnings for the Divine, for God, for the spirit, for the truth, and the desire for what is passing[71]."

CHAPTER SEVEN

Removing Barriers to Growth

Let's begin with a moment of silence. We'll delve into it. We'll focus on the peaceful, calm breathing, and listen to our pulse. We'll imagine our breathing and pulse as anchors of silence. When we focus on these, silence returns to our mind.

Oftentimes, despite our sincere intent, readiness, and behavioral changes, we face obstacles on our spiritual path. Even when we use this or that tool, and understand the role of self-centeredness, we still experience our path being blocked.

What to do? To free these barriers, we need to recognize them and their presence. A central part of the twelve step program has to do with the awareness of barriers hindering our progress, and also contains recommendations for how to break free of them. The twelve step program typically emphasizes practicality. The experience of many people from different backgrounds in using this program, showed that practicality allows for liberation and progress.

It's worthwhile to read the literature of the twelve-step groups, such as from the original literature of AA[72] and learn how to break free of these barriers. What appears below is based primarily on experience accumulated in the steps program, which is further detailed in the original literature of the program. For those who wish to delve deeper in the process, it is highly recommended to go through the steps program in an orderly fashion with the help of those who are personally acquainted with it.

What are the barriers to change? They are the emotional structures or forms of emotional reaction we have gotten used to. Barriers also include habits of behavior and typical thought structures, certain memories, and our social relations which became rigid and prevent change. What all barriers share is they shut us into a certain pattern of thought, emotion, behavior, or in our relationship with other people, and they prevent us from being the grace we wish to encounter. They bring us back again and again to the familiar and the well-known, even if this doesn't help us at all and the results are undesirable.

The barriers are an expression of self-centeredness which has a powerful hold on us, preventing us from progressing. They increase our identification with some aspect of self-centeredness – for instance, with a sense of being hurt by someone else – and therefore prevent us from advancing. The identification of the barriers is effectively a focused identification of self-centeredness, and breaking free of them marks a letting go and transcending the same. To demonstrate, let me open with a parable I once told of the twelve-step program, which describes each and every step and emphasizes the importance of breaking free of barriers[73].

The parable of the swamp

People in distress, who repeat the same mistakes or fall into the same traps and fail to change, are like a person sinking in quicksand. When, how, and why he sank in quicksand are interesting questions, but seeking the answers could delay him; it's a waste of time that's rapidly running out. The heavy, thick mud is covering him from all sides. Slowly but surely he sinks into it, unable to find a stable place to plant his feet.

Surprisingly, he is unwilling to recognize the fact that he is sinking in quicksand, facing great danger. To the contrary, it seems that he is in a warm, protected place, a familiar place. He has gotten used to the typical swamp smell – which for those outside is a stench – but for him it is actually a pleasant one. He might have entirely forgotten what clean air smells like, so for him it's fine that things go on like this.

But he in a swamp, which typically swallows up those in it and does not let go. At some stage, the sinking individual can no longer ignore that he is sinking further and further down, and the thick swamp water is starting to press on his neck. He understands that he is literally up to his neck in trouble and starts a number of hasty moves to extricate himself from the trap. The swamp still seems pleasant and he only wants to get away from the danger zone, not break free entirely. Unfortunately, he is getting to know the nature of the swamp, where every hasty movement escalates the situation, and the distress of the person who refuses to understand the seriousness of his situation, increases.

As time passes, the sinking person sinks further down, and the water and mud now threaten his airways. The suffocation, the distress, and the powerlessness leads to his pride breaking, albeit not easily, and he is now willing to receive outside aid. He finds a thin rope which someone tossed him from out there, holds onto it, and discovers to his disappointment, that the person who tossed the rope stood on the edge of the swamp and slid in the moment the rope was pulled, or they themselves were in the swamp and sank further.

The drowning person's distress increases. He tries and clings to the hands waving around him, of others alongside him in the swamp, but to no avail. Sometimes he causes someone next to him to sink even more and sometimes he gets temporary relief, but when it seems that everything is working out – he sinks again. The situation gets more complicated when others try and lean on him and threaten to hasten his end.

As the swamp water begin to penetrate his nostrils, he, a miserable person in a terrible distress, has one last option – to stretch his neck and tilt his head upward, with a hope for air, a miracle or a last temporary reprieve before the end. His powerlessness is complete.

Everything he tried until now failed, and from the little he can see next to him – so has everything the others tried. He is ready for everything that will happen, with a despairing sense of defeat and the painful understanding that he cannot change the situation himself [this is the first of the twelve steps].

But when he lifts his face upward, toward the distant sky, he is surprised to see a thick rope let down from above, right next to him. Moreover, similar additional ropes are also coming from the sky, on which people are climbing, survivors from the swamp. Until now, due to the habit of years and pride, he refused to look up, and therefore has to yet notice the ropes, and it was almost too late.

But one small thing was still left to do. Close by, he sees someone high on the rope, who points to another available rope right next to him and tells him to hold on tight. His voice sounds familiar. For some time now, that climber has been trying to attract his attention, which he chose to ignore. Since this was an emergency and there was no other option, he clings with everything he has to the rope, making another pleasant discovery: The moment he clung to the rope, it lifts him up, seemingly of itself, with no need for him to climb it, only hold onto it [the second step]. What a relief! With it, a new feeling comes to him –gratitude for the rope, and especially the rope's owner, whom he hadn't recognized until now, pulling the rope upwards without letting go and saving those drowning below.

As he progresses upward, fresh air starts to flow into his lungs. He breathes it with pleasure, understanding just how much he lived within a deep miasma of stench which was the swamp. Most of his body is still mired in that swamp, but the situation is a little less life-threatening with his head no longer buried in it.

He turns to look around and observes the people on similar ropes. Some are quite high above the swamp, while some are still mired like he is. Not far from him, he notices a person who is also suspended on a rope, higher than him, with his entire body outside the swamp.

But that individual sufficed with the short rise out of the swamp and is pretty satisfied with the result. As such, the poor person let go of his strong hold on the rope, and predictably enough – sank back into the swamp. The dive was immediate, and he entirely disappeared in the thick swamp. He made a few waves, which receded. There was a person, who is no more. Sad. Our survivor, who observed the rapid, tragic process from afar, shook with fear, and tightened his grip on the rope, determined to do everything possible not to lose it, no matter what [the third step].

The rope slowly lifts. The hands cling strongly to the rope, the whole body almost outside the swamp, except for the legs which are still drenched in the muck. He feels quite safe, breathing easier. And then the lift stops. He tries and continues to climb on his own, but it's not possible. It turns out when he was mired deep in the swamp, his legs became tangled in the roots and bushes in it, an entanglement which prevents him from advancing.

The one pulling the rope waits for this entanglement to shake loose. The drowned -rescuee looks around and sees that others are hanging onto ropes around him, at the same stage of being lifted up, are holding onto the rope with one hand, grabbing it nicely, while using the other to free all the knots bending downwards right into the swamp [fourth step].

The person next to him, who showed him the rope and who himself broke free of his entanglement, turns to show him what to do. Sure of his hold, he bends down and begins to free himself from the chains of the past which are pulling him downward. This requires that he invests his all and makes an exerted effort – including bending down into the thick swamp, with its many dangers and with his negative memories ; freeing of the roots, and branches, some of which bound him as tightly as handcuffs and which involved pain-ful work to loosen; and in his continued hold onto the rope, which ensures his rescue. Fortunately, the person next to him, who continued to move up on his rope, bent down to him and patiently explained what and how to deal with every knot that reveals itself, and this support provides him relief.

After finishing the work of breaking free of the entanglements of the past, the rescuee asks the guide next to him what to do. He answered that he needs himself to announce to the puller of the rope that he is ready, that he wishes to continue being lifted upwards as much as possible and that he doesn't want to remain in the swamp [fifth, sixth, and seventh steps]. He does what he is told, and the rope continues to go up. The feeling is wonderful, some-thing he doesn't remember ever feeling. A heavy weight that once rested on his shoulders or feet has now gone.

A little more uplifting of body and soul, and the rope stops once again. At this stage, he has already become used to asking the person next to him, who's always a little higher. He explains that in the past, when he lived in the swamp and sank into it, he tied himself to other people there with various strands, so as to stabilize and strengthen his situation. Others did much the same.

To continue to move on up, he must break these ties [steps eight and nine]. This action is slightly more complex than the previous detachment of his legs. He needs to turn to the people, remember moments he'd rather forget, which made sense when living in the swamp, and detach the strands. There is no other choice. These are ties that pull downward, which must be cut. Since they involve other people bound by the same ones, the detachment can only be done with them, not unilaterally.

This is the only option to keep going. In the beginning he is afraid to raise forgotten memories of times and relationships he regrets, but he happily discovers that the experience of detachment is pleasant and is certainly not as threatening as he thought. Every connection that gets cut leads to greater relief, another weight that slides off him. When he finishes cutting all the ties, the rope continues to go up, entirely by itself.

He understands that there is someone who looks at him and cares for him up there, and the feeling is wonderful. The rope continues and rises comfortably and smoothly, and he becomes experienced at lifting up. It does happen that he becomes entangled again with some branches or reeds along the way, or that someone tries to bind him with an old strand, but he knows he needs to quickly break free of them to continue to move on up [step ten]. The direction is clear to him – he wants to advance and reach the one pulling up this wonderful rope which saved his life [step eleven].

Once entirely out of the swamp, it turns out to the person now rescued, again by watching others, that he can move even closer to the one pulling the rope and merits his embrace, which will protect him from any harm and dropping back down into the swamp. All that is needed is for him to agree to bend back down and show the other drowning people the way to the rope, which is there for everyone. Just as he was guided, so can he guide those who want the path of uplifting and overcoming of obstacles and barriers, and helps them as much as possible.

Without hesitation, that person, once drowned ,and now a rescuer, chooses to help others. In doing so, even when he bends down into the swamp to reach them, his stability only improves. The pleasant lightness becomes stronger. Helping others prevents him from forgetting that he was once himself deep in the swamp and how easy it is to fall back into it, to drown and disappear without a trace. So long as he continues such activity, he is strongly supported by the puller of the rope and enjoys fresh air he never enjoyed even before he ended up in the swamp [twelfth step].

As we can see with this parable, the removal of the barriers appears in steps four through nine of the twelve-step program, continuing on to the tenth step. The reason the process is proposed in the middle rather than at the beginning is that progress and stabilization of change is needed before beginning to "dig deep" to remove entrenched barriers. The more advanced steps – eleven and twelve – are the result of the deepening of change, and express the continued progress which is relatively free of barriers. Below briefly and fairly loosely describes the middle steps of barrier removal, according to the formula first proposed in the Big Book of AA[74]. The barriers are tied to our relationship with others, ourselves, and the world, and of course with God, which includes resentments we have accumulated, fears that rule us and harms we did to others.

Examining resentments

Growing up in a social world means being in relationships with people. These relationships include good and wonderful experiences of grace and love, sharing and friendship, but also conflicts, clashes and harm. Sometimes the experience of harm is a product of lack of knowledge, mistaken interpretation or deficient communication. Sometimes the harm is deliberate. Past experiences of harms create an ongoing influence within us marked in different ways, and one of the most emotional prominent is the resentments we develop alongside habits of fear or suspicion.

In this part, we will speak in general of growth from resentment and fear toward forgiveness. We will address harms, but not extreme cases such as sexual, physical, or strong emotional abuse, or indeed any other trauma. Growing from the experience of extreme harm will be discussed later on.

What is harm? Surprisingly enough, understanding the essence of harm is generally secondary to the process of breaking free of the barrier of resentment. It's more important for us to understand what the experience of harm in the past is still doing to us now and most importantly – what can we do to change it, when enough time has passed and the experience has become part of our life story.

Unpleasant events carry an ongoing impact on us depending on the character and the intensity of the harm. However, the main influence the harm carried is not what actually happened, but how we perceive the event when it did, and especially how we respond to it afterwards. In all our relationships, deep and superficial, and even casual and random, different things happen, some we perceived to be harmful to us, sinking deep into our life story. This deep entry is sometimes marked by resentment.

What is resentment?

Resentment in French is ressentir. The Latin prefix "re" marks repetition, and its second part "sentir" – originating in the Latin "sentire" – means to "feel." In other words, a feeling that repeats itself. The resentment belongs to the emotions of anger, and marks a repeating anger. For instance, someone did something in the past we were angry about, consciously or not, and our resentment continues that anger into the present. Whenever we feel resentment toward that person, we effectively regurgitate that initial anger which escalates to the point of resentment, and may even develop to the point of hostility or hatred.

Resentment makes us seek out the person toward whom we feel it. For instance, when that person is successful, our heart aches. When they fail, we take delight in that or feel pleasant relief. Sometimes, the very act of remembering a certain person leads to our rise of resentment. Just a moment ago we were at peace, and now that someone's name has been mentioned, that peace has vanished. There are also cases where the resentment is hidden. Ostensibly, we have good relations with someone, but under the surface is a bubbling resentment which raises its ugly head every so often and comes out in the form of open anger or ambivalence toward the person, or maybe just an unexpected "slip of the tongue" which seems like it came out of nowhere.

When the resentment is toward someone close, such as a parent, then things become more complicated, since it can appear alongside a positive and loving attitude toward them. For instance, someone who loves her father, but also harbors resentment toward him, believing he didn't love her, and was critical, have a very close relationship on the one hand, while on the other often has outbursts toward him even she considers unjustified. After working on herself and developing awareness, the resentment became apparent. There are similar cases where the resentment is hidden and the person is not aware of it, but it still acts and leaves its mark.

Resentment is an emotion which creates a negative experience and influences thoughts and behavior. It can be described as mental poison. The action or situation which led to it has long passed, sometimes really long, but the resentment continues to spread burning poison in our mind. Through it, we re-experience the anger, as well as our vulnerable, weak situation. The resentment, which exists in our mind, is a central component in the process which effectively weakens and harms us, adding to the actual harm done to us in the past. The poison which resentment drips into our mind belongs to the present, while the action leading to it belongs in the past.

Resentment binds us to the person who harmed us in the past as well as strongly binds us to memories and events of the past, preventing us from growing and moving on. How absurd it is – resentment binds us to the very people and memories we would usually want to move away from as much as possible. The more we become mired in resentment toward them, they will become an even more inseparable part of us.

The Big Book of AA states that resentment is the number one enemy that has killed more alcoholics than any other[75]. Resentment prevented them from healing and drove them to back to drinking in a way that led to lethal consequences. Similarly, if we honestly look at ourselves, we can see the serious harm caused by resentment. When nursing resentment, we tend to become deeply mired in the experience of what was done to us, or in negative thoughts about someone else, along with the need to protect ourselves against a harmful world, and self-centeredness has a party.

When our self-centeredness becomes stronger as resentment operates in our mind, we are less and less able or willing to act with grace toward others and the world. Resentment makes us "stuck" and disrupts our ability to live the grace we wish. This is why resentment is considered a major barrier in progress on a spiritual path. It is therefore greatly important to break free of resentments, which we emphasize in the GraceWay.

It is recommended that those interested in the process I will now describe, make use of an experienced person who underwent something similar. This will mean close accompaniment and follow-up, allowing for asking questions and sharing painful things that come up – and they might. If there's no-one around us who has undergone such an experience, it's possible and worthwhile to make use of a spiritual adviser or therapeutic professional who knows this process and can help us.

In any case, it's important that we are not alone in the process. It's also possible to do the process with a close friend or partner who are also following the path. It's even possible to do it in a small group, as a few people together are a greater force than any one of us alone, and if the group forms for the sake of spiritual development, it can advance in a more stable manner than anyone individually[76]. In any event: alone, with help, or in a group, the process is personal, and the help of others only serves as guidance and support.

We'll start the process by listing all our resentments. At first, this listing may seem complex, but if we do it in an organized fashion, it becomes simple. The Big Book of AA suggests dividing resentments into groups based on those toward people, institutions and principles – and starting with the first.

These are resentments which seem pretty clear on the face of it – we feel resentment toward certain people who in our experience hurt us or treated us improperly. To record them all, we need to go backwards in our life story, from today back to our early childhood and write down all those toward whom we have, or had, a resentment. While remembering our life story, we also remember the human encounters we experienced as so harmful that we still have resentments toward those people.

We will also write down resentments which ended, to make sure there is no unpleasant trace left, even if unconsciously. Sometimes we feel resentment to a group of people who harmed us as a group, which we can write down together. For instance, a young woman wrote down: "a group of boys from the sixth grade in my elementary school."

Oftentimes, the resentment list includes people near and dear to us, like our parents. This is common and natural. Close relationships are complex and all sorts of things happen in them, some of which lead to resentments, despite the closeness and love. Sometimes our own name will appear as well, a sense of resentment toward ourselves for mistaken decisions, behaviors we regret, opportunities we missed, and more. In any event, we will build the list without dwelling on any given name and without describing what they did or didn't do to us, or what we did to ourselves. We'll just write the name down and move on.

If we encounter some serious harm we experienced, one we may have forgotten about, during this process, there are two things worth doing at this stage: First, share it with someone as soon as possible. A friend, a partner, a close companion, or a professional therapist, spiritual adviser, or someone we trust and on whose guidance we rely. As long as we do not remain alone with that memory and experience. Second, we will ignore that name temporarily. We'll keep it for future reference, when we talk about healing from harms done, and even then, we will engage in that process only with someone appropriate.

After jotting down the names of all the people toward whom we hold resentments, we'll move on to institutions. This means resentments toward bodies or organizations like the state, the government, a party, the tax authority, the police, court, school, and more. Although these are organizations and not people, we may have developed a strong resentment toward them, which can be marked by bitterness, criticism, and confrontational behaviors toward them.

Obviously expressing an opinion against some institutional body is not necessarily carrying a resentment, which takes over our mind and distorts it. Through self-searching and the aid we receive from the person we chose to accompany us on our path, we will succeed in identifying if this is simply a specific case of expressing an opinion against the institution and understandable opposition, or whether that is simmering resentment. Usually the latter is marked by the strong emotion accompanying our opinions, to the point of internal emotional coercion and a blindness from seeing things differently.

When we finish with the list of institutions toward which we have a resentment, we will then move to principles, meaning abstract things which make us feel resentful. For instance, antisemitism or racism. Obviously, our opposition to something abstract like discrimination does not necessarily express resentment. The accompanying emotions and the intensity of the opposition, as well as our blindness and one-sidedness can tell us of the presence of a resentment. There's nothing like looking from the perspective of someone else or a small group to help us know if we're dealing with resentment mixed with a legitimate opinion.

Resentment toward principles can be identified among people who espouse some ideology considered positive and moral in society, but who are willing to cause far from exalted harm to those who they believe represent a principle toward which they harbor resentment, and in the name of those same exalted principles. They smear, insult, boycott, and what not, in the name of the grand idea of the love of man. That's how resentment works in the mind.

In any event, we will list these resentments. Even if few, they are sometimes significant. We can delve into them and see how they started. They usually involve people, who represent the abstract principle.

For instance, I met a man who felt resentment toward racism, and when we dug a little deeper, he remembered experiences when he suffered from discrimination due to his origins. His resentment began from frustration and anger toward a group of youths who in his eyes were arrogant, discriminated against him, and rejected him when he was younger. At a certain stage, he generalized his resentment toward them to resentment toward the principle, and his attitude was directed toward anyone who seemed to contain racism. Strangely enough, he even felt resentment toward people like him, and his wife told me that he was racist in how he talked to her, even though they come from a similar background and despite his resentment against racism. This is the absurdity of resentment, which pretends to be the pursuit of justice and which effectively serves self-centeredness.

An additional resentment which people sometimes find is toward God, as they understand Him. If it comes up, we write it down. Otherwise, how do we break free of it? One of the strange things about this resentment is that many people claim that they feel resentment toward God and in the same breath don't believe in His existence. A contradiction? Not according to the resentment and self-centeredness.

When jotting down the resentment toward God, it's worth noting whether it's actually against Him, because someone has harmed us, or it's resentment toward someone who represents Him in our eyes. I've met people who declared to have a resentment against God because of the behavior of certain religious people. By contrast, I've met people who were hurt and felt resentment toward God for not helping them, in their view, in their moment of distress and powerlessness in the face of harm.

Stages in breaking free of resentments

What do we do with the list now that we've written it down? First, we'll look at it and see that everyone on it shaped our life story, and indeed still shapes it through our resentments. Is this what we want? Probably not. So we'll continue the process to break free of those resentments.

Let's go over the list, and briefly note what each one did to us to earn our ire. Without getting into long stories or commentaries, but rather in as concrete a manner as possible. This way, we'll know what we're dealing with now, and reduce the interpretations we formed about these people over the years. When we move on to resentments against institutions or principles, we will see with the help of that same concreteness that there were identifiable people involved, who we think harmed us, and that our resentments are against them.

When we finish, we can tell ourselves that our resentments, at least most of them, are due to actions done to us, or not done to us in the case of neglect. Moreover, the resentments are over actions that harmed us and not just general ones. Resentments are our reaction to actions which people (or institutions which contain people) did which harmed us. People, including those close to us, regularly engage in these actions but we don't resent them all, only those who harmed us.

Even we, may sometimes act similarly toward someone else, then we have all the understanding and justification in the world in our biased judgment, but when those same actions are done to us, we naturally develop resentment. When we look at resentments in this way, we see ever more clearly how it is an expression of self-centeredness and works in its service.

Now the fun begins – now we start to break free of the resentments. We're going to let go of and cast off a heavy and needless burden that's been dragging us down into the depths of the swamp of self-centeredness. Even if we think it had some benefit in the past, it has served its purpose and we would like to move on without it. This liberation will happen by making use of a special recipe which includes eight filters. Each time, we'll use a narrower filter, which frees us from deeper resentments, until we reach the "doomsday weapon" which can cut off any resentment – sometimes quickly, sometimes gradually.

We can do this process in two forms, according to our own preference. One is to go over the list of resentments again, name by name, and apply the appropriate filter for each in order to break free. When we reach the filter which detaches us from that particular resentment, we'll list it next to the name, so we know what freed us.

The second approach is to focus each time on one filter, gradually, and go over the whole list while applying it. Every time the filter catches a resentment in its net – we write it down and continue. Each round, fewer and fewer names will be left to go over, until we reach the final filter and then we might end up without any resentments at all. The process below is based on the second approach, but everyone should choose what's appropriate for them, and the methods can even be mixed and matched. What matters is that we go over each of the resentments and happily and lovingly break free of their poisonous effect on us.

The first filter is **the very act of registration**. When we look at our list, we will see while working on it, that there were things that softened inside us. There are resentments where, simply by virtue of having remembered them and defined them, our perspective and understanding of them changes, freeing us from their sting. They no longer harm us, they have ceased to be resentments. What of the people who were involved in these resentments? Let them have a long and healthy life, we have no problem with them, on the contrary. We will mark these resentments that have now expired, thus "airing" out the list a little. There is relief, if relatively small, since these are the easier cases.

The second is **the very understanding of what resentment is and what it does to us**. When we look at the names, one after the other, and we understand that we are tied to a particular name because of the resentment and remain with a high degree of self-centeredness – this understanding is sufficient to end some of them. Understanding frees us from their burden. Obviously, these are still relatively light resentments, but breaking free of them is still an encouraging relief. One person had a list of 180 names, institutions, and principles toward which he bore resentment. 180 resentments that controlled him and his life. After completing the list, he was terrified that he allowed almost every little thing to shape his life and poison his mind with continuous resentment. Just writing these resentments down effectively erased many of them, after a long time in which they were active and poisoned his mind and behavior. The second filter of understanding the nature of resentments, sifted out a large number of them. He fairly quickly experienced a significant feeling of liberation and could now focus his energies on the few resentments which required denser filters.

The third filter raises an interesting question– **maybe the harm wasn't what we thought it to be?** Maybe due to a lack of knowledge or understanding, we built a story for ourselves that doesn't fit the facts? An unbiased examination, viewed from the perspective of time, can allow us to form a new understanding. If we have no clear knowledge of the harm caused, despite the emotional experience that accompanied us over time, then maybe we should let ourselves enjoy the benefit of doubt, and let go of the resentment with the possibility that the harm didn't happen? Even if we thought we'd been hurt for years, memories are not facts, and bravely reexamining matters allows us to tell ourselves a new story.

Say someone was sure their partner cheated on them with a friend, even though everyone denied it. In those far-off days, when the event ostensibly happened, the man was entirely driven emotionally, and without examining matters, , he chose to move away from both and built up a great resentment which influenced his relationships later on. Looking back over the years, he can look at the matter differently, seeing that doubt can go both ways.

He may have chosen one path of being hurt and nursing resentment, but he could have just as easily chosen the second one, casting doubt on the betrayal and the associated hurt. If the choice of the second direction in the present can lead to the end of the resentment, it is certainly worthwhile.

If we are not sure about the details of the harm, we will accept the doubt that maybe it didn't happen, and can finally break free of it. This is not self-deception, but rather an end to the lie we continued to believe in for years, even in favor of the simple conclusion that we didn't really know and still don't know what happened there. The resentment therefore "sat" on something that lacked any real basis, and it's time to forgo its good "services." Good riddance.

The fourth filter is for cases where harm does seem to have occurred. We have clear knowledge based on facts we experienced and still remember, but – and this is a big but – **there was no intent to harm**. Maybe even the opposite. Harm did occur even though the person responsible wanted to avoid causing it, and this understanding creates change.

Resentment is directed at people who intended to hurt us and is a reaction to that harm. For years, we told ourselves a story of deliberate harm, or of criminal neglect, when this story turns out to have been based on partial knowledge of the facts. Now that we are examining matters with all the knowledge we currently possess, it turns out that the harm was not at all intended. Oops, we were wrong, and we can let go of the resentment.

A typical example is someone who was sure her father neglected her in childhood. She remembers how he wasn't present at home and she missed him. She loved him, but because of his ostensible neglect, chose to distance herself and bear a deep resentment. Growing up she learned that the financial situation at home was very bad and their father had to take on another job so she would have everything she needed. That's why she experienced his absence in her life.

She was angry at her father, who had to spend less time with her out of concern for her well-being. But as a child she didn't know the reason, which was kept hidden from her.

When we understand there was no intent to harm, things look different. This different understanding can also be true when it comes to resentments toward institutions, where the resentment is usually not personal. The moment we understand that people acted obtusely and negligently, but that this was due to ignorance or lack of knowledge or "just" because of their own self-centeredness, but without any negative intentions toward us, that understanding provides a sense of relief.

Reality is apparently simpler than the story of the resentment and is usually not due to any negative intent, simply the banality that comes from lack of knowledge, sometimes to the point of indifference. The understanding that the harm had no malicious intent and wasn't personal, frees us from another group of resentments. The relief is usually pretty strongly felt at this stage, and only a few deeper resentments remain to be dealt with. We will continue to advance toward the very possible liberation from them as well.

The fifth filter is aware that there was harm, and the person responsible knows it and may have even intended it, or at least did not care if we were hurt. But when we examine the totality of our relations with them, it turns out that **we also harmed them.** It's irrelevant who struck first or harder – why does it even matter? They hurt, we hurt; we hurt, they hurt back. It's all the same. There was mutual harm here, entirely needless when viewed in retrospect.

The resentment is similarly needless. Let's maintain the equation – there was harm on both sides and that's all. The resentment disrupts and burdens that balance. We tend to think that there is no reason someone will hold resentment against us in a mutual relationship, so why should we harbor one against them?

We often see resentment between partners who separated – mutual harm which led to the destruction of the relationship and resentments that continue to poison those involved. Unfortunately, even couples who live together may suffer from the continuous poison of mutual resentment, and this is where the fifth filter is highly relevant.

For instance, a man who discovers his wife cheated on him. Not just with anybody, but with a close friend. The anger rages, as does the resentment that follows. Very quickly, he generalizes his resentment against all women – they're all unfaithful. But looking at it again, after a while, he understood that his wife's betrayal did not come out of nowhere. He was violent toward her, before it happened. He may not have cheated on her with another woman, but he did betray her trust with his violence and domineering, and the social isolation to which he drove her.

This new understanding changed something within him. Along with the realization that the burden of resentment weighs on him, he was ready to be free, and felt relief. He stopped dealing with her and her betrayal, and mostly stopped his thoughts of revenge, instead focusing on a divorce and later on co-raising the children.

Another example is of a couple that's been married for 25 years. He cheated on her right at the start, in a one-time event about which he confessed to her immediately. In talks between us, as they described the picture of their relationship, it turned out that she may not have cheated on him with another man, but she did cheat on him emotionally by becoming closed off, distant, domineering, humiliating him in front of friends and relatives, and other hurtful behaviors.

For years, they considered separating, but didn't. There came a point where they revealed the reason for their mutual resentments: He reminded her of the pain of her behavior and she reminded him of the pain of his betrayal. In the end, with both taking on the personal work of freeing themselves of resentment, with the understanding of how the harm was mutual, something shifted for the better in the relationship and the issue of separation was dropped. They were able to see the love and support that did exist between them, despite the tension that burst forth from time to time.

The sixth filter has to do with the weightier, deeper resentments. It refers to cases where it's entirely clear that there was nothing mutual about the harm. In no way did we reciprocate do what this person did to us . We had boundaries, and their harm crossed them. But, if we examine ourselves honestly, we discover that once or more, we were as hurtful to others as they were to us. **We've also harmed others in that way.**

Oops. It's certainly not pleasant to realize this. What logic and justice do we have on our side to judge someone else with the severity of a years-long resentment, when we acted more or less the same way, toward others? After all, we would not judge ourselves so harshly, only learn the appropriate lesson. We'll soon see that we can try to fix what we did and the harm we caused. But until then, let's start by letting go of the resentment.

We can think of someone whose partner cheated on him, even though he never cheated on her. They separated and he developed a very strong, ongoing resentment toward her. But later in life, he did similar things to other partners, cheating on them more than once. So what's the difference? She hurt him, he hurt others. This is a somewhat imaginary example, but it's close enough to the reality I've encountered more than once.

What we mean when discussing harm to others is harm of similar severity, but not necessarily the same exact behavior. For instance, someone stole something of emotional value from us, leading us to develop resentment, while we betrayed someone else's trust. Or a case where we harbor resentment toward a parent we believed neglected us, only to discover upon self-examination that our attitude toward our own children was sometimes compulsive. Instead of remaining with the resentment and blaming our parent for the life we built for ourselves and our compulsive attitude toward our children, it's time we took responsibility for ourselves and stopped casting blame and nursing resentments.

The sixth filter puts in the slightly unpleasant situation where we take leave of being the person who's in the right vis-à-vis the person toward whom we feel resentment, instead discovering that we as people are in the same place, offender and offended. There is a mutuality here of our fate as human beings, even if there was none in specific cases of harm. With the understanding of human mutuality, the resentment drops off on its own leading to great relief, as these were quite heavy resentments. When we look at the list of resentments, we'll discover that it has greatly reduced, even entirely deleted.

The seventh filter deals with even heavier resentments, which only a few of us have. It's reserved for our extreme resentments, directed at something that goes beyond legitimate human reactions. We are dealing with painful harm of the sort and level which we probably never inflicted. On anyone. Harm that goes beyond our red lines, and those we think should be everyone's lines. This is the sort of harm which points to unhealthy behavior, driven by a tortured soul. Harm that attests to an illness, certainly a behavioral one, and maybe a moral and emotional one.

This is the seventh filter - an **understanding that the harmful person is sick in the behavioral and moral sense.** Since we are dealing with a sick person, there's neither reason nor justification for resentment. Resentments after all, express a desire for justice, but in fact violate justice themselves. Because of someone else's illness, our mind is poisoned, as intensely as the resentment we are nursing. What justice is there that someone else's behavioral illness binds us to them, poisoning our minds with all its serious effects on us?

Their behavior attests to a tortured soul, suffering which might be healed with compassion or love. True, we who were hurt will likely not be the ones offering them such compassion or love at this stage, and even remain opposed to them and averse to their illness, but in the same breath – we can break off the resentment that binds us. The resentment contains neither justice, nor logic, nor benefit to anybody. It makes the hurt worse.

It's bad enough that the mind of the person who caused the harm was toxic – why should ours be? We also deserve compassion, and certainly love and grace, and the resentment blocks all of these. There's neither justice nor logic here. The change in the story we tell ourselves makes the difference, and I've seen some pretty strong resentments that melted away in this manner.

Miriam was a woman in her forties. When we spoke about resentments, there was one she couldn't dismantle. In her youth, she lived on a kibbutz alone, a new immigrant with no close relatives in the country. There was a cat on the kibbutz which she adopted and loved with the kind of intensity human beings can often love an innocent animal. The cat was closer to her than any human being.

At one time she left to visit relatives abroad and was gone from the kibbutz for two weeks. The cat was left under supervision. When she returned, she discovered the cat was gone. There was a young disabled and a little physically deformed man on the kibbutz, who also lived alone, . For some reason, he thought the cat was bothering him and killed it. Since he was disabled and helpless, his action was somehow forgiven by the kibbutz and the matter was closed without the intervention of the authorities.

But Miriam, then young and alone, was forced to deal with the act and the pain. Her hurt was very deep, and developed into a serious, bitter resentment which continued for many years. Miriam's description told of the offender as being disabled, apparently very bitter of the fact of his disability, whose relationships tended to be shaky. People pitied him, but kept their distance.

I suggested she see him as a sick person which required she cease to view him as cruel and evil, but rather weak and miserable. Not out of some sense of superiority, but simply based on the facts. It took Miriam a few days to absorb this perspective, but with it came great relief. The resentment passed.

Unfortunately, not all deep resentments are caught by the seventh filter. Sometimes we understand that a person is sick, but we also wish them continued suffering in the fires of their personal hell because of what they and their illness did to us. The resentment continues, unfortunately. In this case we have no choice but to deploy what I call the "doomsday weapon," the eighth filter, and I have never seen a resentment that passed through it. I have met people for whom it didn't work, but they probably didn't pick up on something during the process, and need more work to truly break free.

What's the filter that can screen out any resentment? Let's start with a behavioral description of it – for two weeks, for a start. Morning and evening, just when we wake up in the morning and just before we go to sleep, we go down on our knees and ask God, as everyone understands Him, for the following two things:

The first is that He free us from our resentment toward that particular person, something like: "God, please free me from my resentment toward so-and-so, for I have not succeeded in letting it go on my own." The second thing is that we ask God, with precisely the same intentions, that He act for the sake of the person who harmed us, just as we would like Him to do for us.

Yes, you read that correctly, the eighth filter tells us to **pray for the person who hurt us.** If by praying for the person who harmed us, we become free of the resentment, meaning that we break free at least from part of its harm to us, do we not benefit? In fact, the prayer may be for someone else, but their name is just a means, a medium, and the prayer is in fact for us, so that we break free of our resentment. The prayer for them creates the vital break leading us to break free of the resentment. Just as the resentment binds us to the person who harmed us with poisonous cords, so does prayer for them free us with the magic of love. And it works.

Here are two examples:

John was harmed by his mother throughout his childhood both emotionally and some "light" physically, at least as she saw it. She mostly neglected him and ignored his needs. Her needs apparently took priority in her eyes over those of her two children, who experienced this neglect very strongly. It may very well be that she experienced post-partum depression after giving birth to his older sister or him and hadn't recovered, or something else, but the reason didn't matter to him.

John understood that she's sick, because a mother who neglects her kids like this is probably not well. Sick as she might be, he still had compulsive thoughts about wanting to hurt her. He never did harm her or even come close to it, but the poison did its work. He began to pray for her as is suggested – two weeks, then another two weeks, and so on.

About three months after he started, he surprised me with a question: "Should I continue to pray for her?" "Why do you ask?" I wondered. "Because I don't think about her anymore. She hasn't been a part of me for a few days now. I even wish her good health." I pressed the matter: "If you meet her on the street, will you ignore her or greet her?" "I don't know, but the way I feel now, I'll probably say hi and go on my way, I have no interest to be in touch with her." There was obviously no further need for prayer. After years of suffering, the resentment collapsed. A few years later, after he started his own family, he got in touch with her and she turned to be a loving grandmother to his children.

Robert was a recovering addict who participated in a workshop I hosted. When we spoke about ending resentments, he shared a resentment he held against his brother. Since he was a member of NA and was thoroughly familiar with the steps program, he had already tried to break free of the resentment, but didn't "go all the way" with the process.

In a bad joke , he said: "You don't want to know what I told the last man who suggested I pray for my brother." "It doesn't matter," I answered, "what matters is that you pray for him, and you can tell me whatever you want." After some ostensibly joking exchanges between us, he decided it's time to give himself a chance, even though he wouldn't hear of praying for his brother before. Two-three weeks passed and the relief came, as expected.

We'll come back later to such prominent examples when we talk about recovering from victimhood, examples which show how liberation works, almost always. When doesn't it work? Usually when there is a great fear accompanying the resentment, overshadowing it and preventing one from breaking free of it. Therefore, the next step is a process of awareness of the fears and breaking free of these, too.

Before we move on, there are two other resentments to be discussed how to end – toward ourselves and toward God. It may well be that the change we undergo while breaking free of the other resentments will work on these, too, without focusing on them specifically, we will find that they also gradually disappear.

Work on resentments creates a broad range of changes, in addition to breaking free of specific ones. The weakening of the mental poison has a positive influence on many areas, with reducing our bitterness and demanding side, being replaced as these are by an awareness of gratitude. In cases where our resentments toward ourselves and toward God have not yet disappeared, we'll continue with working on ourselves with the knowledge that they will dissipate later on, with our progress, which also includes the development of our ability to accept ourselves and what life has in store for us.

Growing from the fear

What is fear? We all know fear in the experiential sense, to one degree or another. Fear is a universal emotion. There are four related states which clarify what fear is to us.

The first is the sense of danger, even existential danger. We are afraid that we'll fail to cope with the danger and prevent harm, either to ourselves or to those we hold dear. It usually takes over and paralyzes us. The stronger it becomes, the more our judgment leaves us and emotion rules.

The second is caution, a state in which there is evaluation and judgment; we examine the facts we know, and look at various possibilities and meaning.

There may be an accompanying emotion, even a suspicion or fear, but it does not dominate or paralyze us. We retain the power to decide and assess.

The opposite of caution is the third state – haste, the tendency to act without thinking or judgment. Even if the behavior seems brave, it actually ignores the danger and is thus not a sign of courage. What is brave in an action unheeding of danger? Sometimes haste expresses fear, which instead of paralyzing us actually makes us run toward the danger to be rid of the unpleasant feeling of fear itself.

The fourth state is courage, which arises when we deal with a danger in a conscious manner, deciding to act in spite of it. This is a case where we overcome our own natural tendencies, including caution and perhaps also a sense of fear, with the understanding that we should act.

Fear is paralyzing and tends to dominate, and therefore fears which we drag along with us throughout life and over the years are domineering barriers which handicap us and deny us judgment and awareness before action. That is why we want to be rid of them. The process will be somewhat similar to what we did before with the resentments, so we can go over it briefly.

All the caveats I mentioned before apply here, as well – we will not deal with cases of serious harm. If there are such then we will not enter into the process without appropriate accompaniment and support. Indeed, it's worthwhile in any case to have help in the process, preferably by someone with experience and or in a group.

Let's start with the list of fears we had or have from people, institutions, principles, and also situations that typically arouse fear such as fear of closed, open, high, low spaces, and more. It can also be fear of change, or new starts, routine, failure, or other things. It turns out there are many situations which make us feel fear. Here we are talking about the fear we feel and whose effect on our lives we are aware of, not necessarily feelings of paralyzing fear often defined as anxiety or phobias, which usually require professional counseling.

Having finished writing down all the fears we typically feel and occasionally paralyze us, we can see that as with resentments, this is a list of strong influences which ran and still partially run our minds and our life. It's not nice to see it in black and white, but there are things we can do about it. We'll go over everything we listed, and ask ourselves what caused the fear. We will once again maintain a concreteness which creates simplicity. We are not seeking deep analyses of the soul; the simple knowledge of what happened will suffice nicely. If we don't know, it's OK - we'll just note that in writing.

After finishing the list of fears along with what led to them, we'll move on to the process of breaking free of them. Unlike our liberation from resentments, where we checked each resentment against an appropriate filter, the process of freeing oneself from fear has to do with the very idea of fear. We wish to grow from the control any fear has on our mind.

What do we mean by this?

I previously presented four states: fear, caution, haste and courage. These are states which complement one another. For instance, courage and fear can go hand in hand as part of an action to overcome fear or despite it. Fear and caution can also appear together, with both aimed at the same thing, each with its own characteristics – for instance, a logical decision that it's not a good idea to go someplace, alongside a great fear of going there.

To these four states we will add one more, a fifth – faith. Fear is effectively the opposite of the state of faith. In a state of fear, we feel lonely and vulnerable in the face of perceived danger. Sometimes the danger seems to be capable of mortally wounding us, even eliminating us, whether symbolically or in actuality. Therefore, fear is a sense of the temporariness of our existence.

Even if we experience it as a group, such as during war, we feel all alone and vulnerable in the face of great danger which demonstrates our temporary existence. We feel that the intensity of the danger is greater than our ability to cope with it thus, a paralyzing fear rises.

Faith is a state in which we know we are not alone, an intuitive knowledge which sometimes arises along a logical conclusion, changing emotions and a sensual experience, but also goes beyond them. We are aware of a Supreme Power – God as we understand Him – and this supreme power is stronger than the danger. We are sure of this Supreme Power's ability to help us in dealing with the danger, we are not alone facing it, we have something that transcends our temporary nature, invulnerable. The danger is thus less scary, despite our limited ability to deal with it on our own.

Faith is the unique assurance that we cannot be harmed, only our bodies can, for we are not fundamentally our bodies, but something else which can be called a divine element. It's possible that our body will be hurt, as will our condition in the world, but faith helps us see what lies beyond any harm, and this knowledge cannot be taken away from us, under any condition. As a young man once told me after he developed faith: "It's knowing, in those situations which I once feared, that it will all be alright." This means that everything that will happen will be alright. Internal knowledge creates internal peace, despite the sense of danger.

Liberation from the idea of fear is actually the growth of faith. Even if fear rises – and it does – we continue with our actions without allowing fear to direct our behavior. We act according to what judgment tells us, while we devote our action to God. For instance, someone is in a new relationship and is afraid that his partner is not interested in her. Her tendency was to compulsively communicate with him, just to on the safe side.

Instead of this compulsive behavior, she decide to wait patiently, while directing herself toward God and an action which brings her closer to the divine. Thus, she no longer needed to remove the fear from her mind with a compulsive behavior, as she had an alternative, the peace of faith. In this case, peace reached the soul, as fear left, when she knew that whatever comes, it's all for the best. Eventually their relationship did end, but she was at peace with the way she had conducted herself by the time they reached that point.

When fear paralyzes us, we wish to avoid acting until the fear recedes. Fear ostensibly marks out a possible danger and we wish it to end before we act, apparently, we will know for sure that the danger has passed. Since there are cases or situations in which the fear arises anew each time we are exposed to them and does not recede on its own, we distance ourselves from them and effectively avoid certain actions or situations which might be desirable for us. For instance, if we have stage fright which comes up whenever we need to give a speech, and it repeats itself every time, we may get used to not speaking in public at all, even when it is our job.

With faith, our judgment is different. We no longer seek to remove the fear or avoid it. Fear is simply another factor to be considered with cautious or brave judgment, depending on the circumstances. Faith is the foundation for judgment and subsequent action, and it is what supports our courage. We feel fear, and act along with it, instead of waiting for it to end. Gradually, the power of the fear to direct us, decreases, and we grow from within the conception of fear, growing in faith and toward faith. The process is gradual, but the results and the relief are pretty rapid, if we keep at it.

Correcting harms we caused

Relationships with people and the world also unfortunately include almost inevitable damages and harms. An important part of self-change is our complete abstinence from behaviors which might harm others. If we mistakenly cause harm, we fix what we can as soon as possible, as some of the tools teach, and especially the "correcting errors" tool. With the help of this tool, we try and change our behavior and move toward the grace, which never harms.

Despite the change, with a bit of honesty we can see that in the past we did hurt others, sometimes unintentionally or unaware, sometimes as part of a power struggle, and sometimes due to self-centeredness that controlled us. What do we do with the harm we did? On the one hand, what was – was, and we cannot change what happened. We will accept that with serenity and realize there's no point in self-blame. What matters is we're on the path of change.

On the other hand, we nevertheless caused damage. Although time may have since passed, still there are people, institutions, and principles who suffered in ways that may still remain "open" wounds. Maybe something healed and maybe a scar formed, but maybe there is still a wound underneath, and scars aren't pleasant. Just as we had wounds and scars of resentment or fear, which perpetuated the hurt done to us, we wounded and damaged others.

A challenging aspect of our own growth is to correct the harms we caused, as much as possible, so we no longer feel shame, fear, or the temptation or desire to avoid or hide from them. In accordance with the serenity prayer, I described as the third tool, we want to reconcile with the past to the point of peacefully accepting it, along with the courage to correct what we can in the present. This correction strengthens our wisdom of distinction.

The benefit of correction is threefold: First, the very correction of the harm and healing of the wounds we caused others. Second, the change that deepens within us, thanks to the new habit of taking responsibility for everything we did. Third, we free ourselves a little from the negative effects of every harm we caused, such as shame, guilt and more. So how do we fix what has already happened and is done?

Before we get to the important spiritual work of fixing what we broke, let's ask ourselves: Would we want the people we hurt to forgive us, so we can start a "new page"? Accordingly, we'll continue to ask ourselves: Are we willing to forgive those who hurt us? We'll ask the question of forgiveness after we finish removing the barriers of resentment and fear, after we've broken free of most of the resentments and understand the idea of growing from the fear toward faith.

By force of that same faith, we are set to ask ourselves if we're willing to forgive those who hurt us. We still remember what happened, but we forgive and pardon. We don't have to reconcile with those who did us harm, maybe we'll only with some, and maybe we won't go back to being close with others. But we can forgive in the sense of completely freeing ourselves from everything that was and from every negative feeling toward the offenders.

Forgiving and forgetting marks our change of focus – instead of concentrating on the harms done to us, including the pain and the fear and the self-centered focus, we concentrate on the divine and the possible grace. Being the grace we wish to encounter, means forgiving and pardoning harm done to us, forgiving those who harmed us, and hoping that they find the same grace. After we change our focus, we can see to the harms we caused with a relatively clean conscience and try and fix what we can.

As we did before with fears and resentments, we will start the work of correction by systematically writing down every harm we did to other people, institutions, and principles. We will maintain balance and common sense, as well as make use of the outside perspective of an experienced someone.

Still, there were times someone thought we have hurt them though we don't think that was necessarily so. So that we don't err and too easily dismiss such claims, we'll consult with someone experienced in the matter. In other cases we believe we have hurt someone without them actually knowing it, remembering it, or seeing it as harmful. Once again, we will consult with another person for a second opinion – maybe we are too hard on ourselves. On the other hand, we don't want to go too easy either and we should of course be careful about denying harm we caused or make all sorts of excuses for ourselves to avoid dealing with them. We need to balance ourselves with common sense and intuition.

We can start the list by asking ourselves what harms we caused others or the world and then write those cases down. Then we'll examine ourselves according to the moral golden rule which asks[77]: what have we done to others that we would not want done to us? This perspective gives us a good idea of most of the harm we caused. Then we'll ask ourselves if there is something else which others considered as an attack by us against them, or consider harmful even if we don't see it that way. Here, it's worth asking for outside perspective of another person to assess the kind of harm we're dealing with.

Once we have that list, we will add what harm we did to every person on the list. We will try and avoid excessive analysis – just listing the simple facts as we remember or understand them, then moving on to the next name. This chronicling, shows that there are different kinds of harms. There are people whom we harmed in a complex way and there are those where it was a one-time thing. We should note that even the latter can be very powerful.

Another thing worth noting is that harm has to do with the other person and their subjective state, such that our behavior can deeply harm them, even if it would be less so if directed at us, and vice versa. When examining harms we caused, we have to be particularly sensitive about them. At the end, we can see a range of harmful actions on our part, learning something about ourselves from the list, such as repeat behaviors and the like.

In the next stage, we'll ask ourselves and write next to each name: Are we prepared to try and immediately repair the harm? Are we willing to try and repair it afterward, after we've progressed in working on ourselves? Are we presently **unsure** if we'll be prepared to try and fix things later on? And do we think we **don't want** to try and fix things, or do we think **fixing** things **could add insult to injury**, something we don't want, or is there another reason we **cannot** try and fix things? The list we end up with is effectively our work plan for the process of fixing the harm we caused. Especially at this stage, it's worthwhile to get a second opinion from someone else, an "outside perspective," to help us be sensitive and avoid causing more damage.

Having involved another person and consulted with them, we can now start to take action to correct matters. According to the order of correction we noted – we will try and contact the person and meet them, admitting our part in causing their harm and apologize. We can also explain to that person that we are in the process of spiritual change and self-correction, and if they wish to hear more, we'll elaborate.

We will obviously not force ourselves on that person; everything will be done with sensitivity and consideration, as we are seeking to fix things, not dependent on any result or even their forgiveness. True, we can't take back that which caused the harm (or the inaction if the harm was due to our neglecting some vital task) and there are things that can't be fixed, but there is usually a wide berth for improvement, sometimes to the point of restoring relationships.

If the harm was done to property, the solution is relatively simple – we'll return the value of the damage we caused, to the best of our ability. Even if the damage is very high and we can't pay it all back, the very effort to pay it back – and we must stress: effort, and not the perfunctory sort –can already "do it" for those who were hurt and mend the wound a little. If the harm is not to property, but we can still fix things, then we will. For instance, if we told a lie about someone to gain some social benefit – we'll reveal the truth to whoever we need to. What we can fix, we will.

But fixing things means more than that. The important part of it is our very asking forgiveness from the person we hurt, while admitting our role in it. The process of asking forgiveness is important to us and primarily to the person who was hurt. This is the basis of the method known as "restorative justice," which complements and sometimes replaces the processes of law enforcement[78],[78]. Those harmed would like us to take responsibility, admitting our part and making an effort to correct it. This is very worthwhile for us so we can cleanse our life story.

There are many delicate nuances to the work of correction, and all sorts of unexpected possibilities could come up. We therefore stress again that this process should be done with the close accompaniment of an experienced someone and consult with them during the process. We need to be careful with opening up old wounds, as we would not want to cause further harm to someone we hurt in the past. No-one promises that we'll be given warm and fuzzy treatment when we do try and fix things, but the very effort is worth it.

One of the most interesting things I saw more than once at this stage is that when someone is interested in fixing a past relationship , the opportunity seems to come their way unexpectedly, with that very person ending up in their life again. For instance, someone who wanted to return a small debt to a friend who disappeared from his life and he had no way of reaching him, suddenly met him on the street.

Someone else who once cheated a customer in his store, ran into her a few years later in a neighboring store, spotted his opportunity and returned what he owed. Someone wanted to apologize to her divorced husband who'd moved abroad, and then he came for a visit and got in touch with her. And so on.

Coincidence? Perhaps. In my opinion it's the action of the Supreme Power, God as we understand Him, and even a coincidence is His doing, especially when it all comes together so nicely and helps us make progress.

Starting a process of correction is often challenging. We experience embarrassment, fear, and perhaps simple pride , all of which attempt to prevent us from apologizing and fixing what we can. But when we honestly and courageously jumpstart the process, we are unexpectedly helped and receive grace.

In addition, after our initial effort, things usually fall into place, like a puzzle solving itself, and the grace is primarily revealed by us. The cleanliness we merit experiencing within us expresses a grace which becomes a living reality for us. A typical expression of this grace is in our relationships which become calmer and more loving. Another expression is the growth of our ability to be patient, delay gratification, and many other things, all of which involve an increasing ability to let go and transcend ourselves. When we do that – there is grace.

"The feeling of guilt and self-pity are the torturers of man, diverting him from the spiritual path, and love has the power to remove them[79]."

CHAPTER EIGHT

Recovering From a Harmful Experience

Let's start with a moment of silence. We'll listen to it, as though it is beating, in its silence, throughout our whole body ... Into this silence we will raise an experience we heard from someone who was seriously harmed and traumatized. It can also be an experience of someone close to us. We will mostly see how this harm affected the person; there's no need to reconstruct all the details. Did something change in them after that? How did the exposure to what they went through affect us? Now we'll return to the silence.

People harm each other. They cause too much harm and seemingly with intolerable ease. There is hardly anywhere free of cases where people harmed each other. Too often those who have power, or think they have power, abuse it. Even those who don't have power sometimes harm, in an attempt to feel they do.

The different reasons are not so important for us here – the victims are those who suffered relatively serious, traumatic pain. There are those who were harmed by other people, and those who suffered at the hands of what we call a "Supreme Power." For instance, an accident caused due to some malfunction, or a serious illness or early death of someone dear to us. There is a difference in the influence of various factors in the harm done, but it also turns out that people who react to harm have a great deal in common[80].

Traumatic harm has destructive power, creating a reaction which prolongs the pain and suffering. And unfortunately, there is almost always suffering after a traumatic event. But we can enjoy some relief when we know that when suffering is present, there is what to do and change, as we will see below. There is a possibility of change after painful, traumatic harm. In more formal language, we will speak of recovering from victimization, or victims' recovery, of survivors or of overcomers.

When we previously dealt with harms and their effect on us, I strongly suggested that those who wish to go out on a journey of breaking free of influence, should have close accompaniment for the process. When we deal with traumatic harm, that suggestion is not just a strong one – it's unequivocal. The process of working on ourselves meant to help us break free of the suffering of traumatic harm can only be done with the accompaniment of someone who's experienced.

It can be someone who went through a similar process and has already accompanied others, a professional who specializes in this field and who is familiar with the spiritual processes of recovery, or a spiritual adviser who specialized in accompanying people suffering from trauma. The experience and specialization are vital to handle a wound which may be gushing, so that the treatment doesn't lead to additional infection which makes things even worse. In the unique context of healing from painful wounds, the option of trying to make progress on your own is not at all a desirable one.

Primary and secondary powerlessness

Let's start with a statement: Every traumatic harm is forced on the person suffering the harm. No-one wants to be hurt. This needs to be repeated at full volume – no-one wants to be hurt. No-one wants to feel pain. Some may ask – what about those who hurt themselves or keep reentering into painful situations? In my opinion, they also don't want to feel pain. Rather, they are in a paradoxical situation in which their self-harm or reentering into situations of harm, express a desire and attempt to avoid another sort of pain. We'll get to that shortly.

To my understanding, a person who was harmed was powerless in the face of the pain forced on them. This powerlessness exists even in cases where the victim did not openly resist the hurt and even seemed to cooperate with the one causing it. This lack of resistance, to the point of cooperation, was done out of compulsion, internal or external, and not out of freedom of choice. In no way did the harmed person want to be harmed; what they wanted was to avoid it, leading them to act according with their ability and understanding in those moments in a way that would prevent greater harm. This seems obvious, but it turns out it isn't.

Oftentimes, we deny the obvious, and if we were harmed to the point of trauma by someone or something, we seek out a logical explanation to ensure we were not powerless. We try and take responsibility for our scars, caused by a force which was stronger than us at that moment. It seems we cannot admit the fact that this force rendered us powerless at that moment and hurt us. Admitting as such seems to undermine the way things are and should be, seemingly leaving us entirely powerless.

It's easier to blame ourselves, as though our own decisions and choices led to us bringing this on ourselves. When we blame ourselves, we have an almost convincing illusion of control: Since the harm happened because of us, it won't happen again if we change our behavior. Ostensibly, we are now protected against future harm, at least in our own minds, but the price of blaming ourselves is heavy.

Since this is but an illusion of control, we are forced to regularly strengthen and maintain it, with subsequently rising costs. Usually, the more serious the harm, the stronger this tendency. For instance, if someone was sexually abused, instead of accepting that they were not responsible for the harmful actions of their attacker, they may create an imaginary scenario of self-blame, as though they chose this or asked for it.

People blame what they were wearing, the direction they took home, the fact they didn't really resist, and so on. I once heard of a female Krav Maga teacher, teaching young girls self-defense. One day a man unexpectedly fell upon her, dragged her to a hidden place and forcibly raped her. She froze up, forgetting everything she'd taught and knew. Later she blamed herself since she didn't resist, even though this was an entirely natural reaction.

She was in a state of powerlessness in the face of her attacker, who surprised her and overcame her. However we look at it, it wasn't her fault, but it's easier for us to blame ourselves than admit we were powerless. This self-blame tasked her with responsibility which ostensibly ensures that she won't freeze up anymore and know how to fight back, leaving her with the power. But in practice – not really.

Powerlessness in the face of the original harm caused is called primary powerlessness. If we accepted it for what it was, a state of powerlessness forced upon us from an outside force stronger than us at that moment(s), we could feel relief. The harm was painful but even if the pain continued as our life did, it would remain within a specific framework, and the damage done to us would stay limited.

But unfortunately, the typical response of many of us is to try and deny and even fight the fact that we were powerless in the face of the force that harmed us. The effort to deny, which is unrealistic and therefore doomed to failure, leads us to a chain of reactions which slowly leads us to adopt a "victim identity" where we find ourselves in many situations of powerlessness. This time it's not a powerlessness in the face of an outside force, but rather in the face of the memory or pain of the harm and other things we have developed in its wake. Our response, which refuses to accept the primary powerlessness and tries to cancel it out, reflects the internal powerlessness, which I call secondary powerlessness[81].

Here's a simplifying example. Reut is a young woman who was repeatedly sexually assaulted in her youth by three boys in the neighborhood. In addition to the sexual harm, the attacks included repeated humiliations, threats and beatings. When she grew up, Reut was not attracted to men and was entirely uninterested in sex.

But she found herself uncontrollably going with men who focused primarily on sex, during which she would try to control everything going on, with the aim of proving to herself and the world that she is not powerless over men and indeed never was. On the face of it, she was the seducer and the initiator – even though she didn't want the sex itself, and as far as she was concerned the connection between them could end before it even began.

In her view, sex was her source of power over them, and she used it to feel that men are in her thrall. The feeling of control and victory held up until the actual relationship. During sex, she was in a state of internal detachment, dissociation[82], a typical condition for those suffering from trauma. But eventually, the dissociation collapsed and she felt she was once again being violated, again being humiliated. It would end in an experience of terrible heartache and emptiness for her.

She had to scrape herself off in the shower to remove the feeling of touch, and of course prevented men from staying anywhere near her after the act was done. Even if the man himself wanted a deeper or even romantic relationship with her, she pushed him away. The whole process was uncontrollable as far as she was concerned, driven by a powerful internal force, which she was powerless to resist.

Like her feeling that men used her to satisfy their urges, she used them to deal with the powerlessness she felt. The path she took could not truly, seriously, solve her sense of powerlessness. It would awake up every few days and drive her to repeat her actions, out of lack of awareness or the faint hope that this time will be different and she would ostensibly control the situation and her men – which didn't happen, of course.

Her journey to recovery needed to include a stage in which she accepted the fact that as a young girl, she was powerless over those young boys, who hurt her. She understood, agreed, and even resisted out of a natural sense of ambivalence and her struggle continued.

The other hand, I met a man who was raped in childhood a number of times by men in his neighborhood. He entirely accepted that he was powerless. He even surprised me in his ability to accept these painful events, saying "What could I do? I was a kid." Since he accepted his primary powerlessness, his secondary powerlessness was less demanding and took up less space in his life.

When we look at those who are harmed, we see a "power struggle" between two experiences of powerlessness. The more we try and avoid the primary powerlessness, the more secondary powerlessness demands its pound of flesh, and causes us more suffering. By contrast, an acceptance of the primary powerlessness can help provide relief and reduce the pain to the minimum possible.

An extreme example is the story of Eva Mozes-Kor (1934-2019), who became famous on the media and wrote her own story[83]. Eva was a "Mengele twin" – she and her sister Miriam, thanks to their being twins, were saved from immediate murder by the Nazis in Auschwitz – a fate which was the lot of their parents and two older sisters – and were taken for experiments by Mengele and his assistants.

Together, they both underwent ten months of terrible torture, and managed to survive. After forty years of a struggle to commemorate the Holocaust and especially the story of the Mengele twins, Eva surprised everyone when she publicly declared her forgiveness of Mengele.

In an interview and in personal conversations I had with her in 2016 when she visited Israel, she explained the detailed process which led her to express public forgiveness. What was important for her and what matters for us is that her forgiveness for Mengele was a moment of liberation. Eva managed to entirely break Mengele off from her present life, so that he ceased to be relevant for her. According to her, she was a hostage of feelings of anger and hatred toward him for forty years, and he thus became an inseparable part of her identity.

This is an example of secondary powerlessness, which she certainly described as a previous experience of powerlessness in the face of the image of Mengele in her mind. With forgiveness, which happened after a deep process she underwent with herself, this came to an end, and she was free, in a way she couldn't even expect. Mengele ceased to interest her.

The proof of the internal freedom she now enjoyed was an encounter of hers with a former Nazi soldier who was tried at a very old age, when she came to testify at his trial. At some stage, she approached him to tell him something personal. He asked for her forgiveness for the harm he was involved in, and they hugged. She argued this was a simple act of humanity, and she was capable of it thanks to the liberation she felt. We can say she stopped dealing with her own primary powerlessness, and the secondary powerlessness was reduced to a minimum and perhaps even disappeared completely.

To summarize: No-one wants to be hurt. The harm comes even though we didn't want it and did what we could, based on our understanding, to prevent it. Because of any number of reasons, we could not or did not succeed in resisting. We were powerless in the face of a force stronger than ourselves, which hurt us.

There may still be pain, sometimes very strong, which spreads into every part of our life. We were also caused all sorts of additional damages. All this has to do with the primary powerlessness, and it is a natural situation for those harmed. But it's not easy to accept the primary powerlessness, the fact that we were powerless over something stronger than us, and that it might strike again.

We therefore develop reactions which include an attempt to deny or dismiss the fact that we were powerless. This system of reactions creates a kind of internal compulsion within us. By our lights, we cannot react otherwise. We are powerless in the face of an internal force, which operates within us and creates destruction, which continues and escalates the pain of the original harm. Secondary powerlessness is a state of ongoing suffering. The pain of the primary powerlessness cannot be prevented – it was forced on us by something stronger than ourselves. The suffering of the secondary powerlessness can be reduced and maybe even eliminated.

Ravit was in her early thirties when we met, a young mother of two. As a believer trying to apply spiritual principles to her life, she came to me for consulting in the manner of the GraceWay, due to ambivalence about her marriage.

It quickly became clear as we were first getting acquainted that she and her father had consensual relations. Her parents divorced when she was young, and her mother left the country, her and her little brother with her dad. She functioned as a mother to her brother, four years her junior, and a wife to her father, and she said that she also considered relations with her father to be emotionally acceptable.

Obviously she knew this was socially unacceptable but this was cognitive, factual knowledge, not emotional understanding. She loved her father and also agreed to be a spouse to him. The talks with her were generally open and flowed well, and I could ask or say almost anything that came to mind, including "digging" a little deeper.

When I asked her how a girl who wasn't yet ten years old could consent to have relations with her father, she had no answer. When I gently asked whether she knew that legally and emotionally relations with her father were considered rape for all intents and purposes, she of course knew, but denied the action of rape.

One day she surprised me when she said, quite in anger: "He raped me, the asshole." This was a formative moment of the beginning of recovery. Quite paradoxically, so long as she avoided rebelling against the injustice done to her, and even agreed with it, accepting it with ostensible equanimity, she was suffering from secondary powerlessness which affected almost her entire life.

It's no surprise that she also experienced sexual aggression from her husband which she agreed to – after all, her job was to satisfy him, no? This was a paradoxical effort to cut losses by agreeing with what was being done to her, out of a habit she had formed already in childhood. But due to the process she underwent, the change came and she rebelled. The anger which arose toward her father and the recognition that he harmed her and exploited her innocence was an acceptance of her powerlessness as a child. Her secondary powerlessness thus started to weaken, making her able to face her husband and leave him as well.

The possibility of recovery from harm

The distinction between primary and secondary powerlessness is an expression of the serenity prayer: If we accept our primary powerlessness, which was in the past, we can deal better with our secondary powerlessness, which is our continuing reaction, which won't stop if we don't change tack. Acceptance and coping with all this require courage, as well as the help of a force stronger than ourselves.

These are stages in a long process of recovery, which require changes in habits and abstaining from certain things. Recovery also requires the application of "just for today," because denying the primary powerlessness refers to the past, and dealing with its consequences, this being the secondary powerlessness, is in the present, just for today.

Osnat was sexually assaulted and raped in childhood and in her youth by various young boys and men, on a number of occasions. She developed a general defensive reaction in the face of a hostile and hurtful world. For instance, she was a compulsive pleaser. Another thing that was typical of her was that she was constantly feeling tense whether with other people or alone. To calm down, she would harm herself – with pinching, cutting, and even putting out cigarettes on herself.

These are not actions of "self-destructive" as they are sometimes called, but rather the opposite – failed efforts to "save" herself from herself. The physical pain created relative quiet in her tortured mind. The ability to bear pain out of choice gave her a sense of power and capability along with the feeling of control, ostensibly solving her memory of powerlessness when she was hurt so many times.

This is also the movement between omnipotence and impotence, described in a previous chapter – emotionally, she experienced total, paralyzing impotence, but when she bore the intense pain she inflicted on herself, she experienced a moment of omnipotence. But self-harm solves nothing, merely putting off the internal pain, and maintaining a cycle of emotional pain, self-harm, brief relief, emotional pain, and so on ad infinitum.

I suggested she avoid any behavior involving causing herself pain – even avoiding brushing her hair too strongly or pulling it to feel calming pain, and also avoiding showering in almost boiling water so she could have a pleasant burning sensation. Nothing. "Just for today" not to hurt herself, every day anew. Recovery from the self-harm, which contains an addictive component[84]. I also suggested she practice gratitude, to balance out the experience and accumulate positive experiences during the struggle.

She certainly faced a complicated struggle. The challenge it involved stood out even in our meetings, which she usually experienced as a protective and protecting place. But when we touched on an emotionally painful subject, it seemed her hands started to pinch, dig in, wound, and hurt herself on their own, almost.

When I asked her to stop, she said the pain is calming. I told her that if she hurt herself, I would also do so as an act of identification, pinching my hand. She didn't want me to feel pain, so she felt motivated to avoid hurting herself at our meetings. I asked her to abstain from calming herself with the means she was used to, and deal with her sense of chaos in a controlled fashion.

Sometimes we did it together, in real-time. Slowly something started to shift. Gratitude also had an effect; for instance, she was grateful in succeeding in abstinence from harming herself. After a few more months, the need to harm herself declined, bringing a degree of relief.

At the same time, she also took it upon herself to abstain from pleasing or acting like an emotional beggar. This abstinence also required a struggle which made her grateful for her accumulating success. At the beginning of her abstinence, there were times where she tried to "ask my permission" to stumble a little on pleasing, such as pleasing a friend a little, just to sidestep the need to cope. In practice, she was asking for permission from herself and not from me, permission which was not given. We also had to be alert so that she would not try to please me in the same way. For the time she took on a number of big cases of abstinence and held fast to them "like a champ," courageously. Until the change started to emerge from within and the need for such behaviors, all of which caused her harm, decreased.

After many months she succeeded, for the first time in her life, to form a romantic relationship with a man. It did end after a few months, but she learned what she was now capable of. As more time passed, she started to "carry the message" to other young women who were sexually assaulted, meeting and sharing her experience and wisdom with them.

A nice outcome happened after I connected between Osnat and a young woman named Tanya. After they met for a few times, Tanya told me: "Don't be offended, it's not that you don't understand me, but Osnat **really** understands me!"

I stressed the distinction between powerlessness in the face of harm and powerlessness over our response to that harm. These two kinds of powerlessness are typical, attesting to a range of normal reactions. But a normal reaction to abnormal harm is something that's not easy to live with, which is why it's desirable to walk the path of recovery.

At twelve step meetings, the emphasis is placed on the importance of confessing the fact that we felt powerless over something, usually that which brought us to the group in the first place. For instance, AA members confess their powerlessness over alcohol. Correspondingly, recovery from victimization is aided by our confession of our dual powerlessness over both the harm and our reaction to it.

If we understand and admit that we have a reactive mechanism which takes us over, toward which we are powerless – that is the beginning of ceasing to identify with it. When we stop identifying with a particular form of reaction and hold onto it, something in the secondary powerlessness breaks loose, and we have other ways of responding.

Yossi was about twenty five when we met. Some ten years earlier, he had been the victim of a cruel gang rape committed over a period of time by five older boys. Obviously, this had many consequences on his life. Since the rape, life itself has been one huge whirlwind of chaos which he tried to survive as much as he could.

Among other things, he had flashbacks, of the events. The memory of their touch would burst forth in his mind, which he experienced them as though they were happening now. The memory breakouts would appear frequently, sometimes even every few minutes.

This obviously made it hard for him to lead a normal life. Before we met, he tried different ways to deal with the flashbacks, including excellent psychological treatment and heavy drug use. These helped only partially and temporarily. There were periods of some relief, but the live memory would then come back with a vengeance. We tried a couple of means together, such as the serenity prayer – to peacefully accept that he has flashbacks, and not act by them. It provided temporary relief, but didn't really help.

At another meeting, we tried something else. He was scatterbrained more than usual and said that he had strong flashbacks. I asked him to tell me whenever he had a flashback during our meeting.

"Then we'll talk about them all the time," he laughed a little. "It doesn't matter, we'll have what to talk about," we laughed together. Every few minutes, he stopped our conversation, described a flashback, I asked for details so that the description was complete, and we went on as usual, as though there was no disturbance.

I suggested he practice this manner of conversation with a friend who also experienced sexual assault with whom he had shared his secret. He would practice with him during the week, and we continued to practice together during our weekly meetings. At one of the meetings, after a few weeks, I asked him why he hadn't told me about the flashbacks? His answer was surprising. He claimed the conversation was so pleasant and he didn't want to interrupt it, so he simply stopped cooperating with the flashback, letting it disappear as easily as it appeared.

It was the first time he discovered an ability to have some control over his flashbacks. While constantly admitting a flashback every time he had one, he managed to divorce them from himself, gaining the ability to let go and not allow them to develop. Eventually he accepted the ability to choose to break free of them. He gladly chose to do so, and then surprised me when he said he would miss them, because there was something calming about them that gave him a sense of security. More than five years passed, and the flashbacks have gone.

Aspects of recovery

The distinction between primary and secondary powerlessness is central to recovery. We could say that the primary powerlessness is the pain, and the secondary – the suffering. The former is a state in which the self-centeredness of another harmed us, while in the latter our own self-centeredness is harming us and sometimes others as well.

Recovery is a gradual transcending of self-centeredness, like any other journey of spiritual growth. When we begin to transcend the self-centeredness of the secondary powerlessness over the trauma – and this is stated very cautiously, as it should be in dealing with such matters – the primary harm gradually becomes less important in our life. It's no longer the center of gravity pulling us deep into the swamp of self-centeredness, but a memory of a painful past event, with great influence on us and also a challenge for personal growth.

This growth gradually becomes more important than the harm and its consequences. Eva Mozes-Kor demonstrated the idea of growth nicely. For her, what happened to her in the past was less important than what she did in the present. Part of her work was to help a wide range of victims bringing a message of possible serenity and peace to tortured souls.

The basic tool for recovery, indeed for any change, is "abstinence." Secondary powerlessness is expressed in typical behaviors. It's possible to pin these down, and decide what we need to abstain from at the beginning of the process and what to abstain from in the future. The basis for change will be abstention from any behavior which harms us such as self-harm or pleasing behaviors.

Engaging in sex not out of love and choice is very harmful. If there is no meaningful relationship it's worth considering temporarily abstaining from any partnership. As I told someone: "It's not clear if after you changed a bit and advanced, that you'll want to be in a relationship which your powerlessness has created."

The tool that assists in abstinence is "just for today." With its aid and through daily struggle, we become rehabilitated from some of the behaviors of secondary powerlessness. When we take abstinence upon ourselves, the internal chaos screams within our mind with all its might. We can use various tools to make order of this chaos and grow from it.

"Gratitude," for instance, allows us to create a positive space in our mind, which earlier was directed by a strong negative force. "Distinguishing facts" help us stick solely to those facts. The essence of secondary powerlessness is a distorted story we tell ourselves and the reactions which strengthen it. The various characteristics of distinguishing facts, as this tool describes in depth, can answer each and every component of that story. The "finding in ourselves" tool provides a response to the experience of emptiness and shallowness which sometimes arises along with the secondary powerlessness, especially when we avoid its typical behaviors while practicing abstinence.

The negative experience of the harm sinks us deep into the swamp of self-centeredness which I earlier called "victim identity." Some of this identity is a repeat creation of a negative message which is poured in our mind almost unceasingly – by fear, resentments, disappointments, bitterness, and other spices of suffering. The "being positive" tool tries to respond to these by teaching us to replace a negative mental message with a positive one, creating positive anchors. For instance, instead of dependent pleasing, we learn that "We have and need nothing from them"; repeating this has often revealed itself to be a gateway to growth.

This process has a typical complication, which is that the harm discussed in this chapter often becomes a secret protected at all costs. The "finding in ourselves" tool includes looking at ourselves from the outside, by an appropriate person we selected for that end, or in other words: exposing our secret to someone else.

The act of sharing with someone else and breaking the barrier of secrecy, is vital. The secret protects and preserves the secondary powerlessness, and also magnifies the memory of the harm as well as our subsequent suffering. Bringing someone else in on the secret and gaining an outside perspective, creates a degree of balance and opens up the wall of emotional isolation, which is also a typical response. Thus, we can continue using the other tools for change and growth out of the pain of the harm as we move toward the tool "living the spirit."

From a complementary angle, we can view behaviors driven by secondary powerlessness as behavioral spin. I knew someone who showered for a long time with very hot water. To stop this spin, she accepted a form of abstinence on herself – she limited her shower time to fifteen minutes and only in pleasant water, an adjective which made her squirm. "Why should I do pleasant?" She didn't like pleasant nor deserved it. This was her moment of change– pleasant water does not create a spinning out of control or pretend to make her forget what she cannot.

A vital component on the journey of recovery is working on resentments, fears, and forgiveness of those who harmed us. People who were hurt tend to develop a strong reaction of anger to the point of wanting revenge, and they feel that anger drives them to a positive action, allowing them to no longer be powerless. The anger protects them from any possible additional harm.

I've met people who claimed that anger is meant to protect others. For instance, a woman who was battered and whose anger toward her divorced husband continued for seven years after they separated. She claimed she protected her children and their memory of the violence. It seemed to her that if she stopped being angry, she would again expose them to his violence.

In cases like this, the people are ostensibly admitting the primary powerlessness, but have developed a defense, they consider effective, from a repeat of the harm they have experienced, via the anger, resentment and hatred, as well as the desire to take revenge and punish.

I will not address the question of punishing those who cause harm; certainly such a person must bear responsibility for their actions as soon as possible, no excuses. But the offenders are not the focus here. The victims are. The anger which ostensibly protects a person, while admitting the primary powerlessness and declaring it won't repeat, is an attempt to weaken the perpetrator to the point of cancelling them out. Our strong feelings toward them, along with the desire to punish and take revenge, create a magical experience where it seems that the harm or at least its intensity, decline or disappear.

Accepting primary powerlessness in full means knowing that there's nothing to be done about it, despite the ongoing pain. There's no point in trying to cancel out or weaken the harm or the person responsible. If only it were possible. Compulsive preoccupation with the offender and the punishment or revenge, as sometimes happens, leaves the person in a non-consensual alliance, painful and undesirable, with the offender themselves.

The aim of weakening or cancelling the offender, say by imprisoning or killing them, cannot change the severity of the harm done. It may temporarily calm the victim, like any feeling or action driven by secondary powerlessness, but it cannot really reduce the primary powerlessness, and so long as this is the intention, even if implicit, the secondary powerlessness will continue to exact a heavy cost from us. Therefore the GraceWay directs us to work toward letting something go along the anger-resentment-hatred axis, liberation which is primarily meant for us.

The number of times when someone told me of traumatic harm and their stage seemed appropriate, I suggested applying the eighth filter to break free of resentments, prayer for the offender. Moran, for instance, told of a serious resentment she harbored toward her uncle, who abused her emotionally and physically in her childhood, not sexually. It was her cousin who raped her a few times, but she claimed she had no resentment toward him, since he was also a victim of his father.

His father, the uncle, was the head of the family, and they all lived by him. He was a tyrant who oppressed everyone including her, little Moran. According to her story, he destroyed everyone's life. When she grew up, she considered taking revenge on him, even bringing about his death. She said that she thought this a goal worth sitting in jail for. Together we saw that her jail was actually her secondary powerlessness is over the self-story the abuse she went through, and I suggested prayer as a path out of her internal cage.

She was a little angry at me for making such an absurd suggestion, even though she was perfectly acquainted with the steps program and the part referring to ending resentments, but she took it upon herself to apply the prayer. Weeks passed. She prayed for the uncle diligently, twice a day.

One day she arrived excited in a good way. The day before she had a new experience with her uncle, who was now an old, weak, and sick man. It was during a family event. People had fun –ate, drank and danced. Only her uncle sat alone in the chair. No-one wanted his company, he was helpless and couldn't serve himself and eat.

Moran, who saw him in that pathetic condition, felt pity for him. She approached him, gently asked how he's doing, brought him food he likes and fed him. She said that while doing so she found herself almost complaining about me because of my suggestion to practice praying for him, practice which led her to be capable of feeding the poor uncle, even though she once hated him so much.

"And how did you feel?" I asked. "Like a queen!" she laughed, "Entirely free. He was helpless, not me, and it hurt me to see him like that. I even kissed him on the cheek. I'm 'angry' at the path because it worked. I really didn't want it to work, and I practiced a little to fail. But it entirely worked. Because of the path, I have no more resentment toward my uncle, do you get that…?"

Despite that, when I previous described Ravit's change , I noted as a formative moment that day when she said, angrily, that her father raped her – "that asshole." There's no contradiction. To break free, we need to accept that there is resentment. I was convinced that Ravit felt something like resentment and anger toward her father.

My understanding told me it cannot be that someone would undergo systematic, regular raping and accept it as though it was the way of the world without rebelling, even if only in the depths of her soul. Her other responses showed that she simply didn't dare, even to herself, to experience and express anger.

She had an amazing capacity for detachment and dissociation. The awakening of anger signaled that something in the internal detachment was starting to connect. The continued repairing would come via growth from the anger and fear. Her anger at her father was not an end but an initial stage from which it was possible to grow, which is what Ravit later did. She let go of the victim experience, let go of the anger, let go of the husband who hurt her, and today, years later, she is in a stable and excellent, loving relationship with someone else.

Advising those who were harmed

Stories of harm and trauma are not easy to hear, no matter how many times we've heard them. The combination of pain, distress, obtuseness, violence, exploitation and evil intent, hurt us, the listeners, and it is complex and challenging. It sounds like the opposite of the grace we aspire for. When we hear the details from one who was hurt and the painful harm that is their daily reality, it's not easy for us.

Sometimes, when we encounter a traumatic story that someone went through, we are caught flat-footed, and don't know what to do or say. It happens even to experienced professionals. Sometimes the details lead us to feel a deep sense of identification. Sometimes we fear encountering the harder stories of life. Advancing through the GraceWay, which is as openly as optimistic and positive a path as can be, is an acceptance of the pain in the world, without evading or denying it. Accepting the pain allows for relieving the suffering. It allows us to face the pain directly, without blinking, and be there for those who are hurting.

Hagit, a young woman of twenty-two, told me a painful story of systematic sexual abuse in her family by her father and brother. According to her, her mother knew and kept silent. Her older sister, who was apparently their victim before her, also knew and kept silent. Hagit "made progress" and radiated something strong and optimistic at our meetings.

We spoke about it, about her powers. She expressed happiness at her powers being the subject of discussion and not the harm. She told of how a few months earlier, she had met with a therapist working for the welfare services, who cried when she heard her story. Her response was certainly natural, given the painful details.

But not in Hagit's view, who had no pity on her: "Why was she crying for me? I'm not crying anymore, so why should she? In a minute I'll have to console her, instead of her being with me." It's possible to understand the therapist, even though Hagit could not and stood firm when I tried to show her the story through the therapist's eyes. Maybe Hagit's story resonated with the therapist's own personal experiences, or that she was simply a sensitive woman or something else was at play there.

In any event, if we wish to help someone who was harmed, we want to "be there" for them. We want to be able to let go of ourselves, including our identification, personal pain, shock, and even the desire to be the empathetic, good, savior therapist. The person who shares with us needs us to be there for them, without saving them, sometimes that means to create a confidence forming silence.

When people come to me for counseling, I usually ask if they've been hurt in the past. I've found that asking simply and directly about serious pain, certainly while remaining alert and highly sensitive to the matter, but without making a big deal out of it, makes it easier for people sitting opposite me than making it a bigger deal than it already is.

That's how I questioned Doron, a thirty year old young woman who came to me with a desire to stop using drugs. It was easy for her to answer, and she told of sexual assault she experienced in her childhood. I was not surprised, given other traits of hers which fit. She added that with her previous therapist, it took a few months for this trauma to come up; she claimed the therapist avoided asking if she'd experienced something traumatic.

Doron came to me after that treatment and was therefore more ready to open up, but it would seem if was better to speak earlier about the trauma there than wait a few months for her to ostensibly be prepared to speak about it. Based on what Doron described and how, it seemed that the waiting period was more for the therapist than for Doron. That's how Doron had experienced it.

This brings us back to what I said before – when we counsel others, we will be as free as possible for them, so we can show them the grace we all wish to meet. If we have open issues with harm, it will be challenging and maybe impossible to encounter it for others. It's therefore very worthwhile for professionals to do the work of personal progress, and the GraceWay is a very appropriate means of doing so.

Reconnecting life – the story of Yehudit

A few years ago, I met a special woman named Yehudit. Despite her desire to be known by her full name, I promised I would use a pseudonym, to protect her identity and in accordance with the ethical rules of social sciences. Yehudit is a typical Hungarian name – besides being a Jewish one – and she was indeed a native of Hungary, a Jew who as a young girl was sent to Auschwitz during the Holocaust, survived, and built a loving family in Israel.

She was over ninety when she came to the meeting, she did not look it. Even her youth under the heavy shadow of the persecution of Jews in Hungary after the breakout of WWII, the survival in Auschwitz and a German labor camp, and the harsh years spent fighting to survive after the war – all this was not reflected on her face.

She stood tall, with bright eyes and a warm smile, a lucid mind, vital and cheery, loving. We spoke at length and she told me of what she went through in great detail – before the war, during the war with the racial laws and regulations and the violence against Jews in Hungary, her days in Auschwitz and in the labor camp, and after the war, when she achieved relative peace in Israel, and then her husband whom she greatly loved passed away at a young age.

What interested me in Yehudit was the source of her strength. It seemed that her secondary powerlessness was relatively limited and that she had strong resources to deal with the harm itself. She certainly had pain. A lot of it. Even in our conversation, when she told me of her father, the head of the family and the community, whom she greatly loved, and of his murder just before liberation, her eyes watered, and the pain was tangible.

But there was something else in the room, something that went beyond pain. What was it? Yehudit called it hope. She claimed that she was always a person of hope. Already as a young girl, she was optimistic, happy, full of hope for the good life she would live. Even in her most difficult moments in Auschwitz, with her not yet eighteen, when the endless hunger was almost the only voice in her mind, as she saw people dying, suffering, tortured, she felt great pain, but she knew it would all be alright, that it would end.

What was the source of this knowledge? Yehudit spoke of faith. Not religious faith, but faith in God not bound to the establishment or tradition. She argued this faith was the source of her power, an internal source of support that helped her bear the daily challenges. She described the number of times when she felt a guiding hand which saved her from certain death. That hand brought her some relief and managed to improve any complication that arose.

According to her, she understood earlier on that there is a caring Supreme Power, that directed the events in a way which wasn't obvious, given the circumstances. Hope, faith, and another word which she often repeated – love. From her story it was clear that Yehudit was a girl and then a young woman full of love and also privileged to be loved.

Fortunately for her, she was not separated from her mother in Auschwitz, and there was also a young aunt who was close to her and a cousin (not the daughter of this aunt) a little older than her by her side. They were a group of four loving and mutually supporting women led by her mother, trying to protect each other as much as possible, and their love was a protective shield within an impossible hell.

For instance, there was one day at Auschwitz where they were forced to stand for a roll call for hours outside, as part of the systematic, sadistic abuse of the Nazis. When it became possible for her, her mother told her to bend down on the floor and covered her with a broad dress she had on. The image of the mother protecting as much as her limited ability will allow, shows the love that went beyond the painful context of that time and place. That love between them continued during the journey to the labor camp in north Germany, at the camp, and in the days after the war. They were thick as thieves, until the mother's death at a ripe old age.

Another interesting thing Yehudit noted was that she had a younger sister, who was separated from them when they came to Auschwitz and was apparently murdered immediately. Her mother never spoke of her murdered daughter in the camp, focusing instead on protecting the one remaining, Yehudit, and also the aunt, the mother's younger sister, and the cousin, and other women with whom they had a shared fate. Part of how she protected Yehudit was not burdening her with the pain of the bereavement of her young daughter. Together they made it through everything, rebuilding their lives and seeing their family grow in Israel.

Why did I bring up her story? Yehudit is an inspiring woman as is her story. For me it is mostly a story about the human capacity for growth, not just a Holocaust story. The story marks the importance of solid foundations allowing growth despite the extreme experience of challenge, pain, and distress. These three foundations, which gradually emerged from Yehudit's words are tied to each other: hope, faith, and love. Interestingly St. Paul also noted these three elements[85].

In my view, one of our most important sources of study as struggling people, are stories of growth and change and our potential power even in the face of challenges so serious, they seem insurmountable. It's easy for us to get caught up in dealing in depth with the deep sorrow of the negative and the painful, as we see in the various theories of social sciences and humanities.

Yehudit and people like her prove the importance of remembering the strength within us, our wonderful ability, with the grace of God, to rise from any trouble and be love and grace. If Yehudit could be that, then in theory we all can. In practice, this is where the GraceWay directs us, and anyone can advance in it, even partially.

***

If what was said so far touched someone or opened some wound, it's highly recommended to contact with someone who can help and support us as soon as possible. It's possible to bring grace into life in any situation and under any conditions, but when with a great challenge, we will make use of those who can support this process.

Let's take a moment of silence. We'll leave all the pain and suffering revealed here. We'll move away from them and see them from the side, diminishing slowly in the mind. We'll remember that it's all about our journey to break free of self-centeredness and merit grace. Everything that happens to us and to others presents a challenge to us along the way. The challenge is not just what happened, but also our attitude to what happened, and that can always be changed.

Let's think about the serenity prayer, repeating it slowly in our heart three times, while focusing on the content of the prayer.

Let's enter gratitude into our mind – we'll think about the deep gratitude we have toward someone or something or just in general. We'll live the gratitude for a moment and delve into it. We'll return to the deep, softened silence, which fills the mind with its presence.

"You wore flesh, whether you wish to or not, you will have to deal with yourself. If you deal consciously, without the consequence of that struggle arousing interest in you – you are pouring a solid basis for happiness in the future[86]."

CHAPTER NINE

Awareness of Patterns of Activity

Let's take a short-long moment of silence. We'll listen to the silence like we're used to.

Let's continue with the silence and all the while look at ourselves acting within the world. We'll imagine viewing ourselves from above. We'll see ourselves in ordinary day to day situations; for instance, coming to work, getting something done, coming home, eating, having fun; doing something, doesn't matter what. We'll ask ourselves, as we act, when we are diligent, when we are lazy, and when are we idle a little or even a lot?

We'll let the appropriate images emerge – just looking at ourselves acting, without judgment or emotional identification. Images of life, like watching a movie, with ourselves as the protagonist.

When we examine how people act in an impartial and uninvolved manner, we can identify certain patterns of activity which repeat themselves. Examining ourselves through a similar lens, we can identify such patterns in ourselves. Some of these express and even strengthen self-centeredness, while others are aimed to break free of the same. This chapter deals in becoming acquainted with the different patterns of activity which we've become used to, and changing those which do not allow us to advance on the path of the spirit and transcend self-centeredness.

When we encounter people who practice the path of the spirit in their life, and by this we mean genuine practice regardless of the name of the particular path or school, we sometimes get the impression of something which can be called acting through grace. For instance, in various temples and monasteries, in both the east and the west, work is generally done with typical nimbleness, with those who took it upon themselves to do the work in question do so, with a smile or at least with distinct calm, and without complaint.

Such conduct is also visible at AA and NA meetings, such as during the preparation of the room before and after the meeting. Members volunteer to help, cleaning the room energetically and even happily. I can recall an NA member who was starting to get clean of drugs, who would come to the place long before the meeting began, wait with uncharacteristic patience for the door to open, and wash the room on his own initiative – not as part of his official role in the group, so much as to honor the meeting. He would also enthusiastically volunteer to clean up at the end of meetings, as though while cleaning the room he was cleaning up his addiction.

Rabbi Moshe Chaim Luzatto, otherwise known as the Ramchal, in his book of religious moral teachings known as Messilat Yesharim (The Path of the Upright)[87], described the virtue of nimbleness in carrying out commandments as a basic stage in man's spiritual journey. But when we do what we need to do with lack of enthusiasm, or even try and dodge our responsibilities, we do the opposite. In addition to nimbleness or lack of enthusiasm, there are additional typical patterns of behavior, which express our path in the world and in spirit as well as our degree of self-centeredness at a given moment.

We'll learn below of some prominent patterns which repeat themselves, which can be defined as: Acting through grace, trade, laziness and idleness, play and rigidity and also a pattern of struggling with oneself. There are certainly others, such as the pattern of pleasure-seeking, which I later link to idleness for their prominent similarities.

I intentionally defined these as patterns and characteristics of activity, rather than types or structures of personality, as they exist in all of us to varying degrees. At any given moment, there are a number of patterns which drive us, but one of them is usually dominant over the others.

Which one? The one we choose. If we don't choose, the dominant pattern will be the one that chooses us. If we are aware of what drives us we can change that pattern with the help of one or more of the tools offered by the GraceWay.

Doing nothing and having fun

Let's start with idleness. This is a situation where we need to do something but simply don't. We avoid fulfilling our assigned task, putting it off to tomorrow or never, and ignore the consequences. We "live in the moment," but in fact sink into the idleness of the moment without considering anything beyond it. We might eventually do what needs doing, but only partially and with a real lack of enthusiasm. The idle person avoids doing what reality requires of them, without thinking about the future or even hoping there won't be one, and that this moment of idleness will simply go on. Almost all of us are idle sometimes; it's simply a question of degree and timing.

Alongside idleness, we can also note the pattern of pleasure-seeking, where we engage in activity we find pleasant, sinking into it and ignoring everything else, including what we are supposed to do. Ignoring the consequences of our actions and others.

In pleasure-seeking, like idleness we "live in the moment" but in fact sink into the pleasant fun of the moment – sometimes through idleness, sometimes through pleasurable activity. We effectively take everything we can from the moment, the world, and others, trying to take more, trying all the while to reduce what we give to the moment, the world and others.

There can be many reasons for idleness and pleasure-seeking, and a whole range of factors might influence us to fall under their spell, but such an analysis doesn't help us. In essence, idleness and pleasure-seeking express a state of high self-centeredness; the reasons can be many and varied. Sometimes we are aware that idleness involves a great deal of self-centeredness, and sometimes not. We might try to consciously transcend self-centeredness and sometimes even act through grace, but the self-centeredness will penetrate through the small details and activate the idle or pleasure-seeking pattern.

Do you want examples from everyday life? Here we go: The family meal is over, we're all full and satisfied. It's so fun to keep sitting or go about what we consider important. Who'll clean up? How many times are we glad someone else cleans up the mess we left behind? We invent all kinds of excuses and reasons and ultimately we wait for someone else to clean up after everyone. Someone else? Someone we love. Someone we'd be willing to help out a lot. But at this moment in time, we just "feel like" that beloved someone doing what's not convenient or pleasant for us. What matters is this: I'm not doing it. We could just be mired in the pleasant nothingness of idleness at that time, or that we chose some pleasurable activity like talking to someone, watching a movie, and the like.

Similarly – what about the other chores around the house? How nice is it when that someone does them for us.

In almost any area of life, we can see a similar approach in the routine moments of life. Sometimes we'll properly do big and clear-cut jobs, ostensibly even through grace, but idleness will reign in the little things and in moments of pleasure-seeking, the little things fade away. Sometimes we are busy doing good , willing to sacrifice ourselves, "bite the bullet" for others, while neglecting simple things and leaving them for someone else to do, either cleaning or straightening the mess we left.

Even when we are generally diligent people, we sometimes become idle or look to have fun while being unaware of this and usually not admitting it. Sometimes we are idle in things that are not so important to us. Sometimes idleness or pleasure-seeking harms others, perhaps those we love. Are we aware of the pattern which drives us and our self-centeredness? Is it our intended choice?

An interesting characteristic of idleness is the pleasure-speaking spin. Sometimes this spin is acute – we are sucked into a sense of "I don't feel like" doing something, or I just "feel like" continuing and not doing anything that needs doing, or I "feel like" doing what makes me feel good while ignoring everything else, and in face "I feel/don't feel like" effectively runs my life.

We can see this in social entertainment hotspots, where people are sometimes swept up into a pleasure-seeking spin which leads them to atypically offensive behavior. It happens to almost all of us, more than once. As I said, it's a question of degree and awareness – how aware am I of how idleness or pleasure seeking has taken over ? If I am, great; if not – that can be changed.

Sometimes we get used to a certain pattern which repeats itself and becomes a regular, even chronic trait. A fairly banal, but typical example, is someone getting used to their not cleaning their house, leaving it to their partner.

Why? I've met men who explained that cleaning the house has to do with manliness and womanhood and gender roles and the like. But these same people are diligent in cleaning their workplace or their equipment while on army reserve duty, simply because they have no choice. It was interesting to see that their manhood was safely intact even though they were cleaning.

If we look at ourselves honestly, we'll see that almost all of us have repeating patterns of idleness . Maybe we define them differently, seeking out some excuse or imagined handicap that prevents us from doing what needs getting done, but in the end it's still idleness. Even if it shows up in the little things, it's an obstacle in our path of spiritual growth. Since idleness and pleasure-seeking are expressions of high self-centeredness with a typical behavioral pattern, there's no need to analyze the situational, social, or personality-related factors at their root. Suffice for us to want to break free of the self-centeredness or avoid the pattern of idleness or pleasure-seeking.

When idleness leads us by the nose, we feel increasing exhaustion which seems to increase the less we do. We seem to become mired in exhausting inaction, to the point that we have no strength to get up and move. Obviously one can be tired for many reasons, and it's worth checking our physical health, but if there's no clear reason, the exhaustion is likely a story we tell ourselves while becoming mired in idleness. It is the price that idleness collects from us in exchange for the dubious pleasure of using its services. Surprisingly enough, transcending idleness - despite the exhaustion and lack of strength and the pain and all our other fables – can reduce feelings of exhaustion and the like. Fortunately for us, that choice is always available to us at any moment.

Doing as little as possible

The second pattern, a close cousin of idleness, is laziness. We only do what we have to, and nothing more, usually with open or internal lack of enthusiasm. Unlike idleness, we don't avoid what we need to do, but only do what is considered necessary. Despite the difference, the pattern of laziness is somewhat similar to the pattern of idleness. In both cases, we seek out something which is pleasant and convenient, either physically or emotionally, and want it to continue.

In both cases, we don't want to make an effort. The difference lies in laziness being overcome by a sense of necessity that drives us to generally minimal action, in which we do only what we think needs doing. Sometimes laziness is marked by partial action, or procrastinating the matter until the last minute or beyond it, and in neglectful work or what looks like something done just to get it out of the way, without enthusiasm or with complaints, expressed internally or out loud.

Alternatively, we "make a big deal" out of what we did, or how we did it, even if we just did it because we had to. It appears to the outside observer that doing things is about the last thing that interests the lazy person, and they do so only to change a situation they consider undesirable, or prevent a result that they don't want, all the while continuing with what they consider pleasant and comfortable as much as possible.

Do you want examples from everyday life? How do we get up in the morning? Happy, or out of a sense of duty and burden, complaining about having to leave the comfortable bed? How do we clean up or organize things after we and others are done –cheerfully, or complaining, internally or out loud? Or just at the last minute with a demonstrable lack of enthusiasm and aiming to do only the minimum necessary to give ourselves a good feeling for having done the work?

How do we function at the workplace or in our studies – do we do what's needed or go beyond? Do we try to do our best, looking for what else can be done, or suffice only with what's necessary? Do we do it gladly or out of a sense of burden and heaviness? And how often do we do what's needed, or only some of it? And when it seems that we don't have to – it can wait.

We can see this tendency toward laziness in every area of life, even in relationships and in our giving or lack thereof to our partner. In moments when we prefer not to make the effort, but still act out of duty, and it shows in what we do. Laziness is an emotional or behavioral cheapness; we are tight-fisted in our behavior and only "spend" the minimum we consider vital.

This understanding of laziness helps us see how common it is, by almost everyone around us, and primarily – by ourselves. We can pretty easily see ourselves acting in daily life, seeking to avoid what doesn't have to get done as much as possible, and continuing in this way according to this pattern.

Laziness, like idleness, tends toward spinning out of control, including an acute spin which takes over in a particular moment, and chronic spins, which is the burdensome habit of laziness. In both cases, an increasing self-centeredness reveals itself. The lazy spin sometimes leads to miring into idleness and sometimes remains within the pattern of laziness. A laziness spin is sometimes experienced as increasing burden and busyness. The story we then tell ourselves is of doing too many things and yearning to be able to have some rest. When we experience this kind of busy period, it's worth getting the outside perspective of someone we trust, so we can honestly know if we're taking on too much, for various reasons, or if we are forced to bear a heavy burden, or that's it's all an unpleasant mental story of self-centeredness marked by laziness.

In the case of laziness, the experience of busyness is its cost, alongside other similar ones. Our self-centeredness uses it to deepen its hold on us and tell us a pleasant story which tries to bring us to more of the same. Therefore, when we identify a pattern of laziness within ourselves, it's worth for us to do something about it.

We can use a range of tools to cope with laziness. Anyone can choose what's appropriate for their particular situation. For instance, perhaps abstinence in the opposite sense of acting beyond what's needed, and that – just for today. Perhaps distinguishing facts with the knowledge of what's mine or my responsibility, along with deciding on a plan of action in advance which includes initiative that does not depend on what needs to be done, and so on.

Commercial activity

A pattern with a similar, results-focused aspect, but one which appears entirely different, is trade or commerce. This is a situation where we indeed go beyond what is needed so as to receive a reward for our work. It is a typical pattern for all of us which includes good, energetic beneficial work, most of which is done for the remuneration we consider proper. We seem interested in the work and do it with energy and enthusiasm, all of which is aimed at a desired result, with our doing what is needed and ostensibly even more to ensure it.

We trade our work for what we consider a positive result. This result could be material, of course, but there are many other options such as appreciation, attention, or hope for a favor in return. The idle person is of course willing to forgo the result so long as they don't have to do anything, a concession driven by self-centeredness. He would of course welcome the result without the effort, but if that's not possible – then he can do without the reward.

The lazy person, meanwhile, wants to avoid negative situations and results and therefore does things, action aimed toward the reward of lack of harm. The traders act to get the positive result and are sometimes willing to sacrifice of themselves to get what they consider an appropriate or important reward; if possible, it should be more than what their work is worth.

In a state of trade, self-centeredness acts in full force, despite our ostensible giving to others and willing to do something for someone else. The dominant motive is the desire to get something in return. It could be anything from emotional to social to economic or even just something generally pleasurable.

In daily life, the pattern of trade is perhaps the dominant in our routine patterns of activity. We all find ourselves endlessly trading, every day in a natural, normal, and accepted manner. But it's possible to do it differently and it's worth it to know all the options.

Examples of trade can be found in almost all our relationships. Any giving that includes the expectation and even a request for something in return, either immediately or in the future, is a giving which expresses trade, because the promised return is the main reason for the giving. Trade also includes bookkeeping we conduct with others, deep down in our own mind, when we remember whether, when, and how much everybody gave.

Sometimes this trade mindset is expressed when we feel used. Sometimes people do try and even ostensibly succeed in exploiting our work for their benefit, as we try to do to others. But the sense of exploitation demonstrates and expresses the pattern of trade, which tries to create a balance between giving and doing, this time for our benefit and that time at our expense (all of it ostensibly speaking), and trying to ensure it's the former.

Later on, we'll see that things can be entirely different, which is for our benefit, no "ostensibly" about it. At the same time, we'll note that if someone is really trying to take something from us that isn't theirs, in a way that goes beyond what's justified in the situation, and which we have neither the desire nor intention to give, we can choose what to do with this, and if need be – cut them off.

I remember a young woman, exceptionally nice and positive in her demeanor, who was a compulsive pleaser. She would please anyone who seemed threatening enough, which was almost everyone she encountered. There was a purpose to this – to remove social threats and lead to people liking her and saying nice things about her. Emotional begging in full force.

Setting that aside, though, she was definitely a good-hearted woman who was happy to help. She, like all of us, was a woman with many and complex motives, which sometimes contradict one another. Anyone observing her would be convinced that she was a hard-working person always ready to help beyond what was needed, happily, voluntarily, and through grace.

In practice, she was driven by a constant sense of threat from almost anyone, and her charitable behavior was a way to ensure social safety, meaning a desired result, trading in emotion and appreciation and social safety. She revealed herself as a poor trader, giving more than she received, and suffering major disappointment afterward. It's easy to see that abstinence is the appropriate tool for her, in this case abstaining from any behavior or situation involving pleasing someone else.

In a similar context, a wise, good-natured woman told me of how she spent an almost hot night with a nice man, which she might have liked as a friend, but whom she was not at all attracted to in a sexual or romantic sense. In response to my asking why she was with him, the honest answer was painful: "He wanted good sex and I wanted attention." After a brief pause, she added with miserable bitterness: "He got what he wanted."

Emotional begging mentioned before – which describes a situation in which we are looking for attention or appreciation from others, or any positive emotional expression from them, and are willing to do a lot to get it – is a typical pattern of trading.

We see emotional begging in a wide range of daily social situations in which we, flatter someone and suck up to them in order to get a compliment or something else in return. I've met these "serial flatterers," who couldn't imagine how burdensome they are to others, sometimes leading people to respect them even less than they respect themselves.

In other cases, instead of "paying in advance" with flattering words, we trade in self-exposure to others at high levels of self-pity, in order to receive their pity and gain encouragement or simply take pleasure from the attention we received. We complain to someone who can do nothing about our complaint, just so that they reciprocate our emotional begging bill.

It's also possible to identify trading and emotional begging among couples.

When this is mutual, they experience it as a wonderful feeling, a mutual, loving exchange of favors. But over time, the mutuality recedes, replaced by the manipulation of trading in emotions, and then the emotional begging is less wonderful and joyful, it is replaced with disappointment and a sense of emotional distance.

Emotional begging is a pattern of trade, and like all trade it is result-oriented, paying for it in hard currency of some kind. Sometimes the price defines the goods we are looking for, such as a compliment for a compliment. When we give to others without looking for something in return – complimenting, attention, providing, loving, - it is neither trade nor emotional begging. Even when we share others without asking for an emotional reward, this is not emotional begging, and it's worth sometimes to make use of someone else's perspective to tell the difference.

Like our other patterns, trade can turn into spin. When we enter into trading and calculations of whether doing something is worthwhile or not, there's no end to it. This spin is marked by endless social calculations, manipulations,   a feeling of exploitation or emotional begging. The spin of trade can be acute, and can overwhelm us like a chronic habit which runs our lives. Sometimes this spin creates a worldview for us, or reflects an existing one, which argues that "that's life," or "there's no other choice," "everyone's self-interested," and the like.

When the trading pattern runs our relationships, the result is painful and life feels frustrating. This is usually marked by an experience of burdensome and increasing tension. We are seemingly dependent on the result we aim for, and stand guard to get it while using various means, with the cost being tension. In any event, this is the spin of self-centeredness.

We can see how many social relations reflect a pattern of trade: I'll give you attention or respect, and you give me something in return. An ostensibly win-win situation, which leads to the spin becoming stronger as does the self-centeredness. A very common, accepted, and typical state of affairs.

The pattern of trade is predominant in present-day society. We've become so used to it being a given that relationships, distant as well as close, express simple exchanges and we are sure that to receive, we must give, and if we give, then our giving is so that we receive. A person helps someone else, and a common response of the person being helped is "I owe you." An expression of a cultural approach, on which capitalism is based.

But it can be different. Capitalism, culture, and society will likely not change, but we can change ourselves, in the spirit of the serenity prayer and the different tools we've discussed.

The game of life

An interesting pattern of activity is the game. When was the last time we played a game that wasn't competitive? A competitive game is the "commercial pattern" I described above, where we play for a result. But let us now speak of playing solely for the sense of enjoyment. The game is an interesting pattern of activity which sometimes involves a great deal of effort, investment, and even the need to delay gratification, alongside a great deal of enjoyment.

The satisfaction comes in the very fact of doing, without desiring any particular outcome. A pure game done for its own sake, with the experience being focused on this moment. It's like the experience of the idle or pleasure-seeking person, but the player is willing to make an effort and invest, which requires forgoing self-centeredness, and there is no neglect of anything else during the game.

Many types of leisure are game-like, such as going on a trip or hiking through nature. Creative activity is also like a game – things like playing musical instruments or painting as a hobby, and the like. Even the study of a particular topic which is not part of our daily life, which is done for the joy of learning, is a kind of game. For instance, listening to lectures on history. All these examples show us that the game pattern expresses a certain mental state, in which we expect not a result but rather feel glad of the activity.

Since there is a desire for satisfaction and joy in the various kinds of games, self-centeredness might move them over to the point that the game becomes a kind of idleness or pleasure-seeking – enjoying the game instead of doing what we need to do. For instance, we play a computer game while we were supposed to use it for work. Let's be honest: Who can't identify such cases?

Similarly, the striving for a result could dominate the game pattern and turn it into a trading one – investing in order to achieve a desired result, then it's all about the joy of the result, not the activity.

When we clear off some of the self-centeredness, and when it's authentic and not just for show, the game is an important and positive pattern, and one who plays it is naturally happy and radiates that happiness on us and others. It only seems like we're hearing the shouts of children playing, and something within us smiles, too, for their joy is infectious.

We can introduce game-like behavior into our everyday lives, not at the expense of others or what needs getting done. In addition, we can introduce the mental state accompanying the game, that spontaneous joy, into the completion of tasks and duties called for by reality. This is the art of life, which makes life itself into a happy game.

Painful rigidity

Before getting to the important pattern of acting through grace, there's another pattern worth mentioning – acting out of rigidity. This action is done out of the necessity to reach a certain result which includes doing something in a particular manner, and at a particular time and place. The rigid person certainly does more than the lazy one, does not necessarily calculate what they get in exchange like the trader, and certainly does not enjoy the game.

Rigidity is the opposite of the game pattern. I described the game as the art of life, with rigidity sometimes being like death during life. We're all rigid sometimes, to one degree or another, acting like robots with rigidity taking over our vitality.

The pattern of rigidity forces us to sacrifice ourselves. We do not cling to the experience of the pleasant and comfortable and even make an effort for something that seems bigger than we are. Still – this is a pattern where we are self-centered. We try and apply our rigid definitions to all of reality, but we have effectively adopted them for a variety of reasons, all of which reflect self-centeredness. We try and apply a compulsively rigid approach to our surroundings which in fact reflects an internal state we have.

A prominent example is religious behavior, which so often becomes rigid and leads to great disasters. The religious person sacrifices themselves – sometimes including their life – for their rigid belief, usually also willing to sacrifice all those who don't fit their rigid principles or their narrow worldview.

This rigid fanaticism can take on the form of almost any ideology, even one which is ostensibly liberal and humane, being unable in the name of humanism to tolerate a different view than ours. If we espouse a rigid form of humanism and operate according to the rigid pattern, then there is neither joy nor love of people nor humanism, just a situation akin to spiritual death. And that's a shame.

Alongside prominent rigidity and fanaticism, there is also the "small" rigidity in our daily life, marked by things like habits which dictate a certain way of doing things or when we expect others to act in a way we consider to be correct, no matter what. Even aiming at perfection can be driven by rigidity. In the perfectionist state, we need a particular result, which is seen as a nearly existential need, without compromise, without human softness, sacrificing grace for result.

The compulsion of rigidity is actually self-centeredness taking over. One of its expressions, deriving from the same, is the increased anger in our lives, which derives from fear. We are angry and blame everyone who threatens our own rigid pattern, obviously including anger and blame toward ourselves, because our deep experience is that our rigidity protects us from a disaster which could happen if things do not play out in the very specific way it dictates. Self-centeredness becomes an angry dictator seemingly protecting us from a catastrophic danger trying as much as possible to force itself on us and on others.

Although rigidity emerges for many reasons, connected to all sorts of deep issues, it's possible to break free of it, through behavioral flexibility exercises, as shown in the different tools, such as distinguishing facts or the serenity prayer. The use of these tools for rigidity works very well and ultimately allows us to be looser and more flexible in our behavior and ultimately in thoughts and feelings.

From a self-struggle to acting through grace

In the self-struggling pattern, we go beyond what is needed, solely based on internal commitment. This work is sometimes challenging and complex for us, maybe even a burden, as opposed to the game pattern for instance, and it relies on a prominent foundation of overcoming oneself. We act out of a sense of the right course of action, of certain values.

The struggle with oneself is not a pattern of rigidity, pointing to self-centeredness, but it in fact is an attempt to transcend self-centeredness with the hope of breaking free of it. In the struggle with ourselves, we use spiritual exercises, even when we don't find them convenient. Sometimes we do them because they aren't convenient, in order to deal with that longing for the convenient and the comfortable.

While struggling with ourselves, we are faithful to ourselves even in the face of painful internal conflicts. The activity is not necessarily joyful and does not always transcend self-centeredness, but we still fight.

Struggling with oneself is not easy. The opponent, which is in fact us, our self-centeredness, knows all our weaknesses and is quick to use them. It fights for its life against us, with our help. It uses us as much as it can, and we deal with it with the pattern of self-struggle.

Here's one example: Someone decided to get up one morning and practice contemplation through meditation. A nice and respectable decision, but the struggle with himself started immediately the first morning. Early in the morning, he remembers he was very tired because he went to sleep too late, that he doesn't feel like it, that it's pretty cold outside, that these exercises aren't his style, and all sorts of other excuses.

The excuses of our opponent are the closest to us, right there in our head. Accordingly, he also become particularly tired or impatient, or feel anxious. These are the attempts of self-centeredness to "get in its way." The struggle with ourselves shows itself when we don't listen to the self-centeredness but continue to do what was we have decided to do earlier.

It turns out that the pattern of struggle with ourselves accompanies almost all the tools of the GraceWay – from abstinence on down. All effectively guide us, among other things, toward this pattern of activity – to act despite the constant attempt to disrupt our self-centeredness, which is interested in us not acting. Occasionally, the action of self-struggle is also abstinence from undesirable behavior, despite the fierce attraction of self-centeredness to it.

One of the "dangers" of the pattern of self-struggle is rigidity. How do we know when it enters into the picture? According to our response. When a guilt arises at our not having struggled with ourselves enough, when some criticism or judgment we feel about ourselves, or indeed toward others and a sense of "superiority" over them for not fighting like we are, emerges, this is when rigidity comes into play and self-struggle becomes self-centeredness.

For instance, a person starts a diet to lose weight, which is a declaration of war on the self-centeredness which ruled him in his eating too much. The dieter continues to struggle with himself and adheres to the diet, and then self-centeredness, as if lacking any other choice, pretends to be the inner voice preaching dieting. Along the way it becomes a judge and critic of how everyone else eats, creating a barrier and a distance between them, making that person easier to control through self-centeredness.

This is obviously a trick of self-centeredness – when it does not manage to stop our efforts to struggle with ourselves, it starts "speaking the language" of spirituality and self-struggle, thus entering through the back door of rigidity. If we are trying to adhere to any external results – and most of us usually do so even when we try to continue to struggle with ourselves – then rigidity comes in through that expectation, as well as through the criticisms when they don't come as we wanted, and so on.

When we continue with our self-struggle, change happens. Slowly, gradually, or quickly. One of the expressions of this change is the increased frequency of another pattern of activity, which I called 'activity through grace'. Here we go beyond what we need to happily and out of choice. All actions are now done out of that sense of voluntary decision and joy. As though the question of duty does not exist.

There's also no forced commitment from within the struggle, just joy from the very act of doing. We seek to do what we think could benefit someone or the world, without seeking reward or payment or anything else. We don't seek to benefit from our actions. Action through grace directs us to act solely for the sake of worthy action. Activity which stands on its own, free of expectation of any result, freed from the sense of the doer. Action which is inaction in the usual sense of an action leading to a result, as the Bhagavad Gita describes[88]. This has been called wu-wei[89] in Chinese philosophy and Chinese Taoism nicely describes this sort of action[90]. We do because we consider the action right in this moment in time, and do what we consider to be our best.

The pattern of acting through grace is the only one reflecting a moment of complete choice without anything else directing us, and it therefore expresses the self-realization that transcends our self-centeredness. Acting through grace is a state of transcending self-centeredness. In the state of grace, self-centeredness is not the motive or even a consideration for acting. Considerations of self-centeredness are silenced temporarily or entirely, by the grace of God.

Acting through grace continues the pattern of struggling with ourselves, combining it with the game pattern, which is action relatively free of expectation or commitment, but which adds happiness to both of these without burden or conditions, the absence of seeking pleasure or a desire for any result in the world, and the transcendence of self-centeredness. In the game pattern, the prominent motive is satisfaction, which goes beyond overcoming difficulty. In acting through grace, the deep satisfaction already exists, as an experience, and is therefore not a motivation for action. Our enjoyment of the action is simply an added bonus, not a driving motive.

Just as other patterns can lead to spinning out of control, so can acting through grace lead to a behavioral spin – but this time, it's a desirable and positive one. As, the Jewish sage Ban Azzai said[91]: "...for one good deed leads to another good deed ..." and added that "for the reward for a good deed is another good deed[92]" – a positive spin of action whose reward is the very act of doing good, with nothing in return.

We could say that acting through grace is "doing for the sake of heaven[93]." The important reward we receive when we act through grace is grace itself, which is growing within ourselves. When it does, in a positive feedback loop, we feel increased ability and potential. The ability to choose and the sense of self-control strengthens, and we act out of choice independent of anything else.

The missions, which in the past seemed a burden, are easy and joyful , with happiness being the very fact of grace, leading to a nimble action, out of choice, but not driven by result. Such an approach leads to a very fine and a more joyful result, but even if not, the satisfaction is still there – the result was after all not the goal. If we get what we consider a positive result, we will try not to seek it out, because that's when the trading pattern tries to take over.

Obviously what I've presented is an ideal type of acting through grace, but life is complicated, and only have such a capability at times. Still, the very fact that we want it means a change has started within us. There are moments when we see the sparks of this action through grace, truly free, which are wonderful.

Acting through grace leads to an increasing transcendence of self-centeredness, turning into a simple and appropriate tool for dealing with becoming mired in the other patterns involving increased self-centeredness. For instance, instead of delving into idleness or laziness and fighting them, we can seek out acting through grace and strengthen it. It's like doing reverse psychology and using the abstinence tool in two ways – first, avoiding idleness and laziness, and second, acting out of choice, beyond what is necessary, as part of a plan for change.

There is no expectation of pleasure in acting through grace, but if the action through grace reflects what's important to us, how we understand life, it has a silent happiness, freed of self-centeredness. When it continues and expands within us, acting through grace becomes acting through love, to a life of grace and love. Acting through grace expresses the message of the GraceWay and the means to achieve it – to be the grace we wish to meet.

Tamar had a convenient job. She worked for a public company and did a lot of "on the ground" travel, with a car provided by the company, so she could easily get around. When she was on the road, she was entirely independent, and her performance could not be tracked or evaluated. Right from the start, laziness was the prominent pattern of her performance, and she did only what she had to. Like pretty much everyone, no? At least that's what she told herself.

In time, her conception of what needed doing became ever more "flexible," with her doing less and less. A spin process, which advanced from the spin of laziness to the chronic spin of idleness. She would avoid work almost every day, pretend to be busy with field work, but in fact dealt with personal issues on the job and sometimes just did nothing.

Her output dropped accordingly, and her relationship with her superiors deteriorated. If they could, they'd have let her go. This went on for a few years. Tamar enjoyed relative comfort at work, excellent pay, a company car, bad work relations, and most importantly – a bad feeling in the workplace. Even the little she did was of low efficiency – and even that she considered burdensome.

Spin, by its very nature, leads to a crisis or declines on its own. Tamar was near breaking point. The less she did, the heavier the burden at work became . Despite this, in other areas of life Tamar was diligent and effective. When it came to her family, for instance, she was happy to prepare, provide, or clean, with limited expectation of a reward. Despite her minimal functioning at work, Tamar wanted to grow from within her self-centeredness and was ready to make an effort to that end.

Another option that she hasn't thought of arose in our conversations:

create a clear change in her functioning at work. To work "for the sake of heaven," for the very fact of proper work. In practice, it was truly to work for herself, as part of her journey along the path of spirit, and not for her superior. To do her best as part of her use of the "truth only" tool, and bring even more benefit than what was expected of her.

We redefined her workplace as her challenge, and the way she worked as an opportunity to jumpstart herself spiritually. We spoke about becoming mired in laziness and idleness as opposed to acting through grace. These things resonated with her. She was brave and decided to change. After a few months, she felt new and surprising happiness which was an important part of the change.

It was as if she was saying: "I used to go to work with a sense of burden, true disgust. And now – what fun, what happiness." Relationships improved – with colleagues, with superiors, with customers she had to meet, and most importantly, with herself. The goal of the change for her was primarily to learn to do for the sake of doing, acting through grace as a value that stands on its own and expresses a transcending of self-centeredness. She preserved the truth through doing her best, with the positive results being an encouraging bonus. The reward of a good deed – was the good deed, and the rest was gravy. Fortunately for her, she got both.

> *Let's take a brief moment of silence. We'll try and let go of the thought of various patterns of activity and indeed any other activity. We'll listen to the deep quiet, which acts within us and upon us without doing anything.*
>
> *…We'll recall something we wanted to do and did not, for any reason. And we'll try and remember another thing like that, and still another one. We'll see the gap between desire and plans we had and what we actually did. And then we'll let go of that and return to the silence.*

Making plans about what we do in the world is human. The same is true for dreaming about desired plans. Almost all of us plan to do something, big or small, for ourselves or others. Almost all of us can point to the gap between what we wanted and planned – and what we ended up with.

There are many reasons for this gap. Sometimes it's actually good when we didn't follow through with some impulsive plan. But there are unfortunately many cases where we wanted or planned something for the good of the world, others, and ourselves, which we did not end up carrying out for some reason.

The gap between what we wanted to do or become and what we are, creates a feeling of powerlessness. If the gap is small or the plans weren't that important, then that feeling is slight or negligible. But there are times when our desires and plans are important to us, and still – nothing happened. Then we feel a truly frustrating powerlessness.

We offer a whole range of justified reasons to ourselves and the world why this gap exists, with most of them having to do with forces greater than ourselves, such as "I have a lot on my plate," "It's not just up to me," "They didn't let me," and so on. Well-argued, entirely correct arguments that do nothing to reduce the gap.

The twelve tools and patterns of activity in this chapter offer us a new perspective about the gap and primarily about ourselves. Instead of sufficing with the usual justifications directed at the world, we seek within ourselves, just for today, that courage to change what can be changed. Maybe we should want less and be more realistic? Perhaps do just a little to realize our dream, just today, despite our busy schedule?

We can replace the negative thought that explains why we didn't do what we wanted, with the positive thought that shows how we can nevertheless change things. We thus change our typical patterns of activity, letting go of accounts which perpetuate patterns that harm us, replacing them with a new pattern. Action leads to action, and our ability to continue with the new pattern increases.

"To be rid of the image, to go out into a space of infinite light[94]."

CHAPTER TEN

Precious Longing and Cheap Substitutes

Let's begin with a moment of silence. We'll let the silence live in our mind, letting go of what was there before. Into that silence, we will introduce a look at ourselves from the outside, observing ourselves in a particular moment of action, and ask ourselves – what did we seek to achieve? What was our deeper motive, beyond the changing content of the action?

For every answer that comes up, we'll ask ourselves – "Why?" – and even after the additional answer which arises, we'll continue to ask, trying to reach the basic answer lying behind every why.

Let's return to the deep silence without any motive.

When we examine our motives honestly, we can see that deep down, when they are freed of the changing content of a particular moment and the expectation of achieving some result, there are motives which repeat themselves. We want certain basic things from ourselves and from life, which serve as deeper motivation for both action and inaction.

For instance, we yearn for freedom and liberty, long for love, certainty, and security and sometimes also perfection and the like. On the face of it, these basic motives are directed outwards toward the world, others, or even ourselves as objects in the world, and they express our desire to achieve some a result which will benefit us – for instance, that we experience our freedom in full or that we feel loved and accepted, – and also the desire to avoid any painful result, such as feeling limited or rejected.

On the face of it, these motives express self-centeredness or the serpent taking over our mind. But we can look at these basic motives from a different perspective which turns out do derive from deep human yearning for spirituality which has no trace of self-centeredness.

The motives actually express intuitive knowledge we have, about the nature of life, the world, and ourselves, knowledge about our essence and possibility, deliberate disregard, confusion, and typical human error, all of which derive from our self-centeredness, and bring us time and time again, toward action where they will not find a proper and stable response. Leading to the repeated need for action meant to achieve the desired answer, without finding satisfaction.

With the growth of our ability to transcend self-centeredness, pointing these intuitive motives in the right direction, their satisfaction will come on its own. In this chapter, I will describe various motives, their normal expressions and deeply embedded meanings, with an emphasis on our ability to direct ourselves in accordance with this meaning.

Yearning for freedom

Let's imagine a common social situation. Someone tells someone else to do something, and the other guy, almost without thinking, retorts: "You do it!" or "You don't tell me what to do". Even if we don't say it out loud, we'll oftentimes feel rebellion simmer, the desire that no-one tells us what to do, and act as we wish at any given moment, or indeed avoid any action we did not freely choose.

We rack up resistance toward social frameworks or figures of authority, and in relationships we find ourselves competing over the ability to give directions and ostensibly determine what will happen. Similarly, we tend to oppose any limitations imposed on us, wishing to live our life free of any limits. There are situations where our opposition comes into play when someone, in our view, is stopping us by telling us "no." We don't like to hear that, since it stands in the way of our desires, intentions, and yearnings.

This opposition has a number of motives, and when we honestly dig deep, we see that one of these motives, a particularly basic one, is the desire to be free of any limitation, obstacle or hindrance. Logic obviously tells us that we are limited by our bodies, our human nature, social and political frameworks, the environment and existential necessity in which we live, but the yearning has a life of its own. Sometimes it seeks a way to express itself – such as opposing a framework, momentarily fleeing responsibility, or behavior which allows for a temporary but false sense of escape, such as drug use.

David, a young man addicted to sex and undergoing recovery, told of a process of relapse, when he went to a neighborhood where sex services are available. When he got there, he wandered around for a few hours before choosing where to do the deed. He went to various venues, talked to a few of the women there, compared them to other places, continued to make the rounds, left, dreamt, fantasized, and dragged the moment out.

During that time, which went on for a few hours, he experienced complete freedom – the freedom to choose. In a moment he will be able to choose the ultimate gratification and fully experience his freedom as a man and a person.

David usually felt chained, limited, far from free, as though life was crushing him with its terrible weight. In moments of relapse, especially those before the act with the woman, whose services he eventually hired, he lived the dream of freedom he so yearned for. He could act as he wished, no-one told him what to do, and in just a moment, by his choice, he could gratify his virility, out of internal freedom. Predictably, when the act itself ended, the dream dissipated and David felt even more chained than before, as he was aware of being chained to the urges of his addiction, and not just to life and their natural limitations.

With a bit of honesty, most of us can identify those moments of fantasizing about complete freedom to do what we want, the resistance and sense of burden when that yearning is not satisfied, and the price we pay for our attempts to experience freedom at any cost. We'll search for those moments where we cast off our yoke, even for a second, ignoring external limitations, not listening to any negative response or willing to stand a delay in the gratification of something, or simply ignoring something we committed to, or which is our responsibility.

All these express the desire to be free of external limitations, at least for a brief moment. There are small successes here and there, wonderful moments of feeling free running through every fiber of our being. It comes up in those moments of casting off burdens, or when listening to music, or being in a stunningly beautiful place, engaged in a gratifying activity or when we simply avoid any. Such a feeling of freedom is usually temporary and passing.

A natural conclusion is thatfreedom does not seem to exist, as man is a limited creature on every level. Therefore, accepting our limitations seems to be the way to maintain a degree of sanity and proper human relations, and may be a way to achieve serenity, as the serenity prayer directs us to do.

This conclusion is definitely right when we speak of body and mind, and life will lead us to admit this, whether we like it or not. The acceptance of our human limitations and ceasing to resist, as well as breaking free of the fantasy to always do as we wish, is also an important stage in the achievement of serenity.

But all this is only on the surface, as man is fundamentally more than body and mind. Man is first and foremost spirit, "the image of God" as the Bible puts it, or "atman" (self) in Hindu philosophy[95, 96]. Our identification with the body and mind **is** our great limitation, our basic ignorance according to Buddha, from which all our suffering comes[97, 98, 99].

The spirit, as understood by all spiritual traditions and as experienced by those awakened to reality, is unlimited, is **the** unlimited, freedom itself and for itself[100]. By our very spiritual, divine nature, we do live a life of freedom, but are not aware of it. The way of the spirit is the way of freedom, a way of growing awareness of what exists in essence, and with it also a liberation which grows and grows.

The striving and hope to live our free nature is a basic spiritual longing. Due to error, confusion, or an ignoring of our spiritual essence, we turn this natural yearning for spiritual freedom to striving for a sense of freedom from any external limitation, freedom limited to body and mind. These all express self-centeredness and bring about increased suffering.

Reducing our identification with our limited body and mind – a narrowing of our identification with self-centeredness which is both limited and limits us – will lead to a reduction of the suffering. We can get closer to revealing the freedom we long for, which exists in our essence, by increasingly transcending our self-centeredness. It starts on its own with walking in the GraceWay and using its guiding tools. The leading motto of the GraceWay – to be the grace we wish to meet – offers us freedom of existence, which our intuition strives for, a spiritual freedom, aimed for and possible, which is the freedom from self-centeredness.

Longing for happiness

We all want to be happy. It's human yearning, perhaps the most basic one. Longing for freedom is also yearning for happiness. But unfortunately, self-centeredness confuses the distinction between happiness and physical or emotional pleasure or satisfaction on the one hand, and between happiness and flight from frustration, pain, and suffering, on the other.

The natural longing for happiness becomes an unending pursuit of momentary pleasure and an addiction to the pleasure and gratification originating in something outside us. Life and the world present us with a fascinating variety of temptations, and self-centeredness sees them as possibilities for achieving gratification, pleasure and utter enjoyment, thus deepening our confusion and its hold on us.

Actions deriving from self-centeredness cannot deliver on their promises for long. When we awaken from the illusion of the happiness of self-centeredness, we feel despair and bitter reconciliation with the painful, superficial or meaningless human existence.

We cannot ignore that pain, of all kinds, exists in our world. It usually passes, like pleasure or enjoyment, and sometimes does not, but it is always partial. It is only a part of our existence. What part? It depends on the circumstances, most of which are not of our choosing, and which we cannot influence, but a lot also depends on our response to the pain, which is what creates the suffering of existence.

When we change something in our perspective and priorities, there is always something beyond the pain or the joy of the moment, at our disposal whenever we seek it out. When we struggle and try not to be taken in by the temptations of the world and the attraction of self-centeredness to external objects, the possibility of revealing something of our true nature opens up before us. A possibility which was once hidden and is now clear in our eyes or heart.

We do not need to make an effort to get it, it already exists and we need but to act to let go of our holding onto what hides it from us. Then, like a blink of an eye, moments of unexplained and incomprehensible joy appear, independent of the outside world and the gratifications it offers our self-centeredness.

The more we let go, the more those sparks turn into a small fire of internal joy, a happiness we are aware of and can appeal to more and more, even in moments of pain. In such moments, the pain still exists and still hurts, while the flame of joy still burns underneath. If we allow ourselves to be aware of it, we will learn that it is an eternal flame, dependent on nothing but itself, and certainly not on us or our pain or pleasure.

We can direct our attention to it or ignore it; it exists either way. The longing for happiness, when directed correctly, is the yearning to reveal the internal eternal flame. When we try to live the grace we wish to meet, we remove obstacles and merit experiencing increasing sparks of the flame of internal happiness, despite the pain that exists in the world and in life which continues.

Longing for love

No other emotion has been written about in stories, song, film, hymn, poem, and prose more than love. In an ideal world, we are born from love, wrapped in a love that guides us in its soft and loving way toward where we were meant to be, and continue to find more love in our life and create more fruits through it.

At times when this fantasy is realized we encounter and grant love – parental love, friendly love, human love, spousal love, and the love of God, as we understand Him. There's nothing like love to broaden our heart which we naturally want more of. All people seek love.

Animals are also interested in love. At a freedom animal sanctuary where animals are raised in the best conditions, without harm or exploitation, out of devoted concern for their needs, animals seek the love of their caregivers and animals near them and grant love to them. Small and large mammals as well as birds love and seek love.

When we visit such a farm, where people and animals live and love together, the heart naturally opens up and something starts to move. I witnessed a visit of prisoners from the jail's rehabilitation ward in such a freedom animal sanctuary[101], people who had committed serious crimes and were serving long sentences, who reacted to the animals with atypical softness, identifying with their desire to live freely and with love. Our existence contains a desire for love and the knowledge that it is the essence of life without which there is no life.

Our self-centeredness is happy to join in on the love-fest. Self-centeredness loves love – love directed toward ourselves. It's pleasant, it broadens the heart, it loves it, and self-centeredness wants more and more of it. To get it, self-centeredness has many tricks which I've already described, which are primarily marked by a pursuit of people and their attention. With the encouragement of self-centeredness, we find ourselves "bribing" or "winning" people over, sometimes "drawing them in" and subordinating them to our ostensibly loving desire.

For example, a young woman was in a relationship with a man who wanted to break up with her. A familiar situation. She refused. She begged him not to leave her. She swore of her burning love and said she couldn't live without him. She'd call him repeatedly just to hear his voice, which ostensibly gave her confidence, and mostly just to ask him if he loved her, as she declared her own unlimited love.

He found her demands of him impossible to accept which he told her so. This caused her greater anxiety and depression, and that "drawing" and demanding tendency increased. Talking to her, I told her with needed firm gentleness that I think she doesn't actually love him, because she was not at all considerate of him and his desires, only hers. Her answer was simple: "He's my tranquilizer ..."

But that's just it: He isn't. No person we claim to love owes us anything. The desire to earn love, out of an existential fear, out of passion or anything else, leads our self-centeredness to try and subordinate others in the name of love, and there is no love in that.

Much like the longing for freedom or happiness, the longing for true love also becomes something else entirely through self-centeredness – a pursuit of people who are pleasant to be around or who serve some other fantasy of ours. When we identify with self-centeredness and its declarations of love, we are effectively occupied with how to improve our receipt of love or attention from others or the world, and all means seem legitimate to that end.

So long as the world and other people yield to our desires, we're satisfied. Ostensibly, we love and are loved. But in practice, in so many cases, this is but a declaration of love which papers over an encounter between our self-centeredness and that of others. So it was with the woman I described – so long as her self-centeredness and that of her partner aligned, they were both sure of their wonderful love. When the self-centeredness of one of them went in another direction, the crisis became inevitable and the self-centeredness, trying everything possible to draw in attention from the other, revealed itself.

The longing for love is a wonderful thing, like love itself, which is the essence of life. When we live love, we live freedom and happiness. But self-centeredness cannot bring us to this state, no matter how much it tries. The more we seek love, the more we effectively move away from the essence of love. This essence is expressed in a complete transcending of self-centeredness toward others, toward the world, toward God, as we understand Him.

The natural longing for love is a yearning to live our most basic essence, which exists in us despite the barriers of self-centeredness. If we ignore both self-centeredness and its barriers, and live the grace we wish to meet, the love that exists in us, which we yearn for, will be revealed to us. We will meet the grace, deriving from us without any condition or limitation, with love. In every moment in life where it seems we need love, the simplest thing to do is to practice it, to find someone and bestow them with grace, without fear or expectation of any result or condition. Then, we will know that the love that flows within us is the balm for our heart and soul.

Between longing and craving

The human heart, guiding us in the way of the spirit, contains basic yearning. We saw how it expresses itself as longing for freedom, happiness or love. This yearning has other expressions, such as the longing for truth or security, the longing for perfection or eternity. For various reasons, all of which can be marked out as expressions of our self-centeredness in one form or another, our precious basic longing becomes a craving for satisfaction, dependent on something external.

For instance, the yearning for security becomes a desire or even an uncompromising need to control everything, especially that which we can't, instead of finding security where it lies, in God as we understand Him, and in our capability for independent self-mastery when we transcend self-centeredness.

Our self-centeredness leads us to turn basic longing for perfection, the essence of spirit, into high expectations from others, ourselves, the world, or God, and also into systematic criticism when our expectations are not realized – including self-blame.

Similarly, our natural yearning to know and live absolute truth becomes rigidity or stubbornness, when we suffice with our partial conception of changing reality, and treat it as the whole truth. When we see the truth through our screen of self-centeredness, and are sure that absolute truth is reflected back at us, we move away from it.

When we ignore the spirit and entirely identify with the body and mind, even our most natural yearning for eternity, for the spirit itself - the divine - becomes a desire for the eternal life of the body, a fear of death, a fear of losing things or letting them go, to painful longings for what is no longer. We are occupied with perpetuating something in our lives or ourselves or our honor, when we confuse the temporary with the eternal.

It seems as if we live as though eternity is assured us, such as when we "spend" our days to the point of becoming worn out or when we become so mired in nonsense as though we have all the time in the world to choose, with the false belief that we will choose differently someday. If something threatens our self-centeredness' false sense of eternity, we experience deep existential fear, as though we are surprised that our body and mind are temporary.

Eternity exists, it **is** what exists, and it is the eternity of the spirit. When we get closer to knowing it, our perspective of the temporary and the eternal will be shaped accordingly, and we will know peace and serenity.

Jung, the Swiss psychiatrist, described the thirst of the alcoholic for alcohol as equivalent, at a lower level, to the spiritual thirst of our existence, to our desire for perfection and unification with God[102, 103]. We can only quench our spiritual thirst if we walk along the path that leads to the spirit. Jung proposed a relevant formula for breaking free of alcoholism: "Spiritus contra spiritum[104]". This was the first link in a chain which led to the creation of AA and the formulation of the twelve-step program, which the GraceWay warmly adopts. Accordingly, we can offer a formula of the GraceWay which continues Jung's approach: "Grace v contra craving" – any craving.

All the various appearances of craving for something external, express a basic yearning and longing to reveal the essence of the spirit, which alone can satisfy this craving. This longing, which can bring us to a fundamental transformation finding the grace and spirit in life, is changed through the filter of self-centeredness, becoming an experience of fundamental deficiency and craving. Most cravings are for something external which is supposed to satisfy us, however it is but a pale reflection of the essence we yearn for.

Substitutes of one sort or another, quick and easy to get, give us the pleasant illusion of satisfaction, which easily dissipates leaving us with a sense of lack again and again. We are left with a desire for more of that experience and pursue a stronger experience – more interesting, more challenging.

We thus end up in an endless process of momentary gratifications and increased hunger, which grow further. So long as we try and satisfy this craving with external means, the satisfaction we get is temporary while we move away from living with that which exists in our essence. The different tools of the GraceWay direct us to recognize the difference between yearning, which can be the basis of spiritual development, and craving which can at best, leave us stuck where we are and can actually make our situation worse.

The different tools also allow us to gain an increasing ability to realize our yearning. Paradoxical, but true – it is our efforts to satisfy the cravings of self-centeredness which prevent us from finding the right answer for basic human yearnings. By contrast, when we choose grace instead of craving, we experience moments of strengthening, stabilizing satisfaction.

Sometimes things become even more complicated, with our failure to find satisfaction through substitutes, leading us to reach wrong conclusions. For instance, that there is no way to achieve fundamental spiritual satisfaction, and we are therefore left only with temporary, passing satisfaction – which means better to suffice with that than to dream of the precious yearning and its possible satisfaction. Such a thought is a counsel of despair. It turns existence banal and meaningless and creates a painful emptiness.

This conclusion is reminiscent of that which philosopher David Hume called "the is-ought" problem[105], which describes the process by which we deduce what ought to be from what is, learning values from facts we observe. This is also the "naturalistic fallacy" of psychology[106], which deduces what should be from studies based on observation of what is. In other words, we treat the ought and our ego as though it is the only possible reality which requires satisfaction through the senses, and so we are unaware of the ultimate spiritual reality and the exalted satisfaction which is its essence.

A similar mistaken conclusion is that yearning itself is a sign of something unhealthy, for that which does not exist through the senses, the body, and the limited ego, is considered unreal. The deep yearning for the spirit is therefore described in ways which minimize its potential and point at its ostensible visible problems.

For instance, a person's yearning for perfection is called perfectionism, his longing for certainty and security is called a desire for dominance, his yearning for freedom is considered immaturity, and so on. These are definitions which eliminate the basic precious yearning, and their mistaken conclusion seeks to end that yearning. So what's left?

The distinction between the precious yearning and the cheap substitute puts things in order. The craving for substitutes, which expresses confusion, points to deep yearning that is healthy, one which attests to an internal element within us. When we identify a strong craving of ours which repeats a common pattern of craving, we can seek out the worthy and precious yearning which lies at its heart. If we succeed, we'll end up with a different perspective about ourselves. Then we can accept the deep significance of the proper yearning, and change the direction of its search, thus bringing the "is" closer to the "ought".

Obstacles we put up for ourselves

Ostensibly, after failed attempts to achieve satisfaction of the precious spiritual yearning through cheap substitutes, we should have caught on to the principle and changed direction, thus reducing the frustration of disappointment from the false promises of the substitutes, and move closer toward realizing the yearning. But only ostensibly.

In practice, despite our understanding, we still go back to seeking out momentary gratification of cheap cravings, at the expense of strengthening the spiritual yearning. We repeat the same mistakes with the forlorn hope for different results, a condition described as insanity in NA[107].

So why do we cling to this insanity and continue to prefer the cheap substitute to the precious possibility, offered by the way of the spirit? There are a number of forces which we allow to operate within us against the saner possibility of spiritual development.

The first force is a mental expression of the physical law of inertia – we will generally tend to continue with "more of the same" until we can't, and even then we'll try more of it. The steps program calls this a "deviant confidence in familiar pain" - we are sure of the familiar, even if the results are painful, which is defined as a type of deviance[108].

To change familiar habits, we need to demonstrate courage or use strength, as shown by the serenity prayer, which is not a simple matter. It turns out that leaving what we think as our "comfort zone," even when it's not that comfortable, is a challenge that threatens us. Yet, when taking the risk and stopping the continuity of habit, something good happens to us.

The second force which prevents us from seeking satisfaction for the spiritual yearning where it can actually be found, rather than in the cheap substitute, is the power of temptation in the face of our weak points, the chief of these being the desire for power that seeks a sense of honor and external control, the desire for material security and welfare, and pleasure-seeking in all its forms.

When the temptation faces us, it "speaks" directly to those weak points, over our head or our heart, beyond the yearning, making us momentarily forget it and focus on getting easy gratification. It is not an easy task, to control those weak points within us and forgo the temptations presented to them. Yet, letting these temptations go, brings about increasing happiness.

The third force which takes over our mind and confuses it, is the strengthening spin. First, we cut ourselves all sorts of small bits of slack which allow pleasure for a passing moment. But the more we sink into the momentum of the spin, which seems to happen on its own, that slack steadily increases.

Our trust in ourselves, in our ability to stop the spin, shrinks, and so does our desire to do so.

It's easy to lose what we've gained, when we become light-headed and chase easy temptations, discovering, to our disappointment, that in the spin process, these simply grow to dimensions which we ostensibly cannot resist. But let us remember that the very power of the spin effectively derives from us – the choices we made, the slack we cut ourselves, and our self-perception. A slight change on our part can create a positive spin, which will grow to a wonderful impact on us.

The fourth force which can take over our mind and divert it toward pursuing the cheap and quick gratification, is individualism. We identify with our own ego and our experience of self-identity as expressed in our mind – craving, remembering, thinking, feeling, and imagining. The developing ego believes that it is the sum total of human existence.

This is the dominant social worldview in modern secular society – we live in an individualistic society which works to strengthen the individual's egotistical experience. The cheap craving is an expression of the ego which observes the world as external, and wishes to develop in that direction, growing in quick worldly gratification. But the ego is the external expression of something else, that is, the spiritual entity that serves as the basis on which the ego emerges. The precious yearning is for the self to transcend its selfness, which the ego is a barrier to. The understanding that individualistic identity is a private expression of the universal spiritual existence, opens a window for us into ourselves, which can grow as we wish.

The opposite of this individualism is the fifth force, the tendency toward group affiliation to the point of losing one's own way. The way of the spirit offers a transcendence of the ego and self-centeredness, and indeed any social affiliation or belonging, and is a threatening exception in a social landscape that feeds on conformism, with different degrees of freedom, depending on the culture.

It therefore explicitly or implicitly applies social pressure on us, which isn't easy to oppose. Groups of affiliation as such, are glad for our transcendence of self-centeredness, conditioned that it is in favor of social-centeredness, so that the group or the society, or their values and norms will be the higher power in our lives and what we devote to.

The way of the spirit which appeals to God, which yearns for the absolute, which transcends any identification with something else that is not the absolute, is an ostensible threat to sociability. Therefore the sociability creates pressure on us to conform, while sending the message that there is nothing real in the spirit, only in the changing values of society and culture. When we choose to realize the precious spiritual yearning, the social conformism will be reduced. But the more we transcend self-centeredness, we are more social in a way that doesn't require dependence on any group affiliation or conformism.

The sixth force which tries to intentionality block our honest focus toward full satisfaction of the precious yearning, is our limited logic, which relies on intellectual cognitive processes, which are fundamentally material. Logic, intellect and rationality are the limited tools of the mind in understanding and perceiving the world, but we cling to them since they are familiar and faithfully serve our materialistic self-centeredness.

These are all the considered tried and tested means, culturally speaking. They are excellent tools, but only so long as we are aware of their limitations in terms of their scope and capacity for understanding. The moment those limitations are forgotten, they restrict our world and its possibilities. The fact that these means helped science reach impressive-looking achievements, only strengthens their hold on us, while ignoring the simple fact that all the achievements of science are solely on the material level, and have made no progress in terms of human happiness.

The rational intellect offers us material comfort and welfare as a substitute for happiness, which it can certainly gain. But to get to something real, to satisfy the precious longing, we need to transcend the narrow tunnel of the intellect, a transcending which begins with understanding the limitations of that same intellect.

The seventh and last force I will note, is the changing needs and demands of the body, life and the moment. We find ourselves amazed at the way of the spirit and its possibilities, are aware of our deep and basic yearning toward it, understand that it is precious to us, yet the changing moment with its big or small demands, comes and we seem to have no time for the spirit.

We calm ourselves by saying just as things will calm down, we'll get back on the path and delve deep into it. This wish is welcome, but is sometimes just an excuse preventing us from following the path of assured satisfaction of the basic yearning, which can provide an answer to every changing demand of passing moment.

At a group for men batterers, I led some years ago, there was a conversation which demonstrated this in an amusing manner. We spoke about introducing serenity into our life, and one of the men, in a moment of candor, defiantly retorted: "It's all well and good, charming even, but you can't go to the grocery store with serenity!" The other men nodded in agreement, glad at my being "shown up."

When I asked if anyone thinks differently, there was silence. I returned to him: "You are saying you can't pay for groceries with emotional peace? That it doesn't ensure a livelihood?" The man nodded, satisfied at my quick understanding. I surprised him with a simple question, which he hadn't thought of: "How much are you paid at the grocery store for your emotional tension? What credit are you given for the anger, anxiety, and everything that controls your mind?"

It was easy to show him how his financial situation had in fact worsened because of his impulsive reactions, and that if he acted based on that emotional calm, which he desired but dismissed as unrealistic, his situation would probably be better by any measure.

This is all summed up nicely in a short, poem by Rabbi Yehudah Halevi, the Jewish poet, thinker and man of spirit, who lived in Muslim Spain in the eleventh century[109]:

Servants of time are servants of servants;

only God's servant alone is free.

Therefore, when every human being requests his portion;

my heart says: May God Himself be my share.

∾

"A spiritual man, who lives the spiritual, is happy with the spiritual, is happy everywhere, in any environment, at every time, in every circumstance[110]."

CHAPTER ELEVEN

Ho'oponopono – To Know Grace in a Moment

Let's start with a moment of silence. Deep in our mind there is the silence and all we need to do is let it be, in silence.

Let's add something else to the silence. We'll see ourselves out of awareness – how are we when the silence lives within us, and how are we when our mind is noisy? Even in the moments that have passed just now – what was it like when it was quiet, and what was it like without it?

Our struggle to break free of the chains of self-centeredness, powerlessness, compulsive habits or emotions, leads us to seek out tried and tested ways and methods to do so. The search shows interesting phenomenon, almost every culture or time offers methods and ways. Sometimes they are familiar and clear, and sometimes, due to a particular time or culture, they are relatively hidden. But their form is secondary to the way itself, which is shared across the different systems.

One of the interestingly direct approaches is Ho'oponopono, which was developed in Hawaii, and which is close in spirit to the GraceWay, as we will see later on.

The tools in real time

Omer is a young man of about thirty, recently married to Anat for about four years. He believes his is a very good marriage, which lit up his life. Anat seems to see things the same way. They're fortunate. They have a young daughter, who recently celebrated her second birthday. There's also a promising income – Omer is making nice progress as a marketing man and has reached a relatively senior position. There is almost great joy in the home. But only almost.

Despite the goodness Omer has moods. Strong, dominant. Mostly distress, sometimes also anxiety – and many angry outbursts toward his beloved Anat, and even toward the girl. His recent outburst toward his daughter and subsequent fight with Anat led him to seek help.

Omer is a young man with a high degree of self-awareness and a readiness to change, a sure recipe for rapid progress which predictably came. All was well, but only almost. He has strong habits which have been going on for years and which do not let go of him easily, without some fierce fight that shocks him.

The last fight had to do with his mother. He thinks she is mostly loving toward his sister's children, but ignoring his sweet daughter. In his view, and he considers this a solid fact, after so much investment in his sister's children, his mother has no strength or time for his daughter. Here is Omer before us, albeit virtually, but asking for help directly.

What to do? What does the GraceWay offer him?

The serenity prayer, perhaps? To peacefully accept that he can't change his mother but can change his reaction to her. To peacefully accept that it might be that she truly shows favoritism for his sister's children against his daughter. It sounds good. It works for him. But how does he accept the ongoing injustice in the moment of truth?

Yes, he repeats the prayer, but when he remembers the times when his mother shortchanged his daughter, his anger naturally increases. He repeats the serenity prayer, tries to cling to it, while his anger seems to mock him, rising up and taking over, leading to Omer losing control.

"What's mine is mine, what's hers – hers," "I have, and need nothing from her" – here, there are more appropriate tools. Omer learned them quickly and remembers them. Anger is an emotion, and emotion is not a fact. True. It calms him a bit to know this, but not enough. He wants a magic solution, as anger is illogical and bypasses logic.

Just for today to not act out of anger? True, almost a month has passed in which he tried to not act out of anger, and it's definitely wonderful. There's great improvement at home, and even when it comes to his mother, but he's still angry, in his heart, to himself, which he only shares with Anat, to gain a wise external opinion. Sometimes she thinks like him and is also pretty angry and frustrated at his mom, which only increases his own anger.

What is Omer's powerlessness? We can observe an interesting development here. At first, the powerlessness had to do with moods and outbursts. So what did he do? Abstinence, of course – from any outburst. It worked and works great, but the anger is still there, alongside other moods, however weakened. We can say that he is powerless over his moods, especially his anger, and the abstinence is marked by "reverse psychology" toward anger. Initiating entirely opposite actions with the help of the other tools, in addition to taking care to not act out of anger or other moods, definitely improves something.

But there's something else we can see, and this is his victimhood worldview. Regarding his mom, his sister, Anat, and even his little daughter – Omer feels himself a victim to all of them, the man who is hurt repeatedly and has to defend himself.

Is it only regarding women? An interesting point we considered but is apparently not the case. The moment the possibility of ongoing victimhood arose, it turned out that it exists in almost every other aspect of his life: With his direct (male) boss at work, with his friends, his brother-in-law, his dad. In fact, in almost every meaningful relationship , his feeling of being a victim came up.

It turned out that his feeling of victimization is a powerlessness which influences his moods. The moment he finds himself in a state of victimization, when he feels he's being harmed, mistreated or even mocked, he falls into a spin of negative moods which tries to goad him into action. Self-pity opens up the gate of power, honor, and control, inviting the serpent to enter and offer solutions – have an outburst, shout, don't let them hurt you, or perhaps run away, withdraw because it's so dangerous outside, or appease, to avoid further harm. The serpent has many means, and Omer knows them well and how to use them, but he wants to break free of them.

Why did he develop victimization, and what is it based on? Maybe his relationship with his mother, or with his father. We can find something in his past which ostensibly points to this. Maybe there's something else; maybe he was born this way, with this tendency.

In my view, what's best is to leave behind the limited possibilities of maybe, which bind us to ever convoluted interpretations.

Instead, we can take action. Omer must deal with this tendency, to grow from it. For instance, a daily examination of the victimization, sharing this with someone else, either instead of or alongside Anat, avoiding action based on victimization, finding in himself and not being dependent on anything outside himself, and more. And there's something else I will discuss now, which represents some of the tools in a focused way and based on action in "real time."

Clearing the mind in a moment

After being exposed to his powerlessness over his victimization experience, Omer understood and accepted that the experience is his, and is unrelated to other people. Another thing that came up is that his victimization experience was polluting his mind. One moment he's fine with himself and the next, because of the awakening of the victimization experience, it's not pleasant to be Omer at all. His powerlessness is like dirt in the mind – some of it is new dirt, created each time the experience arises, but a chunk of it is old, accumulated dirt.

The accumulated experience of victimization causes him to see the world

through the eyes of a power struggle with the potential for repeatedly experiencing victimization. Since the pollution is in his mind, and he pays an
emotional price for it, to say nothing of his young family and others, Omer
understood that clearing his mind is his mission, not someone else's.

This responsible understanding is the beginning of taking leave of the
state of victimization; instead of dealing with what others will say or do – he
focuses on what he can do to change a given situation. Leaving for a moment
"what they did to me" in favor of "What do I need to do to cleanse my mind."
It is reminiscent of the serenity prayer as well as the other tools.

So, how to start cleansing?

To clean some dirt, the first thing to do is to recognize that it is dirt, that
there is something undesirable in my mind that is polluting. Let's think
about a case where I accidentally spilled crumbs from a nearby plate on the
clean floor. It's easy for me to admit that there's dirt I don't want on the floor
because of something I did.

A practical option for expressing my attitude to the dirt is to say: "Sorry."
A sort of apology for the dirt I caused, in which I confess my part in it and
begin to take responsibility. Sorry there's dirt here, regardless of how and
why it's there. Obviously this is an internal dialogue, expressing the beginning of housecleaning the mind.

But the dirt is still here, and the owner of the mind needs to cleanse it, no
matter how the pollution entered into it. The next stage is therefore taking
responsibility for the cleaning, expressed with the simple words: "Forgive
me," also stated only in our mind, continuing our internal dialogue of
self-cleansing.

Who are we asking for forgiveness? There's practically no end to the
possibilities, with all of them not being important in themselves for the
cleansing process – what matters is the intentionality of asking forgiveness.
This is the way to gather the crumbs and lift them from the floor. We can,
for instance, ask forgiveness in our hearts from the person who is the object
of the dirt in our mind, in this case Omer's mom. He unquestionably had
non-beneficial thoughts toward her.

He can also ask for forgiveness from Anat, who was exposed to his victimization experience, toward God, whom Omer does not notice because of the pollution in his mind, toward himself for suffering from a polluted mind, toward the world, as the pollution of his mind is effectively pollution in the world, and so on. It doesn't really matter, so long as the crumbs are cleared from the mind and it shines with brilliant clarity. Almost.

The crumbs have been collected but they're still there, emanating the kind of radiation any mental pollution radiates on the environment. Mental pollution influences the world, and to free the world and especially our mind from this radiation, it needs to be exchanged for something else.

We need a transformation of the dirt, so that it doesn't continue to attract new dirt into our mind. We do this by replacing the negative pollution and its traces with something which is always positive - with love. Instead of mental dirt – striving for love. This is achieved by simply stating: "I love you" or even just the word "love," obviously said to the heart, continuing the internal process of self-cleansing. This simple statement creates a transformation of the mental dirt into something else, an intention of love.

"I love you" – who? Once again, it really doesn't matter. It can be Omer's mom, Anat, his daughter, God, the world, or Omer himself. All are worthy of love. All are part of it. The honest intention and focus, if only for a moment, is to be love and grace and to increase it in the world.

The moment we mention and honestly express love to ourselves, something happens. The grace acts and the dirt is transformed. It no longer radiates pollution. The relief is immediate and very pleasant.

Now we want to absorb and stabilize the change we've just experienced, and the last stage is thanks in our hearts for the grace, the change, the dirt that is replaced with shiny floors in our mind. Thanks is like mopping the mental floor with a particularly strong cleaning fluid. Even if crumbs drop, and they certainly will because that's life, they'll slide on the floor without sticking to it, with subsequently less lethal influence and greater ease in picking them up.

With Omer, the change happened exceptionally fast. He quickly admitted to himself and me that he felt accumulated mental pollution aimed at his mother, in the context of her ostensible favoritism for his sister's children over his own. "I'm sorry, Mom," and also "I'm sorry, Anat, and I'm sorry for myself."

That's all. This simple confession made him curious to continue, and he was ready for the second stage: "Forgive me, Mom." Since he understood victimization was his attitude to the world in general, he added "Forgive me, world," and also "Forgive me, Omer." He said it out loud, for himself and to me as a witness to the process. We continued the transformation – "I love you, Mom," and here he stopped, embarrassed. "It's strange – I haven't thought about loving her for a long time, and I certainly did not tell myself that. It's actually fun to say it." At once he softened, repeating the sentence and adding his love for Anat, his daughter, God, and himself, and this state-ment was also very strange for him and mostly – very pleasant.

It was such a relief and so pleasant, and all at once. To say thanks was already entirely natural for him – thanks to his mom who showed him his weakness, thanks to Anat who was there for him to love, thanks to God who allowed the grace, and also thanks to himself for making it through. The soft pleasantness only increased, until he sought to immediately bring up another case of victimization which he repeatedly experienced so he could undergo a similar process of soft and silent pleasantness.

Ho'oponopono

The long word Ho'oponopono[111] comes from Hawaii, as we have said. It means "correction" or "making things right" and represents a process of mental cleansing which was common, and still is in Hawaii and other places in Polynesia. It was originally a process of social ironing out, to stop conflicts in the community[112], but Hawaii in the twentieth century witnessed a new style of Ho'oponopono emerge, this being the resolution of conflicts within one's own mind, or as we presented it here, a cleansing of the mind at the moment of truth when the pollution penetrates. What I presented above, what Omer did to immediately benefit from a clean mind, is the process of personal Ho'oponopono.

We can see some proximity between the practical side of Ho'oponopono and the practicality of the GraceWay, as illustrated by the detailed process Omer went through. But let us remember that this is my way of understanding and presenting Ho'oponopono, which I translated to the GraceWay.

Ho'oponopono emphasizes our responsibility for cleansing the mind. According to this approach, every mental state which clings to some content –, emotional, mental, experiential, or other, is a kind of pollution, a condition requiring a cleansing of the mind. Without delving too deeply, we can see that the Ho'oponopono method I presented here is very easy to apply, and experience showed that it much helped those who used it.

For instance, a young man, about twenty-one years old, told me that the moment he realized he was in a state of anger and remembered the word Ho'oponopono, that state immediately dissipated, replaced with an amused smile. The very recalling of the word seemed to do the whole process for him, and he said that his friends also laugh when he says that word, which also eased tensions between them.

Let's briefly repeat the process. There are four stages we undergo to cleanse our mind when we identify what we define as "pollution":

1. We admit to ourselves that there is mental dirt we don't want and which we regret – "I'm sorry"
2. We take personal responsibility for cleansing the mind by asking for forgiveness in our heart – "Forgive me"
3. We create a transformation of the pollution into something highly positive, love, which we declare to ourselves – "I love…"
4. We absorb the change through sincere thanks in our hearts – "Thank you…"

We can use this simple formula whenever our mind contains something that seeks or requires similar treatment, and keep tabs on ourselves to see the change that occurs over time. At the beginning, we will deal with large and prominent dirt, such as anger or frustration toward someone else or ourselves, and over time, when we develop a skill and our mind is cleaner, we can then make time for any dirt, even the most delicate, which arises in our mind.

Every wave of thought or color of emotion which we experience as negative, or which tries to dominate us, can be cleansed in this way. The immediate benefit is a return to a relatively clear mental state, with the more we use this process, the greater the clarity.

Diligent work on one bit of dirt creates change throughout the entire mind, with other dirtying events dissipating and disappearing. Over time, we change our approach to the world and ourselves. By living grace for a moment – and this is one of the meanings of the Ho'oponopono exercise of cleansing the mind – the grace enters our life and stabilizes itself in more ways.

Let's take a moment of silence, bringing up some pollution we have into our mind toward someone or even some idea or body. We will quickly go over the stages.

We'll admit to ourselves that this is pollution we're sorry about – "I'm sorry."

We'll take responsibility for its cleansing by asking forgiveness in our heart from someone relevant, including ourselves or God, as we understand Him – "Forgive me."

We'll create a transformation of the pollution into love – "I love."

We'll absorb the change through thanks – "Thank you."

"Standing before himself, clean of himself, it will become known to him. Asking about himself, it is not known to him[113]."

NO END:

Toward the Endless

Let's begin with a moment of silence. Silence deriving from within us, and when we listen to it, it wraps around our mind with its soft depth. Silence which contains nothing and everything, calm and alert, mired in itself and aware of the world.

Into this alert silence we will add a perspective of ourselves, seeing a prominent tendency of ours, a habit, and perhaps some trait or outline in our character. Without judgment, a perspective that continues the silence, viewing without reacting. We'll try and be aware of our ability to choose between the deep silence and our different modes of mind expressing our tendencies, habits, or traits. We'll choose the deep silence and dwell within it.

At one of the meetings of the GraceWay group for therapists which I moderated, Limor, a professional therapist who was familiar with the path and adopted it in her life and work, spoke of the burnout she was feeling. The workload, the exhaustion to the point of frustration and anger and even impatience toward her patients, was now a part of her life. They don't know it yet, because she manages to hide it, but she does, and it obviously bothers her.

Members in the group asked various questions, got more information and how overburdened she felt and made various suggestions. But something was missing. The suggestions they gave were certainly good ones, made by loving and experienced therapists, and touching on possible behavioral changes, trying to help Limor to accept her temporary weakness. But Limor did not want these. She knew them all; after all, she was an expert therapist herself.

I intervened: "What about your faith, Limor? What about the spirit in your life? How has it expressed itself recently?" It turned out no more was needed. Limor went silent, thought, and admitted: "I guess I forgot it. I was carried away with the workload, with the things I need to get done, and there was no room left for the spirit, and I effectively live without God. Is it any wonder that I feel empty, that my self-pity runs my mind?"

She softened at once, "I understand what I need to do, to return and find God that I left, to give Him the room I gave Him in the past." For her, there was no need to add anything. She had already opened her heart to find God within it, as she understands Him. At a later meeting, she returned to being that smiling and always modest Limor, saying that it was all behind her.

***

People make changes in their life for various reasons, consciously or not. Usually the need for change derives from our habits, behavioral responses, traits, or a particular personality structure. Sometimes the need for change comes from the gap between us and the demands of our environment, or between what we wish to have in our lives and what we actually do.

This is all related to our ego, which is present in the world, acts within it, takes part in interactions and forms relationships with others, feels, thinks, imagines, remembers, and maintains all sorts of other activities. The ego is also centered on itself to one degree or another. The ego, which we are sure is the essence of our existence out of complete identification with it.

When looking at our individual ego, separated from other egos and the world, we can see that it tends to be fairly conflicted, with itself, with the world and the creatures in it, with God, as it understands Him or denies Him. Obviously, not always. Sometimes there's harmony which is wonderful. Usually harmony is possible when the self-centeredness of the ego is relatively low. But even then, the potential for conflict within the ego is there, by the very fact of its separate, individual existence.

The ego's conflict with itself is marked by a restless movement playing around in our mind – the quickly passing thoughts, light or dark, the emotions going up and down, comfortable one moment and disturbing the next, memories, pleasant or otherwise, which influence us in a range of ways, fantasies, expectations, disappointments or passions.

So often our mind is subject to the unending racket of all this, a ruckus expressing the conflict in the changing tendencies of the ego. Here and there we find some wonderful moments of silence, intentional or spontaneous, but then the ego's processes hit us again. This is, after all, its nature.

The conflict of the ego with the world and the creatures in it, especially humans, is marked by disputes, competition or passions, interested in receiving or taking something from others and the world, opinions and feelings toward people, events, and situations and complicated relationships. By the very fact of our ego being individual and separate, it is potentially in a conflict of interest or with everything separated from it, especially other egos like itself.

As said earlier, there are many times when the ego is in harmony with the world, acting calmly and peacefully with love and happiness. But it's very individual and separate nature, along with its clear tendency to be self-centered, means the potential for conflict with the world and others is always in full force. How often has it happened to us that harmonious and loving relationships suddenly exploded into a surprisingly powerful conflict, which destroyed all harmony and made us forget all the moments of love or friendship?

Our individual and separate ego can easily find itself in conflict with God. It doesn't accept Him and His path, is sure it can manage without Him, dismisses Him for its own sake, sometimes being convinced that it is the greatest power, and is indeed sometimes afraid of itself, collapsing without recognition of God, living in an existential vacuum, or mired in the shifting vanities of the moment. Sometimes it is certain it faithfully represents God, being His spokesperson, and does everything possible to force itself on God.

The conflict of the ego creates problematic behavioral patterns, no less problematic personality structures, and mental processes which harm us and lead us to harm others due to various forms of powerlessness. Oftentimes, the conflict of the ego ends badly for it and others. Sometimes it leads us to seek change, to seek out mental relief.

There are many ways of lessening the conflict – tried and tested or innovative and new. Methods aimed at honing, improving, or benefitting the ego in one way or another. But all the methods for solving the conflict in our ego cannot truly end it. Relief is certainly possible, temporary relaxation, clear signs of improvement and progress, but the conflict still exists, actively or potentially, as it is present in the very nature of the ego.

The conflict exists, at least potentially, so long as the ego exists as an individual identity alongside other identities it considers separate – other people, the world, God. Depressing? Maybe, when the ego seems to be all and end all. The individual, separate ego, which is naturally limited and temporary in this world, naturally powerless, subject to the fickleness of the moment and of habit and can always have conflicting interests or struggles with someone or dissatisfied and frustrated, as it pretends to be all that we are. But this is a partial and deceptive picture the ego provides us .

The way of the spirit, any spiritual way, offers something else, which ends the conflict. This is also what Limor, who we mentioned earlier, wanted, and which is why she would not suffice with the good suggestions for relief she received. This is something that cannot be achieved through relief or the ending of the particular momentary conflict, but through a different course of action: Letting go of our identification with the ego, with its tendencies and conflicts – transcending the ego conflicted with itself, to the point of having it annihilated by the spirit. Nothing less.

When we let go of our identification with the ego, the affairs of the ego dissipate accordingly, as the Psalmist says: "Be still, and know that I am God[114]." This is what Limor experienced the moment she directed her attention back to the spirit that she had forgotten with life's pressures – immediate quiet with hope.

And her burden, which took over her life and her mind? It shrunk back to normal dimensions. It became tolerable, smaller. Since the conflict is present in the very reality of the ego identifying itself as an individual and separate entity, the way of the spirit offers the surprising option of ending the identification with the ego as such, and when that happens, the conflict disappears on its own. If there's no-one to be conflicted with– what will a conflict be based on?

This is what the spiritual way, any spiritual one, aims for. For all the spiritual ways are one. Right – time and place create an external difference between what appear to be different spiritual ways, but all the ways are essentially aimed at the truth: Freedom from our false identification with the ego – from what Buddhism calls basic ignorance[115]; then the divine en-lightens us with a loving light that is always within us, with its powerful hope and with no conflict or separateness.

The meaning of ending the ego's conflict by ending the identification with it, is that we have no need to analyze or understand the processes of our ego, deal with them, or find ways to relieve them. Instead, we should make an effort to transcend them toward the ever-present spirit.

This is the way of the spirit as such, and the GraceWay's goal as well. Each one of the GraceWay's twelve tools has a similar principle of action – transcending ourselves, ending our identification with the ego and its ways, and opening our heart to the divine light.

The GraceWay appeals to our ego and offers it the different tools which ultimately help us transcend it. The tortured ego is willing to make an effort to end its torment, and therefore is also willing to practice using the tools which will bring about the end of our identification with it.

Remember, in the spiritual "academy," where different spiritual ways are offered that seem different but are in fact one, the GraceWay is a prepara-tory school, offering vital basic introductory classes to improve the odds of advancing spiritually. Since the GraceWay is only a preparatory institution, we go there, make a progress, and then continue on to the university of the spirit, studying that which fits us best. Everyone should seek out a true spiritual way, as well as a true teacher, and diligently adhere to its recommendations, leading to a transcendence of the ego. When we transcend it a bit, what we see gives us strength to continue on. We will continue on the way and know that the rest is by the grace of God, as we understand Him.

Walking along the way of the spirit reveals a way of seeing the world which offers a different interpretation than the usual ones. Per the way, the world and everything in it is but a reflection of our path to God, as we understand Him. The events of our lives, which brought us to this point, are signposts which guide us to reveal the way and adhere to it. "There is interest in all things turning to the good[116]," there is a guiding hand, such that any who finds us can help us strengthen our spiritual path, that is, to the good.

When I was eight years old, I nearly drowned in the stormy sea. I didn't know how to swim. Along with two friends, we were swept into the deep in the high waves, while our parents, were late in noticing. Out of a resilience driven by lack of options, I managed to jump on the peaks of the waves above me, trying not to swallow too much water, waving my hands calling for help.

What was I thinking about then? I was surprisingly calm, seeing myself sitting in our living room in an hour and drinking hot, sweet tea. With the grace of God, that's exactly what happened.

When I was in Nepal, shortly after the wonderful meeting with Gila – and we have been tight in our path and as one in heart ever since – I suffered from hepatitis that threatened to remove me from this world. I was yellow all over from my eyes to my feet. Despite the terrible weakness, the high fever, the unending nausea, the throbbing headache, the constant discomfort, the bothersome itching, and the not very good conditions for recovery then in Pokhara, my mood was nevertheless great.

Her mood was, too, and she cared for me with grace and devotion I had not yet known, even though we had just begun our relationship. Together, we understood that the fever of the disease was seemingly burning what needed to be burned, leaving behind what should be maintained. My physical deterioration to the point of a tangible sense of the end led me to choose getting back onto the way of the spirit, with her walking beside me.

At the start of this work, I described my own personal spiritual path, in accordance with the development of the GraceWay. Looking back at the events of my own life, the few I described here and many others, I was privileged to observe a guiding hand, soft but determined, behind them. I saw the grace which appeared in moments of happiness and success and in those of challenges, distress and pain, as well as the developing direction I could not escape.

Even when I erred and fell, the grace itself did not. What I once understood as luck, coincidence, a one-time miracle, or out of arrogance, as a successful choice and action, seemed clearly in retrospect to be a supreme spiritual will, which knew what was right, and knew it better than me. Which led and leads me, us, through the passing, finite occurrences, to the infinite, which always lies beyond them, within our reach when we choose it.

All we have left is to let the supreme power continue and lead, enjoying the option of observing it as if from the side, directing us in the best way possible, as we let go entirely, silent in our heart, fully cooperating with it, loving. For we were meant to go there and we are indeed already there, even before we knew it.

"He that is meant for his eyes to open, absorbs the things beyond words. The words cannot touch on even the edge of the truth[117]."

THE TWELVE STEP PROGRAM[118]

1. We admitted we were powerless over alcohol - that our lives had become unmanageable.
2. Came to believe that a Power greater than ourselves could restore us to sanity.
3. Made a decision to turn our will and our lives over to the care of God as we understood Him.
4. Made a searching and fearless moral inventory of ourselves.
5. Admitted to God, to ourselves and to another human being the exact nature of our wrongs.
6. Were entirely ready to have God remove all these defects of character.
7. Humbly asked Him to remove our shortcomings.
8. Made a list of all persons we had harmed, and became willing to make amends to them all.
9. Made direct amends to such people wherever possible, except when to do so would injure them or others.
10. Continued to take personal inventory and when we were wrong promptly admitted it.
11. Sought through prayer and meditation to improve our conscious contact with God as we understood Him, praying only for knowledge of His will for us and the power to carry that out.
12. Having had a spiritual awakening as the result of these steps, we tried to carry this message to alcoholics and to practice these principles in all our affairs.

THANKS

The GraceWay described in these pages was developed over decades of independent investigation, accumulated clinical experience, the reading of innumerable sources, careful academic study, and the many courses and workshops I gave. I have been fortunate to work with many dear people during this period.

It is my privilege to thank them all: Members of the Narcotics Anonymous (NA) groups who opened their hearts and told their life stories and demonstrated to me just how the twelve-step program is practiced as a way of life serving as the initial inspiration for the GraceWay; to the hundreds of therapists and students who took part in the many classes, workshops, and training sessions of the GraceWay, helping me to better clarify the developing ideas; to those who participated in individual or group therapy under my direction, whose healing process contributed to the shaping of the GraceWay.

This book is published thanks to the help of many people and it is my pleasure and duty to thank them all. They include **Dr. Yitzhak Ben Yair**, who helped bring the Hebrew book to print; **Noah Bareket,** who edited the original manuscript's content in an illuminating fashion; **Dr. Shaul Tal**, Director of Focus, who gave home to the Hebrew manuscript and did not hesitate to make constructive comments to improve my work; **Dr. Yafa Shir Raz**, who patiently read the manuscript and added a warm introduction.

My warm thanks to **Avi Wolf**, who patiently translated the Hebrew manuscript into English; the people from eBook Pro, whose dedicated work made the English production available: **Benny Carmi**, the CEO, **Nave Carmi, Kim Ben-Porat, Amir Philos** and all others.

There are many more good people who helped, sometimes without knowing it, and the limited space does not allow to mention them all.

My thanks to the Shnitzer Foundation of Bar-Ilan University's Social Sciences Faculty, whose generous contribution helped make this idea a reality.

Finally, I send my love and warm thanks to my dear family, to my children Dror and Tohar and my wife Gila, whose love, wisdom, and unending support are a constant source of inspiration. My thanks also to Gila for the illuminating cover art for the Hebrew version.

Special thanks to the late spiritual teacher Shlomo Kalo, whose spiritual guidance aided the GraceWay on my own spiritual path.

I thank God for the living grace.

A LITTLE ABOUT ME

I was born in 1958 and raised in Holon, Israel. I received my BA in Psychology and a special Humanities track for exceptional students. This allowed me to acquire the necessary knowledge not only in psychology but also gave me a broader education that included philosophy, some sociology, a taste of mathematics, glimpses of astronomy, an introduction to modern art, as well as a bit of musicology and more.

I received my doctorate from the Institute of Criminology at the Hebrew University, in the direct to PhD track for excelling students. These studies allowed me to expand my horizons again, beyond the fascinating knowledge I acquired in criminology, with basic courses in medicine and advanced courses in psychology.

During my doctorate, I studied the twelve-step program in depth, as well as NA and its groups in Israel. I completed my post-doctorate at the Social Work School at the University of Tel Aviv, which was by then a track of self-learning, where I focused on the development of moral judgment among addicted people in recovery. Between my BA and PhD, I found time to hike around the world for two years and return to Israel with Gila, who has since become my wife and mother to my two children – Dror and Tohar, as well as grandmother to our first grandson – Ma'ayan.

Professionally, I am a clinical criminologist and work as a therapist, as well as a researcher and a lecturer, a full professor, at the Criminology Department at Bar-Ilan University, also serving as head of the department in the past. I have accumulated decades of experience in providing individual and group counseling and therapy to people suffering distress for a variety of reasons including addictions, violence, criminality and victims of abuse.

These are also the topics of my research, thought, and writing. In recent years, I developed the perspective of positive criminology with the help of research teams I directed, which partially continues the idea of positive psychology with an emphasis on criminology. In addition, I developed the field of positive victimology, which offers a new perspective for helping victims of violence and criminality of any kind.

Today, we are working on spiritual criminology and victimology, which aim to bring spiritual wisdom to modern social science. I also initiated the founding of the Bar-Ilan - Retorno University Treatment Center, which I served as its first head. This is a university impact center which maintains a unique interface with the Retorno therapeutic community, much like a university hospital, and helps base the community's work on a continually updating data science - the first of its kind in the world.

The GraceWay presented throughout this book is something I developed gradually based on accumulated clinical, human, and primarily personal experience alongside human field research. From the mid-90s, I gave training workshops for many professionals in Israel on various aspects of the GraceWay and professional application of the twelve-step program, emphasizing the dimension of spiritual change and applying the spiritual path in everyday life.

I have written dozens of academic articles published in scientific journals in Israel and abroad, published a number of books, and frequently lecture at local and international conferences.

My personal site: nattironel.com
My Bar-Ilan Criminology page: https://criminology.biu.ac.il/en/natti

ENDNOTES

1 Ronel, N. (2019). *The twelve tools: From dependence to independence through spiritual change*. Amazon: The Twelve Tools.

2 *Book of Exodos*, 34: 6-7.

3 Freibach-Heifetz, D. (2009). *Secular grace* (Hebrew). Tel Aviv – Jaffa: Resling.

4 Tolstoy, L. N. (1886). *What I believe*. Wikisource: What I Believe.

5 Gordin, R. (2007). *Angles don't dream: The teaching of Ibn 'Arabi – The greatest Sufi sheikh* (Hebrew). Jerusalem: Carmel.

6 *Book of Amos*, 3: 3.

7 Kalo, S. (2000). *Answers* (p. 39) (Hebrew). Tel Aviv – Jaffa: D.A.T.

8 Alcoholics Anonymous (1975) *Living sober*. New York: AA World Service Office.

9 Alcoholics Anonymous (1957). *Alcoholics Anonymous comes of age*. New York: AA World Service Office.

10 Kurtz, E. (1988). *AA the story*. San Francisco: Harper & Row.

11 Karma (Sanskrit) means action, work, or deed. For the believers in spirituality the term also refers to the spiritual principle of cause and effect, often descriptively called the principle of karma, wherein intent and actions of an individual (cause) influence the future of that individual (effect): Good intent and good deeds contribute to good karma and happier rebirths, while bad intent and bad deeds contribute to bad karma and bad rebirths (in Wikipedia: Karma).

12 Maxwell, M.A. (1984). *The Alcoholics Anonymous experience*. New York: McGraw-Hill. Anonymous (1991). *A program for you*. Center City, Minnesota: Hazelden.

13 Ben Zvi , T., & Haimoff-Ayali, R. (2015). The effect of "the good" and the self-centeredness barrier - positive criminology in the lived reality of youth at risk. In N. Ronel & D. Segev (eds.), *Positive criminology* (pp. 32–51). New York and London: Routledge.

Ronel, N. (2006). When good overcomes bad: The impact of volunteers on those they help. *Human Relations, 59*(8), 1133–1153.

14 Kalo, S. (1991). *The self as fighter*. Middlegreen, Slough, United Kingdom: St Pauls Publication.

15 Ronel, N. (1995). *Narcotics Anonymous in Israel: Self help processes and religious faith among drug addicts* (Hebrew). PhD disertation, The Hebrew University.

16 Kalo, S. (2000). Answers (p. 49) (Hebrew). Tel Aviv – Jaffa: D.A.T.

17 Alcoholics Anonymous (1976). Alcoholics Anonymous. New York: AA World Service Office.

18 Sviri, S. (1997). The taste of hidden things. Inverness, CA: The Golden Sufi Center. Kalo, S. (1981). *The brave* (Hebrew). Tel Aviv – Jaffa: D.A.T.

19 Based on Tolstoy, *What I believe.*

20 "Approach" or "tend" in the mathematical sense of "getting closer and closer," a play on words with dual meaning.

21 Ronel, N., & Maor, L. (2012). Grace therapy with recovering victims: Twelve-step based therapy and rehabilitation. In N. Ronel (ed.), *Gone with the spirit* (pp. 215–232) (Hebrew). Ramat-Gan: Israel: Bar-Ilan University Press.

22 Carmell, A., & Halperin, E. (1991). *Michtav me-Eliyahu* (a letter from Elijah) (20th ed.). Jerusalem, Israel: The Committee for the Publication of the Writing of Rabbi E.L. Dessler.

23 *The Bhagavad-Gita.*

24 Ben Yair, Y. (2018). *Jewish criminology - the establishment of theory and practice based on Jewish resources* (Hebrew). PhD dissertation, Bar-Ilan University.

25 *Alcoholics Anonymous* (1976).

26 Ronel, N. (2000). From self-help to professional care: An enhanced application of the 12-step program. *Journal of Applied Behavioral Science, 36*(1), 108–22.

27 Wikipedia: Occam Razor.

28 Simplicity is the ultimate sophistication.

29 Sant Kirpal Singh (1971). *A great saint Baba Jaimal Singh: His life and teachings.* Third edition (p. 5).

30 Wikipedia: Id, ego and super-ego.

31 Frankl, V. (1959). *Man's search for meaning.*

Frankl, V. (2011). The unheard cry for meaning. New York: Simon & Schuster.

Cook, C.C.H. (2003). William James varieties of religious experience and Jungian varieties of human nature: The nature of the relationship between religious experience, belief and psychological type. Journal of Beliefs & Values, 24(2), 139–154.

von der Heydt, V. (2004). Jung and religion: Its place in analytical psychology. In J. Ryce-Menuhin (ed.), Jung and the monotheisms: Judaism, Christianity, and Islam (pp. 7-19). London & New York: Routledge.

James, W. (2017). Varieties of religious experience: A study in human nature. Retrieved: https://doi.org/10.1111/j.1467-8705.1985.tb00797.x

Jung, C.J. (1970). Collected works (Vol. 11), Psychology and religion: West and east. London: Routledge.

Maslow, A.H. (1959). New knowledge in human values. New York: Harper & Row.

32 Pargament, K.I. (2007). *Spirituality integrated psychotherapy: Understanding and addressing the sacred.* New York: The Guilford Press.

Miller, W.R. (2005). What is human nature? Reflections from Judeo- Christian perspectives. In W.R. Miller & H.D. Delaney (eds.), Judeo-Christian perspectives on psychology (pp. 11–29). Washington, DC: APA.

33 Babylonian Talmud, *Tractate Sanhedrin*, 9: 2.

34 Rest, J., Bebeau, J.M., Volker, J. (1986). An overview of the psychology of morality. In J. Rest (ed.), *Moral development: Advances in research and theory.* New York: Praeger.

35 Colby, A., & Kohlberg, L. (1987). *The measurement of moral judgment. Vol 1: Theoretical foundations and research validation.* Cambridge: Cambridge University Press.

Kohlberg, L., Levine, C., Hewer, A. (1983). Moral stages: A current formulation and a response to critics. Basel: Karger.

Kohlberg, L., & Ryncarz, R.A. (1990). Beyond justice reasoning: Moral development and consideration of a seventh stage. In C.N. Alexander & E J Langer (eds.), Higher stages of human d*evelopment* (pp. 191-207). New York: Oxford University Press.

36 Krebs, D.L., & Van Hesteren, F. (1994). The development of altruism: Toward an integrative model. *Developmental Review, 14*(2), 58–103.

Enright, R.D., & The Human Development Study Group (1984). Piaget on the moral development of forgiveness: Identity or reciprocity?, Human Development, 37(2), 63–80.

Enright, R.D., & The Human Development Study Group (1991). The moral development of forgiveness. In W.M. Kurtinez & J.L. Gewirtz (eds.), Handbook of moral behavior and development (pp. 123-152). Hillsdale, NJ: Lawrence Erlbaum Associates.

Fowler, J.W. (1981). Stages of faith. San Francisco: Harper & Row.

Hoffman, L.M. (1984). Empathy, its limitations, and its role in a comprehensive moral theory. In W.M. Kurtines & J.L. Gewirtz (eds.), Morality, moral behavior, and moral development (pp. 177-192). New York: Wiley.

37 Gibbs, J.C. (1991). Sociomoral developmental delay and cognitive distortion: Implications for the treatment of antisocial youth. In *Handbook of moral behavior and development* (pp. 95-110).

Elkind, D. (1967). Egocentrism in adolescence. *Child Development, 38,* 1025-1034.

38 Ben Zvi - Uzan, T. (2016). *Between generosity and self- centeredness in the reality of youth at risk* (Hebrew). PhD dissertation, Bar-Ilan University.

39 Ronel, N. (2006). When good overcomes bad: The impact of volunteers on those they help. *Human Relations, 59*(8), 1133–1153.

40 Ben Zvi - Uzan & Haimoff-Ayali, The effect of "the good" and the self-centeredness barrier - positive criminology in the lived reality of youth at risk.

41 Ronel, N., Haski-Leventhal, D., Ben-David, B. M., & York, A. S. (2009). Perceived altruism: A neglected factor in initial intervention. *International Journal of Offender Therapy and Comparative Criminology, 53*(2), 191–210.

42 Ronel, N., Frid N., & Timor, U. (2013). The practice of positive criminology: A Vipassana course in prison. *International Journal of Offender Therapy and Comparative Criminology, 57*(2), 153–133.

Ronel et al., Perceived altruism: A neglected factor in initial intervention.

43 Ronel, N. & Segev, D. (2014). Positive criminology in practice . *International Journal of Offender Therapy and Comparative Criminology, 58*(11), 1389–1407.

Ronel, N. (2015). How can criminology become positive? In *Positive Criminology* (pp. 13–31).

44 Carmell & Halperin, *Michtav me-Eliyahu (a letter from Elijah).*

45 Lorimer, D. (2015)(ed.). *Prophet for our times: The life and teachings of Peter Deunov.* Kindle edition.

46 Kalo, S. (1991). *To begin allover again* (Hebrew). Tel Aviv – Jaffa: D.A.T.

47 *The Bhagavad-Gita.*

48 Adi Shankara. *Vivekachudamani – The crest-jewel of discrimination.* Retrived 14.1.22: Sri Sankara's Vivekachudamani.

49 Kalo, *Answers*, p. 42.

50 *Book of Genesis*, 3: 5.

51 Alcoholics Anonymous (1952). *Twelve Steps and Twelve Traditions.* New York: AA World Service Office.

52 Sykes, G.M., & Matza, D. (1957). Techniques of neutralization: A theory of delinquency. *American Journal of Sociology, 22*, 664–670.
   Scott, B.M., & Lyman, S.M. (1970). Accounts, deviance, and social order In J.D. Douglas (ed.), *Deviance and respectability* (pp. 89–119). New York: Basic Books

53 Ronel, N. (2011). *Criminal behavior, criminal mind: Being caught in a criminal spin. International Journal of Offender Therapy and Comparative Criminology, 55*(8), 1208–1233.

54 Jerusalem Talmud, Tractate Hallah, 2: 1.

55 Schmidt, P. (1980). Preface. In J. Johnson, *The Path of the Masters: The science of Surat Shabd Yoga* (pp. 15–34). Punjab, India: Radha Soami Satsang Beas.

56 Carmell & Halperin, *Michtav me-Eliyahu (a letter from Elijah).*

57 There is an equivalent here to Newton's Third Law of Classical Mechanics.

58 *Book of Psalms*, 46: 11.

59 Sharp, J. (1984). *Exploring nonviolent alternatives.* Boston: Porter Sargent.

60 Kalo, *Answers*, p. 73.

61 *Book of Shmuel II*, 11-12.

62 *Book of Exodos,* 20: 13.

63 Ronel, Criminal behavior, criminal mind: Being caught in a criminal spin.

64 Bensimon M. & Ronel, N. (2012). The flywheel effect of intimate partner violence: A victim–perpetrator interactive spin. *Aggression and Violent Behavior, 17*(5), 423–429.
   Collins, J. (2001). *Good to great.* New York: HarperCollins.

65 For a summary of the research, cf. Ronel, "Criminal Behavior, Criminal Mind: Being Caught in a Criminal Spin."

66 Babylonian Talmud, Tractate *Yoma*, 29: 1.

67 Kalo, *Answers*, p. 102.

68 Kalo, *Answers*, p. 97.

69 Goleman, D. (2003). *Destructive Emotions: A Scientific Dialogue with the Dalai Lama*. New York: Bantam.

70 A quote said by sixteenth century French author, François Rabelais.

71 Kalo, *Answers*, p. 95.

72 *Alcoholics Anonymous.*

Alcoholics Anonymous, *Twelve Steps and Twelve Traditions.*

73 Ronel, N., & Maor, L. (2012). Grace Therapy with recovering victims: Twelve-step based therapy and rehabilitation. In N. Ronel (ed.), *Gone with the spirit* (Hebrew)(pp. 215–232). Ramat-Gan: Israel: Bar-Ilan University Press.

74 Anonymous. *A program for you.*

75 *Alcoholics Anonymous.*

76 Ronel, N. (1998-9). Self-help groups as a spontaneous Grace Community. *Social Development Issues, 20*(3), 53–72.

77 Reinikainen, J. (2005). The golden rule and the requirement of universalizability. *The Journal of Value Inquiry, 39*(2), 155–168.

78 Braithwaite, J., Ahmed, E., & Braithwaite, V. (2006). Shame, restorative justice and crime. In F. Cullen, J. Wright & K. Belvins (eds.), *Taking stock: The status of criminological theory* (pp. 397–417). London: Transaction Publishers.

Braswell, M., Fuller, J., Lozoff, B. (2001). *Corrections, Peacemaking and Restorative Justice*. Cincinnati, OH: Anderson Publishing.

79 Kalo, *Answers*, p. 74.

80 Batson, N. (2013). *The creation of the victimological self* (Hebrew). PhD dissertation, Bar-Ilan University.

81 Ronel, N. (2009). Spirituality-based therapy with recovering victims: Challenges and opportunities. In O. Hagemann, P. Schäfer & S. Schmidt (eds.), *Vilctimology, victim assistance and criminal justice* (pp. 175–89). Mönchengladbach: Niederrhein University of Applied Sciences.

82 Wikipedia: Dissociation.

83 Kor – Moses, E., & Rojany - Buccieri, L. (2012). *Surviving the angel of death: The true story of a Mengele twin in Auschwitz.* Terre Haute, IN: Tanglewood Press.

Diamond, S., & Ronel, N. (2019). From bondage to liberation: The forgiveness case of holocaust survivor Eva Mozes Kor. *Journal of Aggression, Maltreatment and Trauma, 28*(8), 996–1016.

84 Kurt, H., & Ronel, N. (2017). Addicted to pain: A preliminary model of sexual masochism as addiction. *International Journal of Offender Therapy and Comparative Criminology, 61*(15), 1760-1774.

85 "And now these three remain: faith, hope and love. But the greatest of these is love." I Corinthians, 13: 13.

86 Kalo, *Answers*, p. 63.

87 Moshe Chaim Luzzatto (RaMCHaL). *Messilat Yesharim (The Path of the Upright).*

88 *The Bhagavad-Gita.*

89 Loy, D. (1985). Wei-Wu-Wei: Nondual action. *Philosophy East and West, 35*(1), 87–73.

90 Lau-Tsze. *Tao Te Ching.*

Hoffmann, Y. (1977). *The sounds of earth: selections from Chuang-Tzu* (Hebrew). Ramat Gan, Israel: Masada.

91 The Mishna, *Ethics of the Fathers* (Pirkei Avot).

92 Per his sayings in *Ethics of the Fathers.*

93 Per Rabbi Yosi Cohen in *Ethics of the Fathers.*

94 Kalo, *Answers*, p. 43.

95 *The Bhagavad-Gita.*

96 Sri Sadhu Om (2002). *A light on the teaching of Bhagavan Sri Ramana Maharshi: The essence of spiritual practice (Sadhanai Saram).* Asheboro, NC, USA: AHAM Publications.

97 Kalo, S. (1981)ed.). *Sayings of Buddha: Collected verses from "The way of the Truth" (Dhammapada)* (Hebrew). Tel Aviv – Jaffa: D.A.T.

98 Laura, S. (2006). *12 steps on Buddha's path: Bill, Buddha, and we.* Somerville, MA: Wisdom Publications.

99 Clifford, T. (1984). *Tibetan Buddhist medicine and psychiatry: The diamond healing.* York Beach, ME: Aquarian Press.

100 Kalo, S. (1981). *The brave* (Hebrew). Tel Aviv – Jaffa: D.A.T.

101 Cf. Freedom Farm.

102 Kurtz, *AA the Story.*

103 Leach, B., Norris, J.L. (1977). Factors in the development of Alcoholics Anonymous. In B. Kissin & H. Begleiter (eds.), *Treatment and rehabilitation of the chronic alcoholic* (pp. 441–543). New York: Plenum Press.

104 Spiritus Contra Spiritum.

105 Cf. Wikipedia: The Is – Ought Problem.

106 Kohlberg, L. (1981). *The Philosophy of moral development.* San Francisco, CA: Harper & Row.

107 *Narcotics Anonymous* (1988).

108 Ronel, *Narcotics Anonymous in Israel: Self help processes and religious faith among drug addicts.*

109 Rosenzweig, F. (2000). *Ninetytwo poems and hymns of Yehuda Halevi.* Albany, NY: State University of New York Press.

110 Kalo, *Answers,* p. 76.

111 Cf. Wikipedia: Ho'oponopono.

112 Brinson, J., & Fisher, T.A. (1999). The Ho'oponopono group: A conflict resolution model for school counselors. *The Journal for Specialists in Group Work, 24*(4), 369-382.

113 Kalo, *Answers,* p. 74.

114 The Book of Psalms, 46: 11.

115 Kalo, *Sayings of Buddha: Collected verses from "The way of the Truth" (Dhammapada).*

116 Attributed to Rabbi Nachman of Breslav by his student Rabbi Nathan Sternhartz in a letter to his son, appearing in the collected correspondence volume Leaves for Medicine (*Alim L'Terufah*)(Hebrew), letter 11.

117 Kalo, *Answers,* p. 74.

118 *Alcoholics Anonymous,* pp. 59-60.

Made in the USA
Monee, IL
31 January 2023